The Making of OUR Warrior

Jeff Falkel and the Warriors of ODA 316

More Than a Name Foundation
Littleton, CO

www.morethananamefoundation.org

**MORE
THAN A
NAME**

ISBN: 978-1-60679-056-4
Book layout: Brenden Murphy
Cover design: George Foster
Front and back photos: Courtesy of members of ODA 316

Critical Choice
P.O. Box 1828
Monterey, CA 93942

Contents

What People Are Saying About *The Making of OUR Warrior*

This is an extraordinary story about the true strength of America… A tough, resilient, close-knit fabric of heroic love; Father and Son, Team, and Country.

—Peter J. Schoomaker
General, US Army (Ret.)
5th Commander-In-Chief US Special Operations Command
35th Army Chief of Staff

SSG Chris Falkel would be proud of this book. His father, Jeff, has written a deeply personal story of the brave men that fight the GWOT every day. After every visit in Afghanistan or Iraq to a Special Forces Team at some remote firebase, I would ask myself "where do we get such men?" Jeff Falkel's The Making of OUR Warrior answers that question. It is an intensely personal look at where America gets it's finest Warriors, Army Special Forces - the Green Berets, and the impact on the Falkel family when their son is lost. But, unlike the many War Stories on the shelf, it is the personal story of SSG Chris Falkel's journey to become one of America best and demonstrates his love of country, family and teammates. This book should be required reading for every leader in command of every Special Operations Team worldwide and their families.

—Doug Brown
General, US Army (retired)
Commander—US Army Special Operations Command 2000-2002
Commander—US Special Operations Command 2003-2007

The story of Staff Sergeant Christopher Falkel and his father's love is a penetrating narrative about a

Lakota warrior, athlete, patriot, and son. Heartbreaking at times, it provides unique insight into the Special Forces warrior culture. In Afghanistan, Christopher's Special Forces Operational Detachment Alpha locks on to the Taliban and pursues them for days, fighting engagement after engagement – refusing to break contact. Chris fearlessly exposes himself to enemy fire time and time again with his .50 caliber machine gun, breaking enemy formations and Taliban schemes of maneuver. Frustrated, the Taliban pay Chris the ultimate warrior compliment, sending an internal message that Chris' vehicle is a formidable obstacle and dangerous.

—Geoffrey C. Lambert
Major General (Ret.)
Commander—US Army Special Forces Command (Airborne)
2001-2003

A recommended read without reservation….a story that chronicles the making of a true SF Warrior, highlighting the essence of Why We Fight Now.

—Gus Benton
Colonel, US Army Special Forces
Commander—3rd Special Forces Group (Airborne)

Jeff Falkel has written an original, heartbreaking story of the devastating loss of his son, SSG Chris Falkel. Chris was a member of our country's first line of defense— the amazing men of the Army Special Forces. This is a beautiful book about those most important heroes: those we don't hear about on the evening news but go about their commitments of courage and tenacity without fanfare. The Making Of OUR Warrior will stay with me always.

—John T. Carney, Jr.
Colonel, USAF (Ret.)
President/CEO
Special Operations Warrior Foundation

The Making of OUR Warrior is the heart-wrenching and ultimately enlightening story of SSG Chris Falkel and the family he left behind serving his country against the ruthless Islamic extremists who attacked us on 9/11. In the wake of that travesty, Chris was one of the few who volunteered to take up arms in defense of our country as a Special Forces Soldier, knowing full well that meant he was going to war at the tip of the spear. The Making of OUR Warrior is the tale of a Warrior's valor and the special bond between a father and his son. As a Gold Star father, Jeff shares some of the intimate conversations he had with his son and his teammates with a passion that is hard to capture on paper. No parent should ever have to bury their child. The Making of OUR Warrior shows how this tragic loss can ultimately be an empowering tribute to his son and his memory.

—Joseph J. Martin
Lieutenant Colonel, US Army Special Forces
Congressional Fellow
Author of Get Selected to Special Forces

An inspiring journey of faith, courage, determination, friendship, and the love of a family.

—Steven L. McLeary
Major, USAF (Ret.)
Special Operations Warrior Foundation
Executive Director

Dedication

… Whom shall I send and who will go for us? Then said I, Here I am; send me!

—Isaiah 6: 8

We would like to dedicate this book to the men, the warriors, the heroes of 3rd Special Forces Group (Airborne)–Past, Present and Future. Our country is safer because of the dedication, commitment, loyalty and love that these brave men demonstrate everyday. We are forever in your debt and you will forever be in my heart and prayers.

I would also like to make a special dedication to the warriors of 3rd Special Forces Group (Airborne) that have paid the ultimate sacrifice and gave their lives for their brothers next to them and for our country in either Operation Enduring Freedom (OEF) or Operation Iraqi Freedom (OIF). You served with honor, you fought with glory, and you will NEVER be forgotten.

To these warriors who gave their all for us–we owe them a sacred debt to live EACH day to the fullest!

1st Battalion

SFC John Edward Taylor BN S-2
KIA 17 May 2003 OEF

CW2 Bruce E. Price ODA 313
KIA 15 May 2004 OEF

SFC Robert J. Mogensen ODA 311
KIA 29 May 2004 OEF

CPT Daniel W. Eggers ODA 311
KIA 29 May 2004 OEF

SGT Jason T. Palmerton ODA 312
KIA 23 Jul 2005 OEF

SSG Christopher M. Falkel ODA 316
KIA 8 Aug 2005 OEF

CPT Jeremy A. Chandler ODA 334
KIA 11 Aug 2005 OEF

SSG Kyn H. Chay SOT-A 302
KIA 28 Oct 2006 OEF

SFC William R. Brown ODA 331
KIA 6 Nov 2006 OEF

MSG (R) Donald A. Barger ODA 333
KIA 10 May 2008

SSG Marc J. Small ODA 3123
KIA 12 Feb 2009 OEF

MSG David L. Hurt ODA 3123
KIA 20 Feb 2009 OEF

SSG Jeremy E. Bessa ODA 3123
KIA 20 Feb 2009 OEF

2nd Battalion

SFC Peter P. Tycz II ODA 365
KIA 12 Jun 2002 OEF

SFC Mitchell A. Lane ODA 365
KIA 29 Aug 2003 OEF

SSG Robert S. Goodwin ODA 345
KIA 20 Sep 2004 OEF

SSG Tony B. Olaes ODA 345
KIA 20 Sep 2004 OEF

SFC James S. Ochsner ODA 344
KIA 15 Nov 2005 OEF

SFC Tung M. Nguyen ODA 356
KIA 14 Nov 2006 OIF

SFC Justin S. Monschke ODA 354
KIA 14 Oct 2007 OIF

3rd Battalion

CW2 Stanley L. Harriman ODA 372
KIA 2 Mar 2002 OEF

SSG Paul A. Sweeney ODA 371
KIA 30 Oct 2003   OEF

MSG Anthony R.C. Yost ODA 375
KIA 19 Nov 2005 OIF

CW2 Scott W. Dyer ODA 384
KIA 11 Oct 2006 OEF

SSG Robert J. Miller ODA 372
KIA 25 Jan 2008 OEF

SSG William R. Neil ODA 3332
KIA 22 Mar 2008 OEF

SGT Nicholas A. Robertson SOT-A 3301
KIA 3 Apr 2008 OEF

Acknowledgments

The strength of the wolf is in the pack, and the strength of the pack is in the wolf.

—Rudyard Kipling

No book is written by just the author or authors. It is a work that takes the knowledge, skills and abilities of many, MANY people, and OUR book is no exception. I use the word "OUR" because this book about Chris was written by so many people that have impacted Chris' and my life. Some people actually wrote parts of chapters, some people shared their stories with me and allowed me to share them with you. And some were there whenever I needed a shoulder to lean on, and a heart to open mine up to. It is difficult to put into words how grateful I am to these people, for I would not be where I am today were it not for these people—my family.

First, I want to thank my ODA 316 family. You took Chris in, made him part of your lives and loved him as I do. And now, you are MY family. I never truly understood what love and family were all about until I became part of OUR family. Thank you for loving Chris and loving me as only you can. The hole in my heart can never be filled, but having you and all you mean to me and to Chris, helps it to heal each and every day. I have said this to each of you so many times—I can never thank you enough for all you are and have done for Chris and for me, but I will spend the rest of my life trying.

I want to thank LTC Joseph Martin for being there for me every step of the way in this journey. He did not know Chris directly, but was the Company Commander of the Special Forces Preparatory Course that Chris went through in 2003. He took his passion for Special Forces and wrote the best selling book, *Get Selected for Special Forces* to help other young men, like Chris, prepare themselves for the greatest military unit the world has ever known. His insight, wisdom, encouragement and love helped make this book what it is.

I want to thank Dr. Jim Peterson, Ms. Megan Comstock, and the amazing staff at Critical Choice Publishing for putting up with me and producing OUR book with the honor and reverence it deserves!

I want to thank George Foster who took the cover design that LTC Martin first provided and turned it into a work of art. George, thank you for all the love you put into your work so we can show OUR love for Chris.

I want to thank my "Brotherhood of the Barbells" who have been there for me, in good times and in bad, and whose strength goes beyond what they are able to "lift":

To Dr. Thomas Baechle, one of my oldest and dearest friends, and the first person I called after I got the news on 9 August—you have been my beacon in the storm.

To Dr. Anthony Abbott, a retired Special Forces Captain, and my brother. You have given my life the grid coordinates I needed to follow.

To Dr. Avery Faigenbaum, Coach John Taylor, Mr. Roger Earle, Coach Dan Wathen, Dr. Don Chu, Dr. Dave Pearson, Dr. Dan Wagman, Coach Joe Owens, Dr. Tom Wilson, Dr. Mike Greenwood, Coach Bill Allerheiligen, Dr. Jaynie Bjornaraa, Coach Bud Bjornaraa, Dr. Larry Meadors, Coach Steve Plisk and Dr. Bob Chen—thank you all for always being there for me, and there have been MANY times that I have called on you for your strength and your love, and will for the rest of my life!

To my California and New York families—you have been with me through thick and thin, and having you all there at Arlington meant more to me than you can possibly imagine. But Arlington was just the beginning, and we will continue to travel the path together, forever!

I want to thank Mr. A.J. Laguardia, my Sprint representative. After Chris got out of Basic Training, our cell phones were like a life line between us, and A.J. set us up with a plan that didn't cost me a fortune so that Chris and I could talk when ever and for as long as we needed to talk—and believe me, we talked!!! Then, after Chris died, I was literally talking to people all over the world, and A.J. and Sprint took care of me so I could take care of so many others.

I want to thank my Fox Hollow family. Much of what I taught Chris was made possible by having this special, sacred place, that I was able to share with both Chris and Tim. For all you have done to help me see "straight" again, I can never thank you enough!

I want to thank my father, Harmon J. Falkel, for teaching me how to be a dad. He gave me my vision. He taught me how to laugh, how to cry, how to be a man. He was an integral part of the U.S. Army Air Corps, initially teaching flying at the beginning of World War II, and then flying throughout the European Theater. He was one of the first helicopter pilots, but learned very quickly that when they crash, you get hurt! The smart gene in our family stayed with my dad! Chris never met his grandfather in that he crossed over when I was 14. But I know that he was the first one to meet Chris on the other side, to give him a hug and a kiss, and to welcome him and introduce Chris to the rest of the warriors waiting for me now. Chris knew all about his grandfather from everything I told Chris. My dad used to use me for his strength training, and I did the same thing with Chris and Tim doing push-ups with the boys sitting on my back, training on the slide board giving the boys a "ride", and doing "Fazzenie's" on shoulder day—tossing the boys up in the air as high as I could and then catching them before they bounced off the ground! When the boys were little, I would toss Chris for as many reps as I could and then "super-set" with Tim, as he was smaller and lighter. Amazing training sessions!!! I loved my dad, and I miss him. But I know he is with Chris and Jay now, and I will be there soon to be with you again! We will have a good time.

Finally, to the rest of my family—this book is for you, because of you and all that you mean to me.

I love you ALL, just as Chris loved you and you loved him.

Foreword

There are two types, at least, of fighting men who serve their nations with honor. The first is the citizen-soldier. The citizen-soldier is, to my mind, the soul and beating heart of a free republic. His type goes back as far as ancient Greece, to the freehold landsman who takes down his shield and armor from above the hearth, kisses his wife and infants' goodbye and marches off to defend his city from her enemies. Closer to our era, citizen-soldiers were the "embattled farmers" of Lexington and Concord who took up the same defense with flintlock, powder and ball. The citizen-soldier is a reluctant fighter. War is not his element. When summoned, he rises to the occasion, visits hell upon the enemy, then returns to his true life at home. Probably the most vivid example of the citizen-solider in recent fiction is the character of Capt. John Miller, played by Tom Hanks in "Saving Private Ryan." The citizen-soldier is the first line of defense of any free society, and the man who, throughout our own country's history, has preserved her liberty time and again.

This book is not about citizen-soldiers. Its subject is another type of fighting man, for whom the proper term (overused and misused as it is these days) is "warrior."

The warrior and the citizen-soldier are not the same. I honor both and place neither above the other, militarily or morally. It's an exercise that will reward our attention, however, to consider the differences between the two.

The citizen-soldier fights to defend his country, his family and the values he holds dear. The warrior fights for the fight itself. A warrior does not participate in the fight; he is a fighter. That's who he is. It's all he wants to be. A warrior is not himself, apart from war. Like the priest or the holy man, a warrior is "called"—often at a very early age. Chris Falkel was. So were all the men of ODA 316.

Warriors recognize one another without words. Their type is ancient; it pre-dates nations. Before there were civilizations, there were warriors.

The Warrior archetype arose out of and is only a half-step removed from the Hunter, which is the most ancient archetype of all, excepting only Eve. The warrior has not changed in fifty thousand years. His skills are primordial. His being is tribal. His calling transcends patriotism. His love is for his brothers of the group, the clan, the band. He lives and breathes honor and fears only one thing—that he will prove unworthy of his comrades-in-arms. He will die first, gladly. A flag doesn't mean so much to a warrior, nor does the identity of his enemy. Any enemy will do, as long as he has inflicted harm on those of the warrior's blood. The warrior respects his foe, even honors him, but he lives only to kill him.

The warrior's mythology is not really Christian. His gods arise from cultures like the Lakota, the Native American; from the ancient Spartans, Macedonians and Romans; and from the Vedic precepts expressed in the Bhagavad-Gita. His spiritual home lies in those warrior societies in which the acts of killing and being killed were viewed from a sterner, and some would say more profound, perspective than in our own. I was not surprised to learn that the warriors of ODA 316 elected to tattoo their flesh with the Greek letter lambda, with which the ancient Spartans inscribed the surfaces of their shields to identify their country, Lakedaemon. The hearts of these Special Forces men beat more in synch with Leonidas and Dienekes, perhaps, than with their own countrymen. MAJ Jim (whom you'll meet in these pages) tells the story of the 135 soldiers aboard the homeward-bound jet from Baghdad International Airport. As the wheels lifted off the ground, 134 cheered. Only Jim wept. He hated to leave the fight. That's the difference between a citizen-soldier and a warrior.

Jeff Falkel's tribute to his son Chris is aptly titled. Because Chris' story is that of the making of a warrior. A strong father-son bond is common among warriors. The love flows both ways. Pride is a huge part of it. The father reveres the son and vice versa; each burns to live up to the other and to make the other proud of him.

When you read Jeff's stories of Chris as a young boy, of his stashing of weapons in hidden caches when he was five years old, of training himself to hit hard, hold nothing back, operate without food or sleep, you'll see a warrior in embryo. Chris knew. He saw his own death coming. The passages in this book when Jeff tells of hearing the news, of telling Dianne, of Arlington and of Fort Bragg are heart-breaking but brutally true, not only to Chris' life and death but to the lives and deaths of warriors since time immemorial.

Warriors inhabit this material sphere differently from the rest of us. Their life unfolds on different planes simultaneously. Death is ever-present to them. They live on this side of the curtain and on the far side too—sometimes they live more vividly on the far side than they do here, in life. A warrior looks into the eyes of his brothers and sees their deaths, as he sees his own. Death doesn't mean that much to him. Those who love warriors must make their peace with this. When you read this book, you'll encounter numerous incidents involving falcons. ("Falkel" means "little falcon" in Lakota.) This is no accident. Hawk and falcon are messengers in Native American mythology. Like the Greek god Hermes, Falcon shuttles between the lands of the living and the dead. Falcon is a warrior bird, who is equally at home in both dimensions. He carries messages. No brother-in-arms can ever die, a warrior believes (and his experience bears this out). The spirit of a fallen comrade remains vivid and communicates continually from the other side. In these pages, Jeff recounts dozens of such messages from Chris. Are they fanciful? The fictitious creations of a father's grieving heart? I don't think so. I have another friend who recently lost his son. For him, the totem animal is a dolphin. My friend has stories too, one after the other that defy all rational explanation. What I admire most about Jeff's achievement in producing this testament to his son are his own efforts to remain rational, to keep a cool, reality-check head. Have you read Joan Didion's "The Year of Magical Thinking?" Then you know how difficult that can be.

My own life in recent months, as I said, has brought me into contact with three fathers who have lost grown sons. One is a dear friend from high school, one a famous personage whom I've never met but whose life I've studied. One is Jeff.

Sons should bury fathers, not the other way around. A father never recovers from this loss. There is no healing. One of these fathers wrote,

"All kind and well-intentioned words bring little consolation. Nor can I say that time heals the wounds in such a case. On the contrary, the older one becomes, the more he realizes how much he has lost."

This book is by definition personal. It couldn't be more personal. It's Chris' book, it's Jeff's, it's Tim's, it's Dianne's, it belongs to everyone in the extended family. It's not really a book in the sense of a crafted "work" produced by a coolly detached professional. This material is raw. It's as fresh as a fatal wound. Touch it and your hand comes away sticky with blood. It's not a book, it's a document—a testament etched in acid but with every cell penetrated and permeated by love. It will be as real and immediate a thousand years from now as it would have been a thousand years in the past. Is it too long? Yes. Is it extreme? Yes. Excessive, even obsessive? Yes. But when Jeff asked me, I told him don't change a word.

The person who touches my heart most in these pages is Tim, Chris' younger brother. Chris is fine. As tragic as it is that Chris' life was cut short, that he will never experience the joy of having children or loving a wife or any of the other sweet fulfillments of life, still he stepped out of this world the way he wanted to, in a blaze of glory, doing what he was born to do, among friends he loved and who loved him, comrades-in-arms whose lives he helped to preserve by his valorous actions in the face of mortal peril.

Tim, will you stand to your detriment in your brother's shadow? I don't think so. My instinct tells me that your destiny will be loftier and more complex than any other in this broad, wide family. You may have the trickiest path, to remain part of this sage and to transcend it. Your road may be one of art. I know a little about that and I can tell you: it is transformative, and its gift is meaning. I salute you, Tim. Godspeed.

Lastly, to readers of this Foreword, will you forgive me if, to honor Chris and Jeff, I end with a passage from one of my own books? I wouldn't do it if I didn't think it was appropriate.

The passage concerns another animal, not a falcon but a horse, perhaps the noblest and most celebrated warhorse who ever lived, Alexander the Great's Bucephalus. This steed carried Alexander into battle at the Granicus River, at Issus, Gaugamela, and in a hundred other clashes, until he fell—at the age of twenty-four, legend says—at the battle of the Hydaspes River in India. Bucephalus was a warrior. From "Virtues of War," this is the peroration of Alexander's eulogy:

> *My friends, many of you have sought to console me for this loss. You have recalled to me that the wide world is mine to search, and from its precincts I may select any horse I wish and train it to be a second Bucephalus. I don't believe it. In all the earth I shall not find his fellow. He was, and is no more. My own end, when it comes, is by his passing rendered less hateful to me in that hope, only, that I shall meet him again in the life to come.*

—Steven Pressfield, best-selling author of *Gates of Fire*

Prologue—The "OUR" in *The Making of OUR Warrior*

For anyone that has ever been in the military, there is a very special bond that is developed between the men that belong to a team or unit, doing what ever is necessary to protect the warrior standing next to them. This has never been truer than for the men, the warriors, the Spartans that fought next to SSG Christopher M. Falkel on Operational Detachment Alpha (ODA) 316. Chris was attached to 3rd Special Forces Group (Airborne) in January, 2004, and his job was as a weapons sergeant (18 Bravo) on ODA 316. On a Special Forces "A" team, there are several MOS (military occupation specialty):

- 18 Alpha—the team leader, usually a Captain
- 180 Alpha—the warrant officer that is second in command
- 18 Bravo—the weapons sergeant
- 18 Charlie—the engineer sergeant
- 18 Delta—the medical sergeant
- 18 Echo—the communications sergeant
- 18 Fox—the intelligence sergeant
- 18 Zulu—the team sergeant

Throughout OUR book, we will refer to Chris' teammates by the rank and first name only to protect their identity as almost all of Chris' teammates are still on active duty in the United States Army Special Forces, taking the fight to the enemies of our country, doing what they do like no others!

These men are the true definition of a warrior. Combined, they have more than 100 years of service to our country, dating back to before Operation Desert Storm in 1990. They are some of the most decorated warriors in Special Forces, and I want to introduce them to our readers now to set the stage for how Chris became the warrior he was. While I started Chris' military education, it was these men, these warriors, these Spartans that stood next to Chris, who loved him as their brother, and are the warriors that I love now as my brothers and my sons.

LTC (P)

LTC (P) was a Lieutenant Colonel who was promotable (P) but retired from Special Forces prior to his promotion to Colonel.

LTC(P) has held a myriad of positions in Special Forces ranging from a Team leader of a 5th SFG(A) ODA during Desert Storm in 1990 to Deputy Commander of 3rd SFG (A) until his retirement.

Thank you, Sir: for ALL you have done for OUR family and for being there for me when I truly needed you the most! I love you.

MAJ Jim

MAJ Jim was Chris' first team leader on ODA 316. Words are not sufficient to describe the relationship that both Chris and I have with MAJ Jim.

- 18 Echo on a 5th SFG (A) ODA during Desert Storm in 1990
- Commissioned as a 2nd Lieutenant after graduating from New Mexico State University
- Infantry Rifle and Scout Platoon Leader for 25th Infantry
- First 18A Team Leader for ODA 316
- ODA 316 team leader in Asadabad, Afghanistan in 2003
- ODA 316 team leader in Gereshk, Afghanistan in 2004
- Team leader for a Special Projects Team 2005-2006
- Combat Advisor for an Iraqi National Police Commando unit 2006-2007
- Cadre instructor at Robin Sage—the final phase of the Special   Forces Qualification Course 2007-2008.
- MAJ Jim is preparing to head back to Afghanistan in the summer of 2009.

MAJ Jim was awarded the Silver Star for his heroism and valor in Iraq in 2006. The Silver Star is the third highest award in the United States Military for valor in combat. MAJ Jim was also awarded the Iraqi Medal of Honor and an ARCOM with "V".

I love you, Jimbo as no other, and you ARE.....

1 LT Dan

1 LT Dan was Staff Sergeant Dan, one of the 18 Delta's on ODA 316 with Chris for two tours in Afghanistan.

- One of the original members of ODA 316 as the 18 Delta—medical sergeant
- 18 Delta in Asadabad, Afghanistan in 2003
- 18 Delta in Gereshk, Afghanistan in 2004
- 18 Delta in Deh Afghan, Afghanistan 2005
- 18 Delta in Deh Afghan, Afghanistan 2006
- Commissioned as a 2nd Lieutenant (2LT) 2006, and assigned to 82nd Airborne Division as an infantry battalion medical platoon leader
- 18 months in Baghdad, Iraq with the 82nd Airborne Division from 2007-2008
- Promoted to 1 LT 2008 and volunteered for MMIT, currently serving in Afghanistan
- Scheduled for promotion to Captain in summer 2009.

1LT Dan was awarded a Bronze Star with "V" for his heroism during the Battle of Mari Ghar 7-9 August, 2005. He was also awarded an ARCOM with "V" for a combat action in Iraq.

I love you, my brother and I will never forget all you did for my son.

CW3 Chief

CW3 Chief was the company warrant officer for A Co, 1st battalion, 3rd SFG (A) for ODA 316 in both deployments to Afghanistan. It was Gereshk, Afghanistan where Chris and Chief first met in 2004.

- Forward Observer in the 2nd Ranger Battalion 1984-1989
- 1st Platoon Alpha Company Forward Observer
- Charlie Company Fire Integration Support Team FIST NCOIC
- Battalion Combat Observation Laser Team (COLT) Leader (HALO)
- 18E C/1/1
- ODA 131CIF Assault Troop 1990-1993
- ODA 134 RST 1994-1995

- Warrant in A/1/3 1996-2005
- ODA 314 Commander
- ODA 314 Assistant Detachment Commander
- ODB 310 Company Operations Warrant
- ODA 316 Assistant Detachment Commander, Afghanistan 2002
- ODA 316 Commander
- ODA 311 Assistant Detachment Commander
- ODB 310 Company Operations Warrant, Afghanistan 2003 and again in 2004

CW3 has served in every tactical capacity as an operator in the SOF community. His professionalism, leadership, and technical and tactical competence played a key role as a mentor to the warriors of ODA 316.

CW3 Chief retired from Special Forces in 2007 and is now working with LTC (P).

I can never thank you enough for all you have done for me and all OUR brothers, Chief, but I will spend the rest of my life trying. I love you with all my heart.

CW2 Shawn

CW2 Shawn was formally SFC Shawn on ODA 316.

- 18 Delta on ODA 316 in Gereshk, Afghanistan in 2004
- Promoted to Warrant Officer in 2005.
- Re-joined ODA 316 in September 2005 in Deh Afghan, Afghanistan
- 180A on ODA 316 in Deh Afghan, Afghanistan in 2006
- 180A on ODA 316 in Afghanistan in 2007
- 180A on ODA 3116 preparing to leave for Afghanistan in early 2009

Cato hnake, kola!!!

WO1 Markus

WO1 Markus was SFC Markus on ODA 316 when Chris first arrived in Gereshk, Afghanistan in 2004

- 18 Delta on ODA 316 in Asadabad, Afghanistan in 2003
- 18 Delta on ODA 316 in Gereshk, Afghanistan in 2004
- Promoted to Warrant Officer in 2005
- Special Assignment 2006
- Special Assignment 2007

In January 2008 WO1 Markus was diagnosed with Multiple Myeloma; an enemy that none of us saw coming. He attacked this foe with the same force and lethality that he uses against the enemies of our country!!! He battled and beat that enemy in just one short year and is now cleared for redeployment. WO1 Markus will return to the battlefield in March 2009.

I love you, Markus, with all my heart, and will for the rest of my life.

CSM Buzzsaw

CSM Buzzsaw was the Battalion Sergeant Major when Chris arrived on ODA 316.

- 18 Bravo during Desert Storm in 1990
- Instructor in SWC (A) 1991-1994
- ODA Team Sergeant A/3/3 SFG (A) 1995-1998
- 1SG NCO Academy 1999-2000
- Civil Affairs Team Sergeant 2000-2001
- United States Army Sergeants Major Academy
- G-3 NCOIC SF Command 2002-2003
- Sergeant Major of A Company, 1st Battalion, 3rd SFG (A) in 2003 to 2006
- Command Sergeant Major of 2nd Battalion, 3rd SFG(A) from 2006 to 2008
- Command Sergeant Major of 95th Civil Affairs Battalion 2008 to present

CSM Buzzsaw was awarded the Bronze Star with V for his heroism during Operation Desert Storm.

CSM Buzzsaw has been awarded 3 Bronze Stars.

CSM Buzzsaw has been awarded 7 Meritorious Service Medals.

Even though you are a "Chefs" fan, you did more for Chris, and more for me, than you can ever possibly know. I love you, my brother!

SGM Big Ron

SGM Big Ron was the team sergeant 18Z on ODA 316 when Chris arrived in Gereshk in 2004.

- Team SGT on ODA 316 June 2003 - July 2004
- 1SG C-2-3-SWTG July 2004-Aug 2006
- SGM Academy Class 57 Aug 2006-May 2007
- Promoted to Sergeant Major Mar 01, 2007
- SGM for "Chaos" Company, 2nd Battalion, 3rd SFG(A) in Afghanistan 2007-2008
- S3 SGM for 3rd SFG (A) 2008 to present, preparing to return to Afghanistan in Jan 2009

SGM Big Ron has been awarded 3 Bronze Stars for his heroism.

I love you, Big Ron, as Chris did! Your smile will always be in my heart.

MSG Big Al

MSG Big Al was SFC Big Al when Chris arrived in Gereshk in 2004.

- 18 Fox on ODA 316 in Gereshk, Afghanistan in 2004
- 18 Zulu on ODA 316 in Deh Afghan, Afghanistan in 2005
- 18 Zulu on ODA 316 in Deh Afghan, Afghanistan in 2006
- First Sergeant of the SWC Language School 2007 to 2008.
- Retired from Special Forces in 2008

MSG Big Al was nominated for the Silver Star for his heroism, bravery, and professionalism during the Battle of Mari Ghar, 7-9 August 2005, but withdrew his nomination so his brothers would have a better opportunity to receive their awards.

Thank you, my brother, for bringing our brothers home. I will never forget what you did, and I will love you forever!

MSG Tony

MSG Tony was SFC Tony when Chris got to Gereshk in 2004.

- One of the original members of ODA 316 as the 18 Charlie
- 18 Charlie on ODA 316 in Asadabad, Afghanistan in 2003
- 18 Charlie on ODA 316 in Gereshk, Afghanistan in 2004
- 18 Charlie on ODA 316 in Deh Afghan, Afghanistan in 2005
- 18 Charlie on ODA 316 in Deh Afghan, Afghanistan in 2006
- 18 Charlie on Special Assignment in Baghdad, Iraq in 2007
- 18 Zulu team sergeant for an ODA in 2nd Battalion of 3rd SFG(A) 2008 to present and went back to Afghanistan in early 2009

MSG Tony has been nominated for the Distinguished Service Cross—the second highest medal for valor—for his bravery, heroism and professionalism during the Battle of Mari Ghar 7-9 August 2005. We are still waiting for MSG Tony to be recognized, but we know what OUR brother did during those battles.

MSG Tony received ODA 316's first Purple Heart. He also won an ARCOM with "V" device for actions taken that same day in the Pesch Valley in Afghanistan.

MSG Tony brought my son home to me, but he has given me so much more, just as he did for his little brother, Chris. His son has my son's name now, and I will love you and your children as no others!

MSG Chuck

MSG Chuck was SFC Chuck when Chris first arrived in Gereshk in 2004.

- One of the original members of ODA 316 as the 18 Echo
- 18 Echo on ODA 316 in Asadabad, Afghanistan in 2003
- 18 Echo on ODA 316 in Gereshk, Afghanistan in 2004
- 18 Fox on ODA 316 in Deh Afghan, Afghanistan in 2005
- 18 Fox on ODA 316 in Deh Afghan, Afghanistan in 2006

MSG Chuck retired from Special Forces in 2008.

MSG Chuck was nominated for the Silver Star for his bravery, heroism and professionalism during the Battle of Mari Ghar, 7-9 August 2005, but like MSG Big Al, Chuck requested that his nomination be withdrawn so his brothers could receive the awards they were nominated for.

MSG Chuck won an ARCOM with "V" while fighting with ODA 316 in the Pesch Valley in Afghanistan.

I will never be able to thank you, my brother, for what you did for Chris, but I will spend the rest of my life trying. I love you with all my heart!

SSG "JT"

SSG "JT" is a member of 19th Special Forces Group (Airborne) which is one of the two Army National Guard Special Forces units. SSG "JT" was attached to ODA 316 when Chris arrived in Gereshk in 2004.

- 18 Delta with ODA 316 in Asadabad, Afghanistan in 2003.
- 18 Delta on ODA 316 in Gereshk, Afghanistan in 2004
- 18 Delta on ODA 316 in Deh Afghan after the Battle of Mari Ghar—deployed in September 2005
- SSG "JT" is still a member of 19th SFG (A).

My brother—your actions speak louder than words can possibly express. Thank you for loving both my sons as I do. I will love you for the rest of time!

These are the men that legends are made of. These are the men that keep us safe and secure at home. These are the men that have done things and continue to do things that no one would believe, but we KNOW what they have done together.

They make Special Forces truly SPECIAL, and I can never thank them enough for EVERYTHING they did for Chris. You took him in, helped him grow into the warrior he became, and you loved him as I do.

You are ALL my heroes.

You are ALL my brothers…and I will love you all with ALL I am for the rest of my life!

Preface

There is a choice you have to make, in everything you do. And, you must always keep in mind the choice you make, makes you.

—Anonymous

This book was almost never written. Chris' best friend and our next-door neighbor, SSgt Matthew Sagahun, was coming home on leave on 9 August 2005. He called home from an airport somewhere between Camp LeJune and Denver and his younger brother Thomas told Matt what happened to Chris. Matt initially told Thomas that was NOT a joke, because in Matt's mind, nothing like this could ever have happened to Chris. I will never forget sitting on my front porch and the look on Matt's face as he got out of the car and ran to me that fateful night. We sat there alone for several hours—laughing, crying and trying to come to grips with the reality that OUR Chris was never coming home again.

My younger son, Tim and I had to leave the next morning for Honolulu to get his things out of his apartment and moved into another. So Matt told me not to worry, that he would handle everything while I was gone, and he did, like the warrior he is. One of my biggest concerns about leaving home right then was the media onslaught that I knew would be coming. So, I talked to Matt about it, and we agreed that we would not talk to ANY reporters, and Matt would handle any and all that came to the house while I was gone.

While I was flying that next day, for some reason I started writing down memories of Chris. I am not exactly sure why, maybe it was for the Memorials, maybe it was for the "Boys" of ODA 316, maybe it was just for me so I would not forget all the wonderful, funny and tremendous things that I had experienced with my son, because my head was spinning in complete and utter disbelief that he was gone. But, being at 33,000 feet, I felt so close to Chris, and the thoughts just poured onto the paper along with my tears. When we arrived in Hawai'i, I called home right away and talked to Matt. He told me about the media circus outside our homes and that he had been thinking that maybe we

SHOULD talk to the media, and tell the world about Chris. It was then I knew why I had been so compelled to write down all those memories.

So, The Making of OUR Warrior was started on 10 August 2005. It has been "written" in so many, many places: from the seat of my stationary cycle ergometer in the weight room of my basement; from the greens and fairways of Fox Hollow Golf Course in Lakewood, Colorado; from 30,000 plus feet on airlines literally flying all over the world, from the ski slopes of Colorado, from the homes of his teammates at Fort Bragg in Fayetteville, North Carolina and from the battlefields of the Global War on Terror in Afghanistan and Iraq. This is OUR story about OUR warrior, OUR hero, and OUR brother and son. Chris touched so many people's lives while he was here with us, so it stands to reason that his story, this story, will touch that many more.

I have done many things in my life. But I have never done anything like OUR book. I have gone through every emotion you can imagine, and many that I never knew even existed. It has been a journey like no other I have ever taken. While I miss Chris more than I can possibly express, my life is so much better and full of love because of what Chris meant to so many people, and now what those amazing people, my family, mean to me.

This book is something I NEVER wanted to have to do, but it is something that MUST be done.

Writing this has been the hardest thing I have ever done, but it is probably my best work.

This is the story of a father's love and a son's life…the story of my warrior, my hero, my son!

1

Getting Ready

The eagle gently coaxed his offspring toward the edge of the nest. His heart quivered with confusing emotions as he felt their resistance to his persistent nudging.

"Why does the thrill of soaring have to begin with the fear of falling?" he thought.

This ageless question was still unanswered for him. As in the tradition of the species, his nest was located high on the shelf of a sheer rock face, hundreds of feet from the dangerous rocks below. Below there was nothing but air to support the wings of each child.

"Is it possible that this time it will not work?" he thought. Despite his fears, the eagle knew it was the time. His parental mission was all but complete. There was one final task...THE PUSH!

The eagle drew courage from an innate wisdom. Until his children discovered their wings, there was no purpose for their lives. Until they learned to soar, they would fail to understand the privilege it was to be born an eagle. The push was the greatest gift he had to offer. It was his supreme act of love. And so, one by one, I push each of you—here—today!

—Unknown Author

This is the story of my warrior, my hero, my son. He was Staff Sergeant Christopher Matthew Falkel. Chris was a member of Alpha Company,

1st Battalion, 3rd Special Forces Group (Airborne) on Operational Detachment Alpha (ODA) 316, who was killed in action on 8 August 2005 during a 54 hour gun battle in Mari Ghar, Afghanistan, as part of the United States Military's Global War on Terrorism (GWOT). And while he was only 22 when he died, he lived his life preparing to become the soldier, the warrior and the hero he became.

Chris started his journey to become a Special Forces Warrior on 24 September 1982. At 1831 (6:31 PM) local time in Boston MA, Chris was born. However, while most babies are born screaming and kicking, Chris didn't make a sound! As soon as he was born, he opened his eyes and looked all over the delivery room—his first recon mission! In fact, he didn't cry, even once, for the first few days of his amazing life!

Chris was always observant and not much escaped his view. When we would bring him to the store, people would always come up to him and tell us, "What big eyes he has," and my response was always "Yes, he DOES have big thighs!" But his eyes always told what he thought, what he felt and what he was up to. From the time he could talk, he could never fool "the old man," mostly because I had more than likely done what he was about to attempt, and paid the price for it. One of the phrases Chris used to say to me, probably only second in number to "I love you, Dad," was … "I hate it when you are RIGHT, Dad!!!" And, it was your eyes that always gave you away, my son!!!

Chris learned to walk when he was nine month old. He learned to climb about a day after that!!! And once he learned to run, there was no stopping him! He was one of the happiest babies I have ever known. His first word was "broccoli" (???), even though it wasn't until he got to Ft. Bragg that he liked eating it again. We lived in the Boston area until Chris was two, and then moved to Athens, Ohio where our youngest son, Tim, was born 20 May 1985.

Chris was a great big brother! In fact, Tim didn't learn to walk until he was almost 14 months old because he had Chris to run and get him WHATEVER he wanted! Our house in Ohio was out on an old farm, and we had a huge front and back yard, and even bigger empty lot next to us. There were not a lot of kids Chris' and Tim's age in the neighborhood, so they mostly played with each other, but also learned how to play by themselves—again, a skill Chris would need in the future for his profession as a Special Forces warrior.

The field next door became the boys "battleground." They would dig "foxholes," set up "ambushes" and use the natural grasses for "cover." One of my hobbies is woodworking, and every once in a while, I would go to the shop to make something, and one of my tools would be missing. I am rather "particular" about my tools, and the first time this happened, I got rather upset. Well, Chris could hear me yelling all the way out in our back yard, and so he came running into the shop and asked what I was looking for. As I recall, it was just a chisel, but Chris was off like a shot out into the field and in a couple of minutes he came back with my chisel! He told me that he had put it out in the field "as a weapon in case we would be under attack"—he was about 4 or 5 at the time—and as soon as I was done with the chisel, could he have it back so he could put his "weapon" where it belonged!?!?!

What do I say to that? My first question to him was where there any OTHER "weapons" he had out in the battleground? Of course, his answer was an empathic "NO!", but yet, every time I went to the shop and couldn't find a tool, Chris knew RIGHT where it was out in the field! One of the first things that MSG Tony, Chris' brother that brought him home to me after he crossed over, told me was that when Tony was gathering Chris' personal items to bring to me, he found an entire case of grenades under his bunk in Deh Afghan (...which, of course, were "disposed" of properly!). When Tim and I were packing up Chris' apartment, we found hundreds of different rounds in every possible drawer, cabinet, etc.—even in the bathroom medicine cabinet!

Chris developed his love for the outdoors and for nature while we were in Ohio. At the end of the road in front of our house was a forest, or "woods" as they say at Ft. Bragg—that always used to make Chris laugh when people called the forest—"woods"! We would go for hikes, looking for some particular tree, or animal, and just enjoying being outside and part of nature. Once we moved to Colorado in 1989, our love for the outdoors became even more a part of Chris and my time together. But I have so many fond memories of Chris and I, and many times, Chris, Tim and I playing in the "battleground" and the forest in Athens, Ohio.

Chris and Tim also learned about strength and conditioning while we were in Ohio. We had a strength and conditioning lab at the university where I worked—it was REALLY a weight room, but by calling it a "Lab" we got more money to buy more "toys" for the weight room. Every Saturday, the two other men I lifted with used to bring their kids to the weight room. It was just a great time bonding and interacting with the kids while we pushed the plates! Next to the leg press machine we had a sign on the wall that was the quote from Nietzsche—"That which does not kill us makes us stronger." Well, one day when Chris was just learning to read, I was on the leg press with a VERY heavy load when Chris read the sign out loud for the first time. Dan, my friend and lifting partner, asked Chris what he thought that saying meant. After a couple of seconds of deep concentration and thought, Chris told Dan—"Well, if we do leg presses, and we get stronger, then the witch won't kill us!" And, with that, what ever load I was lifting came crashing down on my chest because I was laughing so hard!!! But, Chris and Tim started their love of exercise and strength training back in our "lab" in Ohio, and it was something that carried both of my boys on to becoming the professionals they became.

Another aspect of Chris' conditioning was when he started playing soccer in Ohio. Chris really wanted to play, even as a very young boy, and that was fine with me. I had played soccer most of my life, and I knew what a great game it was for kids. However, in the mid 1980's, American soccer had not learned the value of small-sided games where the field is smaller for the younger players, and there are less players on each team so that EACH player gets more touches on the ball. So, Chris' first experience in soccer as a 6 year old was playing 11 players on a side on a full size soccer pitch or field! It involved LOTS of running and not a lot of soccer!!! But he loved it, and he was very good at it. When we got to Colorado, one of the first things we did was find a team for Chris to play on. It was late in the summer, and most of the teams had full rosters, but there was one coach that made room for Chris. I asked if I could help coach, and they were grateful for my volunteering. I can remember vividly that Chris didn't like being a substitute, and not getting to play all the time. One of our defenders got hurt, and so Chris asked to be a defender. He was an incredibly physical player, even as a young boy.

There are two memories of Chris and soccer that I will treasure forever: The first was the championship game our first season out in Colorado. Chris was only 7 years old, and again, we were playing with 11 boys on each team on a full size soccer field. The weather in late October/early November in Colorado can be magnificent or brutal, and on this particular Saturday, it was miserable! We played that game in a cold, freezing rain—a cross between sleet and snow, and a wind that would almost knock the boys over. We were dominating the other team, and as such, got little or NO action down in our defensive end of the field. While most of the other boys were BEGGING to come off the field, Chris stood there, shivering like no one I have ever seen before, but not complaining, and there was NO WAY he was coming out of the game! I remember trying to get him warm after the game with towels, blankets, and the heater in the car on full blast, but he never once complained about being cold, and he was so happy to have won the championship!

Just to show how tough Chris was as a player, and how much he loved the game—late on a Sunday evening when Chris was 11, he came downstairs from his room complaining about a pain in his abdomen. If Chris was complaining, it must be something, and my diagnosis was an acute appendicitis—and as Chris would say, "I hate it when you are right Dad!" So, that evening he had an emergency appendectomy. The next Saturday, I could not keep him out of the game!!!

My other memory of Chris and soccer in those early days was driving to an early game, and Chris realizing that he had left one of his boots (soccer shoes) at home. I wasn't too happy with him as we turned around and raced back home. I had him stay in the truck and put the rest of his gear on while I ran in and got his shoe. I was very surprised to see that on all of the adidas stripes on his boots, there were black and red hash marks. So, as soon as I got back in the truck, I asked Chris what all those hash marks were. I will never forget the look in his eyes and the devilish smile on face when he told me, "Those are the guys I have taken out tackling the ball, Dad—and the red ones are for the guys that went flying through the air!" Yes, Chris was responsible for more frequent flyer miles than I have with all my international travel, as it related to other players flying through the air when Chris tackled them (tackling in soccer is getting the ball away from an opponent). I still laugh to this day every time I think of that! In fact, at his Memorial in Littleton, one of his teammates from youth soccer all the way through high school soccer told my wife and I that he HATED when he had to go up against Chris in a soccer drill because he KNEW that Chris was going to go as hard as possible, EVERY TIME, and that it was going to hurt!!!

But even as hard as he played the game, he NEVER even once received a yellow card from the referee for a foul—something I can not say I was able to do in my soccer career! He was a clean player, but very, VERY physical. I loved watching Chris and Tim play. They would KILL each other in the backyard, and part of the reason Tim was such a great soccer player was because he learned to play going up against Chris! Chris showed him NO MERCY even though Tim was 2 years younger, and it made Tim a much better player!

Chris also showed me that he was a "man" of principle and integrity at a very early age through his soccer experience. The first team that he was on in Colorado was a recreational team, and when the boys became old enough for competitive soccer—where there are various levels based on skill—the coach that I had been working with became the coach of the first team, and he asked me to be his assistant coach. That was an honor and I had learned a great deal about coaching from him, so I said yes. But during the try-outs, this particular coach did not think Chris was ready to play on the first team. While I disagreed, I knew that Chris would not get to play much if this particular coach did not think he was capable of playing at that level. I talked to Chris about it, telling him that I would go coach what ever team he was on. He told me that he wanted me to stay with the first team coach, and that we wanted someone else coaching him, at least for a while. I had to respect his request, and so for the next couple of seasons, Chris was on the second or third level team, and I helped coach the first team. It was hard for me to not coach and be with Chris, but he was insistent that he wanted to be on the other team. So, instead of having soccer together, which I did with Tim as the head coach of his team, Chris and I started working on other things so we could spend time together.

It wasn't until I was driving back to Ft. Bragg with Chris on our last "road trip" together over Christmas leave in 2004 that I learned why he didn't want to play on the first team. The head coach's son was also on both the recreational team we were first on and then on the first team, and Chris did not like the way the head coach treated either his son, or me during practice and games. Chris did not want to be around him, but he knew that I would learn a lot by coaching with him that I could pass onto Tim's team. Once again, my son, you saw things that I never looked for—not bad for a 10 year old!!!

When we got to Colorado, we moved to Littleton, and the town literally ended about 3 kilometers (1.8 miles) from our house. That is where Chris' education about tracking, stalking and land navigation skills really started to develop. Because we all had soccer practice during the afternoon, Chris and I would head out at night to work on his skills. Night operations are a hallmark of Special Forces, and by the time Chris was 8 years old, he knew that he wanted to become a Special Forces warrior. In fact, he stuck a "Long Tab" (Special Forces patch) and "Arrowhead" (Special Forces Unit patch) on the wall over his bed. They are still there today and will be as long as I live in our house! He used to tell me that every night when he got into bed, he thought about being in Special Forces, and about what he could do the next day to be even more prepared for his eventual job!

That is the dedication that is so desperately needed in SF and I am so VERY grateful that Chris found a team of equally dedicated and focused brothers on ODA 316!!!

So, several nights a week, most weeks, we would "sneak" out at night after everyone else was asleep and head down to the open space at the end of the main road in town. I had pretty significant arthritis in my knees back then, and it was difficult for me to sleep. Therefore, I would wake up after only about an hour or two of sleep, and do my writing, etc. When Chris found out that I didn't sleep, he asked me to wake him up so we could go "train." Most parents have found memories of tucking the children into bed at night, and I do have many memories of doing that with Tim. But my fondest memories were of waking Chris up, and the look of absolute joy and excitement that he was getting to do something with me that NO ONE else was able to do! There were several times that we took Tim along on our "night ops" (operations), but most of the time, it was a special, a very special time for Chris and me together.

Thank you, my son—I will never forget those amazing nights with you!!! Some of the BEST days of my life were my nights "training" with you!

However, there was one night that Chris did NOT enjoy having me wake him up…I had gotten up early to work on an article, but when I turned on the computer, there was a message that a password was required, and I was unable to get into my program! It wasn't like that 6 hours earlier, and the ONLY other person in the house that used the computer at that time was Chris. So, I went up to his room and barely touched his shoulder. I no sooner touched him and he shot out of his bed and literally "flew" down the stairs! When I got to the computer, he was so apologetic! "I'm sorry Dad; I put that password on the computer so Tim couldn't get on and play a computer game!!!" Chris ALWAYS had more computer expertise than I did—something he reminded me of even on our last phone call together!!!

We would track antelope and other animals that roamed in the open space. We would work on "cover and concealment" to try and get as close as we could to the animals, and to avoid the local law enforcement! We worked on land navigation skills and map reading. We worked with and without a compass, using the stars in the Colorado sky as par of our land navigation "FTX" (field training exercise). We worked on developing sleep deprivation tolerance, but most of all, we just had FUN being together!!! Again, I never really knew how much it meant to Chris until our last road trip back to Ft. Bragg when we talked about it most of the way through Missouri!!!

There was another thing I learned on our last road trip together that makes my heart smile even today. There was some construction on the interstate, and we decided to get off the highway so we could continue pressing east. I was driving and so Chris took the map, flipped it around 'upside-down' and look for a new route. I asked Chris why he flipped the map around, and he told me, "Well that is how you do it, and if YOU don't get lost…" That was my Chris!!!

Throughout this book, I will share with you and the world much of the relationship, the time, the memories and the love that Chris and I had. But there are certain things and stories I will keep to myself, and much of that road trip and the conversations we had, I hold in my heart just for me. I have never shared some our talks during those 26 hours of driving with anyone, and I never will. It was one of, if not the, most special times we ever had together, and for those memories and for all your love then and NOW, I am forever grateful and love you more than you can possibly know, my son!!!

The other thing I will not share are my dreams about Chris. I don't sleep very much, and I rarely remember dreaming when I wake up. But since Chris crossed over to be with the Spartans, the Lakota, and the other warriors he is now making laugh with his antics, I have had many dreams about Chris. Some of them are so real, I wake up and look for him in the room. But, those dreams are mine, and mine alone—I only wish they would come true. Chris used to love to surprise every one and any one! And even three years later, there are some days that I expect him to sneak up behind me and surprise his old Dad.

I have done a lot of things in my life. I have survived even more. I have experienced pain that few people ever have or can even begin to understand. I have done things I never talk about, and done things that make my heart swell with pride. But the most difficult and most painful thing I have ever done or will ever do, is living the rest of my life without you, my son! I miss you more every day, and that is something I did not think was humanly possible. As I said at the first Memorial service we had for Chris in Littleton, Colorado, there is a hole in my heart that will never heal.

However being part of Chris' 316 family has done more to fill that hole than can possibly be described, and that is one of the reasons we are writing OUR book about Chris. It is OUR story because Chris was who he was and BECAME because of the men, the warriors, the brothers that made not only his life "special," but who put the SPECIAL in Special Forces. It is the ODA 316 family that have written this book and shared Chris' life with me. There have been times as I have written OUR book that I couldn't even see the computer screen for the tears in my eyes and the pain my heart. And just sitting down to write OUR book was like getting hit by a truck—I actually know what that feels like!!! But, after I got the words on the page, the healing actually started. This has been the hardest thing I have ever done, and it is my best work. When they say this is a "labor of love," they have no idea!?!?!

So this is OUR story—the story of a Special Forces hero, a Special Forces Warrior, a Special Forces brother, and the story of my son.

2

What Made Chris—Chris!

Eagles don't flock. You have to find them one at a time!

—H. Ross Perot

As I have told OUR family, even though we miss Chris more than anyone else, we are really the LUCKY ones—because we have such wonderful memories of what made Chris—CHRIS! Here are some stories that will give a better insight into who we loved, who we miss, and who Chris was and is to us…

When Chris was old enough to learn to ride a bicycle, we lived on a road that was not conducive for bicycle riding, so I would take him to the local elementary school and he would practice in the parking lot. We did the stability progression of two training wheels, to one, to one barely touching, and eventually no training wheels at all. Finally Chris was ready to go solo, so we got up at the high end of the parking lot, I gave him a running start and he was off. He started pedaling, and started gaining confidence. As he got toward the end of the parking lot, he turned to look to see if I was looking. He had the "Classic Chris smile" going from ear to ear! But, while he was looking at me, he failed to see the light pole directly in front of him until he got to meet it "up close and personal!" He bounced off the pole, got up, started laughing even more, and told me, "Let's do that again, Dad!" I had to convince him that while crashing might be fun, it wasn't fun for his little bicycle, so we tried to avoid the light poles in the future!

I can only remember one time when Chris was REALLY mad at me! Chris, Tim and I were skiing up at Keystone ski area in Colorado. The boys were probably 9 and 7, respectively, and they loved going off the side of one of the trails and skiing along amongst the trees. Well, Tim had gone off to the right, and I told Chris we would ski to the left, go down this little section, and we should be able to cut through right in front of Tim. He thought that would be AWESOME, so we took off as Tim went through the trees. Well, Tim skied a little faster than I had calculated and as I was heading up the slight incline to cut Tim off , I quickly realized that I was going to run right into Tim—so, I jumped over Tim as he skied underneath my skis! Well, Chris thought was about the coolest thing he had ever seen up to that point in his young life, so he wanted me to do that to him! When I told him "NO!" because it was so dangerous and I almost killed his little brother, that wasn't a sufficient reason for NOT doing it to him! He was so mad at me; he didn't talk to me for a couple of days!

When Chris was old enough, he started wearing my BDU's (US Army Battle Dress Uniform) to school. He was the first kid in town that wore old Army uniforms to school, but no one dare tell him that he could not wear them. By the time he was a sophomore, he had the same size foot that I have, so he started wearing my old boots as well. One day, in gym class, the physical education teacher was having the students run a 40 yard sprint for time. So, when it was Chris' turn, he got on the line with 'his' combat boots on, and crushed the competition. The teacher could not believe it, so he had Chris run another sprint against the football star in the school. Beat his socks off as well. The teacher then had the reigning state champion in the 440 yard race 'challenge' Chris, and it only motivated Chris to run the 40 even faster than he did before. The teacher kept trying to convince Chris to run on the track team, but he had more important things to do—like getting ready to go into the Army!

Chris had a movie line for every and ANY situation. But, he not only knew the line, but he could practically imitate the voice, inflection, and timing of the movie line. And, I can't tell you the number of times in the past 3 years that one of Chris' brothers has commented to me that Chris would have used a particular movie line in a certain situation. It always makes me smile to think about that, and we all laugh at Chris making us laugh even still!

When we moved to Colorado, we used to have an Easter egg hunt around our house for Chris and Tim. If the weather was bad as it can be in the spring, we would have the hunt inside the house. But, if the weather was good, I would hide the eggs all over our yard. Well, the first time we hide the eggs, Chris found about 90% of them, and poor Tim only got about 10 percent! So the next year, we put a "C" or a "T" on each plastic egg so Tim was not at a tactical disadvantage! But, after a couple of years, Chris got bored with that scenario, so I let Chris hide the eggs! He loved that, and he was very good at it. How good was he? In the summer of 2005, we had the house sided. During the course of removing the old siding, we found four eggs that Chris had hidden over eight years earlier!!!

Over the past three years, I have done a tremendous amount of traveling, mostly via aircraft. Normally, whenever I fly, for what ever reason, I sleep on the aircraft, and actually get some great rest. But, since Chris left us, when ever I fly, I have found a closeness to Chris that I have never experienced before. It is also a time when I seem to miss him the most. I miss his laugh. I remember some goofy thing he used to do. I think about the places we used to talk about visiting together, and now I have to go there by myself. I have spent the majority of most flights writing notes about Chris, laughing to my self, and normally at some point in the flight, crying almost uncontrollably. But the feelings I experience on those 'birds' and the memories I cherish, have helped me heal like nothing else I have ever done.

Chris used to get so mad at me because I would not let him have a toy gun—not even a squirt gun. I would tell him, from the first time he asked for one at the toy store, that guns were NOT toys, and that when he was old enough to respect a weapon and to use it and take care of it properly, I would buy him as many weapons as he wanted. So, when he was about 12, I gave him a pistol BB gun. We set up a "range" in the basement, and we learned to shoot. Right handed, left handed, one eye, both eyes, even eyes closed as long as Tim was not around! Even today, there are still BB's on the floor in the weight room at the house. When I see them, it brings back so many amazing memories. Chris' next weapon was a .22 caliber rifle. For his high school graduation present, I gave Chris a sniper rifle. In fact, true to my promise, I bought Chris every one of the weapons in his "arsenal!"

And, I will NEVER forget the conversation we had after Chris finished Robin Sage, and received his Yarborough knife and his Green Beret! The first part of the conversation was about being assigned to 3rd Special Forces Group (Airborne). Chris wanted to be assigned to 10th SFG (A), which is stationed in Colorado Springs, Colorado and their 1st BN is located in Germany—some place Chris always wanted to be!!! Chris was told that if he could find another 18 Bravo that wanted to change assignments, he could swap groups. There were three 18 Bravos that received assignments to 10th SFG (A), who HATED the snow, so Chris thought for sure he could swap with them. But, they told Chris that as much as they hated snow, they liked Fayetteville even less, so they would not swap with him. He was so mad!

That is the first time I told him that he was DESTINED to be in 3rd SFG (A)! The colors of the 3rd SFG (A) flash, or group insignia, are yellow, red, white and black. Yellow is for 1st SFG (A), Red is for 7th SFG (A), Black is for 5th SFG (A) and White is for Special Warfare Training Group (A). But these four colors are also the four colors of the Lakota—the Native American nation of our ancestors! 3rd SFG (A) was EXACTLY where Chris belonged! I had seen in a vision when he was in SFAS—Special Forces Assessment and Selection—that Chris had a Green Beret on with the 3rd SFG (A) flash, and when I told him that, it changed his facial expression dramatically. Chris knew of many of my visions, and he understood their meaning. As it turned out, 3rd SFG (A) was indeed the place for Chris; for he would never had been a member of ODA 316 if he had been able to swap for the assignment to 10th SFG (A)!!!

We then talked about another reason that Chris was destined to become SF—on the unit patch, there are three lightning bolts over a fighting knife. The three lightning bolts represent the rapid infiltration by either land, sea or air that SF warriors can use to complete their mission. Chris had 3 experiences with lightning over the course of his life. The first was when he was about 10 months old. We were playing out side of our house in Hopkinton, MA when a storm moved in and without any warning, a lightning bolt hit a tree on the edge of our property! The hair on both of our head's stood up on end! The second was when he was in elementary school and Chris went to a 3 day outdoor learning class up in the foothills of the Rocky Mountains. Chris and his teacher wanted to climb to the top of a 13,000 foot peak, but as they got to within several hundred feet of the summit, a thunderstorm moved in. This is a very common occurrence in Colorado, and you need to respect "Mother Nature," particularly when it comes to lightning. Well, the students were so close to reaching the summit, they decided if they RAN up to the top and then RAN back down, they would be "OK"—NOT! Chris again had his hair stand up, and this time he told me he actually felt the electricity go through his feet! The third time was when Chris was in high school, and I was conducting a goal keeper clinic. Chris and Tim would come to my clinics and take shots at the keepers. It was a beautiful day, not a cloud in the sky, but there is a meteorological phenomena called "blue sky lightning" where a lighting bolt can come basically out of nowhere. We had one of those hit the far end of the field! Three lightning bolts...

The most amazing lightning storm I have ever seen was the night of 10 August 2005 when Tim and I arrived in Hawai'i to move him out of his apartment. We stayed up on the North Shore with some of our relatives, and we stayed up late that night talking about Chris. As the evening progressed, a thunderstorm rolled in off the North Shore of Oahu and it lasted for almost 3 hours! It was the most amazing lightning "show" I have ever seen! All I could think of was Chris letting me know he was not only "OK", but he was already test-firing the weaponry in his new firebase!!! I will never forget that storm.

After we talked about his new Group, Chris turned and looked at me and said, "Well, I made it as a weapons sergeant—not BAD for someone YOU never let have a toy gun!!!" I sat there in his car, looked him straight in the eye, and smiled. We had an amazing way of communicating with each other without saying a word at times, and THIS was one of those times! He looked at me and said, "What...," but I just sat there and smiled. After about two or 3 minutes, he got this look on his face, and I heard the words I had heard Chris say so many, MANY times before..."I HATE it when you are right, Dad!!! NOW I get it—the 'guns are not toys' thing! I HATE it when you are right!!!"

He had that pissed off look on his face, but his eyes told me he truly DID get it, and then we both laughed and gave each other a hug! It was an incredible moment in both of our lives. I then gave him his graduation presents: (1) a Falkel tradition 'paper gift' of money for his .45 caliber pistol, and (2) a necklace that my dad had given to me, and I was now giving it to my son! When MSG Tony brought Chris back to me, one of the personal items he handed me was that necklace. I will never forget the look on Tony's face when I told him to give the necklace to Tim.

There has always been a special form of "comms" (communication) between Chris and me. There were at least five times that when he would call me, we were watching the same DVD! (There were also two separate times that Chris and Tim bought the exact same style of running shoe without the other knowing!!!) We would use hand signals to communicate with each other while we were skiing. Chris was always there, by my side, when the arthritis in my knees was so bad that I could barely walk. He would just show up at the hospital after one of my many surgeries, even though I had told the family I didn't want any visitors. We had so many amazing conversations over all the years! Chris always thought it was such a "treat" for me to wake him up so we could go "train," and we would have such great talks. I remember one conversation we had while we were laying by the side of the road in the middle of Utah on our way to a soccer tournament, watching the meteor shower, and all the millions and millions of stars. I remember one conversation when Chris wanted to quit his little league baseball team because he made a couple of errors in one game, but that how he had made a commitment to his team, and he had to finish the job. I remember our conversations at the local high school track while Chris ran and I rode my bicycle along side to help him with his pacing for the 2-mile timed run component of the Army Physical Fitness Test. I remember Chris calling me from the middle of Kansas on his On-Star feature of his truck because he was in a blizzard, but didn't want to stop—so we talked for almost 6 hours to keep him company and awake on his last trip home. I remember talking about what his dream car would be—either a 1968 Camaro or a 1969 Chevelle—and what color he would paint it, what size engine, what type of tires, even what kind of steering wheel would look the best!

But there were also times we would "talk" without saying a word! There were so many times in our amazing conversations that we would not say a word to each other, for lengthy periods of time, but we would stay connected on the phone because it was our way of staying linked together. Our hearts had a way of talking to each other without saying a word.

Chris and I had an uncanny sense of knowing what each other needed, what each other was feeling. And we STILL have the ability to "talk" to each other. There have been many, many times over the past 3 years that I needed to talk to Chris, and some how, some way, I was able to hear what he had to say to me, and I knew what needed to be done. Thank you, my son, for loving your old dad as ONLY you could!

One of Chris' other "skills" we worked on was being on time! I have few "pet peeves" but being late is one of them. There was actually a time I left the rest of the family and went to a game without them because I had told them we were leaving at a certain time, and when they were not in the vehicle, and it was time to go, I went!!! Chris and I used to play a game of calculating or predicting what the exact time would be when we would arrive somewhere. I had forgotten about that "game" until the first time I drove back to Fayetteville with Chris. He had figured out that the driver could "hedge the bet" in regards to controlling the time it took to arrive somewhere—so I had to pay for lunch because he predicted when we would arrive on-post!

There is a Falkel family tradition that my dad passed onto me, and I passed onto Chris, and that is the gift of giving. I can remember the joy in my father's eyes watching his kids receive a gift, no matter what the gift was. And the greatest gift I get is the look on the face of the person I have given something to. Well, once Chris had a job, and was making money, he would love to spend his money on someone else, getting them a gift that ONLY Chris would have thought of getting for them. For Chris knew that the gift of happiness is the greatest gift of all!

One of the greatest gifts that Chris ever gave me was during a phone call just before he left for Gereshk in 2004. He called me relatively late at night in Colorado, which was even later on the East Coast, and he asked if I could send him all my "FALKEL" name tags off my old uniforms! As Chris told me, "They are the only ones ever made, so it is just right that I should wear them next!" Thank you, my son for giving me that amazing gift that I will cherish forever!!!

Chris also received some amazing gifts. The gifts of "his kids" and being able to be part of their lives were the greatest gifts he had ever received—just as having those wonderful kids in my life now is my greatest gift. But one gift Chris received from one of my dearest friends, from one of my brothers, occurred after Chris had crossed over. Chris, Tim and I used to love hiking in the Colorado Mountains until my knees got too bad to allow us to hike. And whenever we climbed one of the 54 mountains in Colorado that is over 14,000 feet high (we did a total of eight together), Chris would pick up a rock, write the name and date on the rock, and then keep it for his collection. When MSG Tony brought me Chris' personal items, there were two rocks in his "stuff"—one from Gereshk and one from Deh Afghan.

But, the 14,000 peak we never climbed together was the closest one to our house—Pike's Peak. Every time he came home on leave, we would say we would hike up Pike's Peak, but we were always too busy, or just never got around to it. Well, my brother Bob, whose son SSG Cody was in 10th SFG (A) and whose son SP4 Bobby is in the SFQC right now, went up to the top of Pike's Peak with his dear wife and their youngest son one Sunday in the fall of 2005 before the snow started flying. While Rhoda and Colin were in the gift shop, something compelled Bob to go exploring around the top of the mountain. Bob was looking down over the "fruited plain" when he suddenly stopped, and picked up a particular rock. Something told him he needed to pick up that rock and that he needed to bring that rock with him on his trip to the east coast that next week for a business trip to Washington D.C. After his meeting, he went over to Arlington to see Chris, and again, he had this incredibly powerful feeling that he needed to leave that rock from the top of Pike's Peak on top of Chris headstone. As Bob was waiting for his plane, he called me to tell me what had happened. I listened and told him there would be an email waiting for him when he arrived home. That's when I told Bob about Chris picking up rocks from our hikes up the other "14'ers," and that we never got to climb Pike's Peak.

Chris had that kind of influence on so many people. SSG Cody, in part, became SF because of Chris. Cody was a couple of years younger than Chris, and there were many times that Cody and Chris would come to soccer practice with Bob and me when we trained Tim and Bobby's team. Chris and Cody would always play against the younger kids, and show them no mercy! So, when Chris became SF, it was something Cody wanted to do as well.

Cody was on a HALO—High Altitude Low Opening—team, and that was one thing the Chris was very envious of!!! He always wanted to go to HALO school—he now has his own set of special HALO wings. But, after one training exercise, Cody called me up to tell me about an amazing story that had happened to him. They were in a foreign country, training the special operations soldiers of that country in various military techniques and tactics. Cody was out on the range, and was not shooting particularly well. But, after taking a break, Cody started thinking about Chris. He looked up, and saw what he thought was a falcon or an eagle, as the beautiful bird was quite far away. However, after seeing that bird, Cody started shooting "lights out," making shots he had never made before. Cody told me that he felt Chris there out on the range, and it was like Chris was 'willing' Cody to shoot better!

One of the things that Chris and Tim learned at a very early age was the value of fitness. Tim had amazing skill as a soccer player, but it was his fitness that allowed him to use his skills and abuse his opponents throughout his soccer career. Chris also realized at an early age that fitness was not only important, but that it could be fun! We used to have a ball training together, and Chris had the discipline to train even if I was on a trip. The best example of that was the rule about Game Boy video games. We did not allow video games in the house when the kids were little, but when we moved to Colorado, and we had longer flights to get to the east coast to visit family, I got each of the boys a Game Boy hand-held video game. But, there was a rule—if they wanted to play their video game at home, for every 30 minutes of playing a video game, they needed to give "me" 30 minutes of exercise! Now that was not very hard in that they had two hours of soccer practice 3 or four times per week, and if they were not at practice, they were playing in the back yard, or training with me. Well, one night I came home late from a trip, and everyone was asleep. But as I got into the house, I heard a strange noise coming from the basement. I went down stairs, and Chris was sitting on my stationary cycle, playing his Game Boy while he was riding the cycle! That was Chris!!!

Chris was always telling me that he was going to buy me a vehicle when he could afford it! Well, in 2004, Chris spent WAAAAAY too much money on a new truck! He LOVED his truck! And it had all the stuff I would NEVER have had as accessories on a vehicle—leather seats, seat warmers, fancy CD player, the WORKS—some of which I STILL can't figure out how to use correctly!!! Well, after we got back from Arlington, Tim and I drove Chris' truck back to Colorado. we decided to give Tim my old Tundra, and I would keep Chris' truck for my vehicle—like I said, Chris was always telling me he would get me a vehicle I would have never gotten for my self! To this day, we all still call it "Chris' truck," because that is what it is. It is still registered in both of our names and always will be.

Well, in early 2006 when I was still doing home physical therapy, I had another amazing coincidence with Chris in his truck. Here is the email I sent to OUR family that day:

> Today, 20 January 2006, I was driving to my next to last patient's house. It had snowed yesterday and last night, and some of the roads were still snow-packed and so I was listening to a particular radio station that has the best traffic reports throughout the day. It is a country station and they were playing a Kenny Chesney song, "Who You'd Be Today?" that reminds me of Chris every time I hear it. I happened to look at the clock on the radio, and it was 1:36 PM. Ever since Chris became a member of ODA 316, the numbers 3, 1, and 6 seem to continually appear and be part of my world (i.e.: the last four digits of my cell phone number are 3166!)

> Where the radio is located in Chris' truck is in the blind spot of my right eye, and so I rarely look at the clock on the radio to see what time it is…I usually just look at my watch. The other thing about the radio in Chris' truck is that the name of the song that is playing will scroll across the display just below where the clock is located. Again, I rarely look at this screen because it is in my blind spot, and to look at it and read the title of

the song that is playing, would require me to turn my head and look with my left eye. But, for some reason, at 1:36 while listening to that song, I saw on the screen an amazing thing. There was only one word, and that word was, "Chris." I did a double take and the word "Chris" just stayed there, it didn't move. I immediately pulled off the road and keep looking at the digital display. For the remainder of the song, over 2 minutes, the word "Chris" was displayed. Then, when the song was over, rather than the word "Chris" scrolling off the screen, a new word instantly appeared, and it was "LOVE" with an * next to it. At this point, I don't know what to think or do, except stare at the digital screen to see what will appear next. The word "LOVE*" stayed there through the next song, a Tim McGraw song called, "My Old Friend" that I have shed more than a few tears over, again, because it reminds me of my warrior.

Then, just as fast as it appeared, it was gone, and the title of the next song scrolled across the screen just as it is supposed to.

I have had many visions in my life, and many of them have come true. But sometimes, even I can't explain what happens, and this is one of those times. However, I do know with all my heart, that my son is with me, now and always, and at times, I feel his presence so strongly that it seems like if I turn around fast enough, I will see him there smiling at me with that beautiful smile and laugh of his that would light up a room! While I miss him more every day, I am also so lucky that I have him in my heart and in my soul, and that is what helps me get through days like today.

I wanted to share this with you, my family, because you are all so special to me, and to let you know my son is making sure the "old man" will get through this. And, I

have all of you to thank for that as well. For that, and all
you do for me, I love you all so very much.

Just some of the hundreds of stories I hold in my heart and that
flow through my mind of what made Chris—Chris!

3

Fox Hollow Golf Course

Lessons in life—Lessons for life

I started working at Fox Hollow Golf Course, in Lakewood, Colorado in the summer of 1998. I had a patient whose husband worked there, and he suggested that I might enjoy it. He mowed fairways every morning, and even though I did not play golf, the thought of getting out on a fairway mower every morning, watching the sun rise, and just being out in nature was very appealing to me. So, I applied for a part time—"mow and go" job, where I would come in, mow what ever they wanted me to mow, and then head to "work."

The Assistant Superintendent at the time was Mr. Mark Krick. He started me mowing greens with a walk behind mower, because, as he put it to me, the most important thing for golfers to have mowed is the greens. The mowers we use are Toro 1000 Greens Mowers, and while there is a drive mechanism, you still have to walk back and forth to mow the green. At the time, the arthritis in my knees was pretty bad; in fact, I had a hard time even getting up from a chair! I pretty much had to stop all other exercise that I normally would be doing such as lifting weights, in-line skating, playing soccer and skiing with Chris and Tim, because my knees wouldn't let me.

Well, after mowing four greens that first day, and walking about a mile per green, I could barely get out of bed the next morning! But I had made a commitment to Mark and Fox Hollow, so I went into work the next day, planning on telling Mark that mowing greens just wasn't going to work for me. I never got the chance to tell him that because I no sooner got to the shop and he helped me load my greens mower on a trailer, took me out to the Meadow greens, and left me there. Again, as much as I enjoyed the beauty of Fox Hollow, the walking was killing me. But the next day, I was not nearly as sore. And the next day was better yet.

Now, you couldn't pay me to mow anything EXCEPT greens! Sure, I know how to mow fairways, tees, step-cut and some of the rough, but I love mowing greens most of all! Every day that I am home in the spring, summer and fall, I head out to the golf course to mow, and most days, I am mowing greens.

One of the main reasons many of the "mow and go" guys are out at Fox Hollow is for the "golf benefits," as they get to play golf several times per week without having to pay for it. I had never played golf before I started working there—golf is a sport that takes a long time to learn to play, particularly if you want to play well. But it takes even longer to play a round, and I didn't want to take that time away from Chris and Tim, so I never played. But by 1998, Chris was 16 and Tim was 13, and they wanted to learn to play golf. So, my brother got the boys their first set of golf clubs, and we started playing. I didn't play too much, as the rotation in the golf swing made my knees very unhappy. But, I would take the boys to the practice area, and then we would play 3-9 holes after all the paying customers were done.

Some of the most enjoyable and memorable days of my life with my sons were out at Fox Hollow. Tim is my "technique" son—he would practice what ever sport he played for hours to get his technique just right. Chris was my "power" son—he liked to hit the cover off the ball, each and EVERY time he hit a golf ball. So, our golf outings were always entertaining, to say the least! Tim would be concentrating on playing as well as he could, hitting just the right club for the particular shot he had. And Chris would step up and smash the ball as hard as he could every shot. I remember a particular "discussion" on a par 3 hole where Chris wanted to use his driver for his first shot. Tim went ballistic because you are not SUPPOSED to use your driver on a par 3 hole!!! Well, Chris teed the ball up, took out his driver, and with a half swing, put the ball about 3 feet from the cup! He was going bananas, and Tim was ready to throw his clubs in the lake! We had so much fun together, playing golf out at Fox Hollow.

Chris' favorite hole at Fox Hollow was a par 3 on the Meadow nine. We have (3) nine hole courses at Fox Hollow: the Canyon, the Meadow and the Links. To avoid confusion over a particular hole, the maintenance crew uses the numbers 1-27 to identify each hole. The Canyon contains holes 1-9, the Meadow holes 10-18 and the Links we call 19-27.

Well, Chris' favorite hole is number 16 on the Meadow. It is a par 3 hole, between 100-160 yards long and there are some beautiful trees along a river to the left side of the green. I am not exactly sure why 16 was Chris' favorite hole. It might have been because he almost got a hole in one there. Or maybe because Tim once had put his golf bag on the side of the green and just as he was getting his putter out of his golf bag, a sprinkler head popped up, and absolutely soaked Tim from head to toe (golf bag as well)! Chris' near hole in one occurred one late afternoon when we were golfing together, and as soon as he hit the ball, he started screaming that it was going in the hole!!! Well, it rolled up to the pin, and stopped about a half an inch away from going in! I am not sure if Chris was more excited that he hit the ball that well, or upset that it didn't go in, but it was a great day on the golf course for both of us!

Number 16 is also the hole where several falcons live, so it has even more meaning to me. Several amazing things have happened to me while I was mowing that part of the golf course that I talk about in the chapter on falcons. But, 16 is also a very special number for not only Chris and me, but for all the members of his ODA 316!!! That too, is for another chapter in OUR book.

Golf Course Training

One of the things I love the most about mowing out at Fox Hollow is being on the greens the first thing in the morning. The sun is starting to rise, the colors are magnificent, and there is a peace and quiet about that time of the morning that is very special. I particularly like it when there is dew on the greens. First of all, it makes mowing straight lines that much easier because you can clearly see where your last line ended. But there has always been something fascinating to me about seeing my footprints in the dew on a green.

After I had my knees replaced, I utilized the dew on the greens to "evaluate" my gait or walking pattern, in an attempt to try to learn to walk "normally" again. I would get to a green, and before I would start mowing, I would walk back and forth for a couple of minutes, and then evaluate my step length and various other aspects of my walking pattern. Doing this "drill" probably helped improve my walking more than anything else.

Well, when Chris was ready to really start learning Land Navigation, I thought, what better place than the golf course to teach him how to measure and evaluate his walking patterns as they applied to moving through the woods. One of the keys to successful land navigation is knowing how long your stride is. Having dew on both the greens and the fairways made it real easy to measure how long Chris' stride was, and then to see how reproducible it was. Chris became a master at knowing how long each stride was, and then we would walk over fairways, rough and greens to make sure it stayed consistent. We would also have "competitions" while working on developing stride and step lengths. One of the games was to walk a set distance on the green, and then try to repeat those same steps while blindfolded, and then we would see who was closest to their original footsteps. We would also have a trial of walking with half the distance between strides, again, seeing who could be closest—two guesses who ALWAYS won!!!

One night, after one of the land "nav" tests in Selection, Chris called me to thank me for all the nights and all the time we spent working on his pacing and stride length, because he was spot on in his evaluation!

Today, there are many times when I first get to a green to mow, after I remove the flag and check for ball divots, I see two sets of footprints on the green. And there have been so many times that while I am mowing, I feel Chris' presence like at no other time. In fact, there has been more than one time that I thought I saw someone else out there on the green, but when I quickly turn to see who it might be, there is no one there. Chris used to love to play hide-and-go-seek, and every once in a while, I feel like he is going to pop out from behind something and "surprise me!" Oh, how I wish that would happen...

We also used the golf course to calculate distance. There is a set distance from each tee box to the green on every hole at every golf course. And then, at various locations on each fairway, there are yardage markers telling how far it is to the green. So, Chris and I figured that if I were to stand at a particular place, Chris could gage how far away I was standing, and then I would "tell" him where I was so he could hone in his distance estimation skills. We would communicate with each other on our cell phones, and once he guessed the correct distance, I would move to another location and he would figure out what the new distance was. This skill proved very useful in making Chris the tremendous sniper that he became. While a sniper and his spotter have sophisticated scopes and tools to calculate distance, there may come a time when those instruments and tools do not work. So, Chris was prepared and skilled at distance estimation like no one I have ever known. He had a gift when it came to sniping, and part of that gift was developed and perfected on the greens and fairways of Fox Hollow Golf Course.

There were other skills we worked on out at Fox Hollow as well. The humidity in Colorado is very low during the day, so we used to go out at night, and the early morning to work on Chris' skills. I have never been a great sleeper, and I have always been a "morning person," so getting up at 0200 or 0300 has been easy for me. Chris loved getting up with me and heading out to the golf course—as he got older, many times he would still be "up" when I got up, so we would head out and do something together when everyone else was asleep. We would work on his sleep deprivation skills. I firmly believe you can develop the ability to function at a higher level in a sleep deprivation state, as long as you become accustomed to the sensation, fatigue and functioning while sleep deprived. Chris and I would work on developing his abilities to keep his wits, and thinking at their highest level during a state of sleep deprivation. And, we had a ball doing it!!!

Learning to see in the dark and develop his night vision was also developed at Fox Hollow. Learning to function in a sleep deprivation environment was started out at Fox Hollow. Learning the skills of land navigation was perfected at Fox Hollow. Learning distance estimation was developed at Fox Hollow. Getting ready to "own the night" was started at Fox Hollow. And I got to go along for the ride!!!

Fox Hollow at Lakewood is a VERY special place for me, and, other than being "home" at Ft. Bragg, it is the place that I feel closest to Chris because of all we shared there!

4

Tim—Chris' First Brother

Men are haunted by the vastness of eternity… And so we ask ourselves, would our actions echo across the centuries? Will strangers hear our names, long after we're gone? And wonder who we were, how bravely we fought, how fiercely we loved?

—Odysseus from the movie *Troy*

On 20 May, 1985 at approximately 1100 EDT, I saw Chris' eyes light up as I had never seen them light up to that time, nor after that day. I also never saw his smile as bright, ever again, because that was the day I came home from the hospital and told Chris he had a little brother! Chris was only about two and a half, but he was a very intelligent, intuitive and loving little guy, and he ONLY wanted a little brother—having a little sister was just "unacceptable" to Chris. So, when I came home that morning, he was so excited—he ran around the outside of our house in Ohio several times because HE had his little brother!!! I can also remember the day we brought Tim home from the hospital, and Chris giving Tim his first kiss on the top of his head—a "target" Chris would later use on several other occasions! He loved his little brother as ONLY a big brother can!

In fact, Tim didn't learn to walk until he was about 14 months old. Chris was less than nine months old on that Saturday morning when he looked me in the eye, stood up, and after smiling as only he could, started walking on his own. No, Tim didn't NEED to walk because he had Chris to go and get anything Tim wanted! Tim would sit on the floor, point to a toy, and make some grunting noise—Chris would sprint to the toy to "retrieve it" for his little brother.

But once Tim did learn to walk, he almost instantly had to learn to run to keep up with his big brother. When we lived in Ohio, there weren't many kids in our neighborhood, so Chris and Tim spent most, if not all of their play time together. And, for the most part, they were more than just brothers—they were best friends. Of course, Chris would get mad if Tim took something of his. Tim became a tough kid because of the "training opportunities" that Chris used his little brother for! Remember the "target" on the top of Tim's head—Chris had gotten a "junior medic kit" for Christmas one year, and he decided that the toy syringe would look good sticking out of the top of Tim's head! Fortunately, no blood—no foul was the rule around our house—but somehow that syringe seemed to vanish after Chris' first cranial evaluation!!!

Chris was seven and Tim was five when we moved to Colorado. I decided before we moved in that Tim would get the room on the front of the house, and Chris would get the room on the back. There was a partial roof just below Tim's window, and I knew that if Chris had that room, he would have been practicing his "PLF"—parachute landing falls—and Tim would not even think about jumping off that roof. Plus, Chris' room did have a beautiful Aspen tree right outside his window that would have been much "safer" for Chris to use for his escape route…and that tree was well used over all the years Chris lived at home!

Our house in Colorado had a small backyard, but it was at least level—and that was actually one of the criteria we used to decide which house we would buy. It was the training ground for soccer, baseball, badminton, tetherball and even golf chipping drills. All of the homes in our neighborhood have wooden fences between the yards, and so the wood slats became "fair game" for the boys as they practiced their soccer skills. After about 20 or 30 replaced slats—how could their "coach" get mad at that kind of power—I finally put up plywood over the "goal end" of the yard, and even though a soccer ball has not been fired at that wall in over six years, I just can't bring myself to take that wall down. We also had a badminton net strung between the deck and the fence. When I was an undergraduate physical education student at Cortland State University in Cortland, NY, the TOUGHEST course that I have EVER taken, including my Master's in physical therapy and my Ph.D. in exercise physiology, was Badminton 156!!! Badminton is a phenomenal sport, and it is the perfect cross-training sport for soccer. So the boys and I used to play badminton every chance we could—even in the snow! Some of our most fun games were when there was snow on the ground to cushion our diving for the shuttlecock! We had some great times in the backyard, and Chris and Tim's skill, determination, and tenacity were cultivated pounding on each other in our backyard. Chris did not care that his brother was two years younger, and Tim did not care that his brother was older and stronger—they would go after it, AND each other, every day.

One of my favorite stories and memories of Tim growing up was when we went to Europe in 1998 to play in an international soccer tournament. Tim was a defender then, and he was tenacious to say the least. Chris and Tim used to play soccer in our backyard for HOURS, almost everyday, and because Chris was older and bigger than Tim back then, it was a great training opportunity for Tim to become the tremendous player he became.

Now, while Chris and Tim used to train for hours at a time, there was rarely a "training session" that did not end with one or both of the boys ready to kill the other! They were VERY competitive and the competitive spirit that they forged playing soccer, and every other sport they played AGAINST each other, helped both of my boys become the athletes and the men that they became.

Well, Tim's team played a team from Northern Ireland in the preliminary rounds, and then again in the semi-finals of the Paris Cup tournament. The Northern Ireland team was one of the best sides I have ever seen, and their star player was a young MAN named Alan. He was "supposed" to be under 14 years of age, but my guess and the rest of the teams in the tournament suspected that he was "significantly older." He was physically and talent-wise, a man playing against boys (Alan is now playing professional soccer in Scotland). Tim was our left defensive back, and Alan was their right forward, and so it was Tim's job to mark Alan, and mark him he did! Alan could do nothing all game, and you could see him getting more and more frustrated as the first game progressed. He tried to physically overpower Tim but it did no good, because Tim would beat him to the ball almost every time it was passed to Alan, and if he couldn't beat Alan to the ball, Tim stole the ball from him at the most opportune time. I have always been incredibly proud of my sons, but watching Tim play these two games against Alan were some of my most proud moments coaching soccer.

After the tournament (we beat Northern Ireland in the semi-finals, but lost to a Tampa team in the finals), the coach from the Northern Ireland team asked if he could have Tim's jersey to frame in their club house because Tim was the ONLY person that had ever shut down Alan completely! It was a great honor and Tim gladly gave up his jersey and received a prized Northern Ireland shirt in return. Later, after we left the field, I told Tim how proud I was of him, and how great it was that he played so well against Alan. Tim looked me in the eye and simply said, "Chris is tougher than Alan, and I can beat Chris anytime I want!!!"

We also loved to in-line skate together. By the time we moved to Colorado, the arthritis in my knees was getting worse, and I couldn't run anymore other than short distances at soccer practice. So, I started in-line skating for fitness, and the kids wanted to learn to skate as well. There is a 25 mile bike trail very close to our house, so the three of us would go over to the bike path to train. But, because the boys were still pretty young, they would get tired before my training session was over. So, we improvised—I put on a weight training belt with two waterskiing ropes attached, and then when the boys got tired, I would tow them down the path. I got a better workout, and they had a ball being towed. Once in a while, they would not be paying attention because they were having too much fun, and they would get tangled up, or roll off the pavement, and one of them would crash, then the other, then Dad! But we had many great training sessions on that bike path.

When the kids were old enough, my brother and I taught them how to ski. Part of the reason I moved to Colorado was for the skiing. I love skiing, even after my knee replacements, and I wanted my boys to share my passion for being up in the mountains and flying downhill! When they first learned to ski, Tim would shadow me down the hill, practicing his turns right behind me. Not Chris—his goal was to beat everyone, and I mean EVERYONE, to the bottom of the hill! Everyone on the slope was fair game, and it was his mission to beat everyone to the bottom of the hill. Every year for Christmas, I would give each of the boys a "Super Ski Certificate" as a Christmas present. They would get a day off from school, they would get to go to what ever ski area they wanted to ski at, they got to eat what ever they wanted. One year, Tim and I had licorice and jelly beans for breakfast on the way to Breckenridge! And THEY thought the Super Ski Certificate was "their" gift!?!? We had so much fun skiing when the boys were little. But, once my knees would not allow me to walk, not to mention ski, there came a time when it was not safe for me to ski, and as such, there was a period of about five years before the boys could drive that we didn't head up the hill at all. When Chris and Tim renewed their love of flying downhill, they started snowboarding instead of skiing. By this time, Tim was taller than Chris—a fact that used to bother Chris more than you can possibly imagine—and after Chris left for the Army, his opportunities to snowboard were limited to his time on leave at home, and an occasional trip to the "mountains" of North Carolina. The elevation of Chris' bedroom in Colorado is 6,016 feet—the highest point in North Carolina is less than 4,000 feet, so Chris used to love calling them "the mountains—NOT!" But Tim and his friends would snowboard almost every weekend, and Tim became a terrific snowboarder. All his time shadowing me and learning to turn must have paid off because Tim is such a graceful and yet powerful snowboarder. He has also become very proficient at "survival in the terrain park" where he would perform on the rails and obstacles throughout the snowboard park.

The last Christmas Chris spent at home in 2004, the boys wanted to take a trip to Crested Butte, Colorado for their Christmas present. When Chris was in his final weeks in Gereshk, he had emailed me to ask if I could buy him some freestyle skies when they went on sale at the end of the ski season in Colorado. Chris wanted to eventually be assigned to 10th Special Forces Group (Airborne) so he could "be paid to ski" and as he had not skied in many years, he wanted to relearn. The skis he wanted were called "Public Enemy" skis and I am convinced that the only reason Chris wanted those particular skis was because they had three .45 caliber shell casings in the tip of the ski!!! Tim agreed completely! As we were loading up the truck for our ski trip, Tim asked Chris if he was going to bring his snowboard. Chris said no because he wanted to re-learn to ski, but Tim convinced him that he should throw the snowboard in the back of the truck "just in case." Little did I know that Tim KNEW what was about to happen.

We stopped at one of our favorite ski areas—Copper Mountain—on the way to Crested Butte for a day of skiing before heading southwest to Crested Butte. Chris and I had our skis and Tim was on his snowboard. After we get off the lift, Tim takes off like a shot—Chris had not seen Tim snowboard in over a year, and Tim wanted to show Chris "what he had," and Chris noticed. He was amazed at how fast and how smooth Tim was on his board. But, Chris was also very excited about trying his new skis, and so he took off. Tim was about 200 meters below us on the slope, and he stopped and waited for us—something the boys got used to doing while skiing with old Dad!

Well, what Tim "knew" that Chris and I didn't, was that skiing and snowboarding are COMPLETELY different! Tim tried skiing one time after he started snowboarding, and it only took once to drop skiing like a bad habit! So, when Chris goes to make his first turn, his muscle memory had completely forgotten how to turn!!! I could hear, as could everyone else on the slope, some rather loud profanity coming from my oldest son, and rather than relying on his athletic ability, Chris started to panic. His stance became as wide as possible—his arms and ski poles were straight out to the side for balance, and he was doing everything he could to not crash! After seeing Chris have such a difficult time with that first turn, I knew he was in trouble, so I skied down as fast as I could to help him down the slope. Tim, already being down below us, had the best seat in the house, and when I looked up to see where Tim was, he was literally lying on the snow laughing his ass off—watching Chris and me trying not to kill each other!!! We finally made it to the bottom of the slope. Chris took his skis off, we walked back to the truck, and got his snowboard. After that, he NEVER skied again! To this day, all Tim or I have to do is to think of Chris going down that slope at Copper, and we instantly start laughing uncontrollably! Even Chris, who had a hard time laughing at himself, was amused at how he got down that slope.

The rest of that trip was very special for Chris and Tim. They had such a great time snowboarding together, and, I had the time of my life watching my sons truly enjoy and love being with each other. Little did I know then that it would be the last time the three of us would do anything together—and as such, it means that much more to both Tim and I that we did have that time all together. We talked, we laughed, we cried—it was one of the best times we ever had together! I am so lucky to have two terrific sons, and even luckier that Tim and I have those memories of our last trip skiing with Chris.

Tim's last day with Chris was 2 January 2005. Chris and Tim are huge Denver Bronco fans, and I was able to get two tickets to the Broncos vs. Indianapolis Colts game. I gave my ticket to Tim and I am so glad I did, because Chris and Tim had one of the best days of their lives together! When they first got to Mile High Stadium, they went to a McDonald's booth in the parking lot where you could make a sign to hold up in the stands. Those who know Chris and Tim have seen first hand their opportune and hilarious Hollywood antics! So, while Chris was thinking of something witty to put on his sign, Tim came up with, "Hey Peyton, Now I Know Why Tigers Eat Their Young!" (a classic line from the movie, "Caddy Shack.") Well, Chris was PISSED because that was such a great saying!!! Tim told me Chris didn't talk to him for half an hour because Chris was so mad that Tim thought of such a classic line!!! Chris eventually decided to put "316" on his sign, and I was so glad he did, because when the camera scanned the fans at one time during the game, I saw on TV the "316" sign, as did several of the warriors from 3rd SFG(A) back home at Ft. Bragg! The Broncos beat the Colts that Sunday, and even though they lost to the Colts the next weekend in the playoffs, it was a day that Tim will never forget, and there have been so many times since that day that Tim has thanked me for letting him go to the game with Chris. No, my son, thank YOU for sharing that day with your brother. When Chris and I had our last ski trip to Utah, Chris told me over and over again how much fun he had with Tim at the Broncos game—from the face painting, to the near fight, and yes, even the McDonald's signs! So, all "three" of us had a great day, that last day Chris spent with Tim.

After Chris crossed over and we were done with the Memorials and the interment at Arlington National Cemetery, Tim and I drove down to Bragg with Jim, Tony and JT. We spent the night in Chris' apartment, loaded up his truck with the things we wanted to bring back to Colorado before the movers came, and we left for home. We drove 26 hours straight to Littleton. We took a shower, loaded up my old truck, and drove another 16 hours for Santa Barbara, where we put the Tundra on a boat so Tim would have a vehicle in Hawai'i. In those 42 hours of driving literally across the country, we had some great talks, just as Chris and I had had over our many trips back and forth from Littleton to Bragg. When we got to Honolulu, the semester had already started, so Tim and I went to his professors and explained the situation. They were all terrific about the situation, and each professor told Tim that if he needed to take a leave of absence, he had until the week before final exams in December to decide if he wanted to continue with his classes. But, as great as his professors were, his housing situation was that much worse! When the Suburban came down the street on 9 August 2005, Tim and I were on our way to Honolulu to move him out of his apartment and to find him another place to live. At that time, there were hundreds of places available, and there should not have been any problem finding a place for Tim to live. But, because of all that happened over the following three weeks, all, and I mean, ALL of the apartments and living areas were taken. My cell phone records showed that on that first day we were back in Hawai'i, I made 87 phone calls trying to find Tim a place to live while he went to class. The same thing happened the second day, and the third day, and the fourth day!!! We were able to stay up on the North Shore with relatives, and they very graciously told us Tim could stay with them for the entire semester if we wanted, but it would have been a very difficult commute for Tim to go back and forth every day from the North Shore to the University. I had to get back to Colorado to go back to work right after Labor Day, and so the last day I was there, Tim and I had another of our great talks. I was so frustrated because we tried so hard to find a place for Tim to live—there was one place that I found for $1000 a month, but when I called to say, "we'll take it" because we were so desperate, the woman asked how tall Tim was because the ceiling height was only 5 foot, 8 inches high and Tim is 6 foot 2 inches tall—so I told Tim that if he wanted to come home with me, he could go to school for a semester in Denver, or he could take a semester off and work. After thinking about it for a few minutes, Tim told me that Chris wanted him to stay in school, and that it would be the best tribute to Chris for him to stay in school and do the best he could with his studies. Of all that I have to be proud of Tim for, that day and that decision are one of the things I am most proud of—few people I know would have made that decision, but not Tim. It was easy for him because he knew that is what Chris would have wanted him to do, and so, it was simple—he would stay in school. On Saturday, 20 December 2008, Tim graduated from the University of Hawai'i—Manoa in Marketing and Sports Management, and I know Chris was looking down and smiling with pride as his brother crossed "his" stage to get his diploma.

Chris bought me my first Hawaiian shirt. Chris liked wearing Hawaiian shirts every once in awhile as he didn't need to be "covert" ALL the time, and he wanted people to know I was coming, so he thought Hawaiian shirts would do the job! He also wanted me to wear something for Tim—to honor him—and Chris knew how much Tim loved being in Hawai'i. Chris never got to go to Paradise with us, but he always wanted to see the Hawai'i that Tim talked about constantly. Every time I go there now, I feel Chris with me and Tim feels the same way. So, one of the things Tim and I have done to honor Chris is to give Hawaiian shirts to all of Chris' teammates. Every time I go to Arlington, I wear one of my many Hawaiian shirts. When we had the family visitation the night before Chris was interred, ALL of the boys wore their Hawaiian shirts for Tim, for Chris and for me! Tim has had several surfer memorials with his friends to honor Chris, where they go out on their surfboards, sit around in a circle and remember someone. It is a great honor, and Tim is so very proud of his big brother, and he knows how lucky he is that Chris was such a big part of his life.

In our last conversation before Chris left for Deh Afghan in June 2005, we talked about Tim. Chris was always riding Tim's ass to get "some ink"—a tattoo—and Chris told me that if something happened, one of the first things I was to do was to get Tim some ink. So, in May 2006 when we went to Ft. Bragg for the Memorialization of the Special Operation warriors that were lost in 2005, Tim and I went to Smokin' Guns Tattoo to get his ink. We will talk about Tim's ink in OUR chapter about Liz, but Tim's ink is on his back, just as Chris always had Tim's back in good times and in bad while they were growing up.

Chris also told me in that last talk that he wanted Tim to get the best education possible and that I was to use his Soldiers and Government Life Insurance money for Tim's education. So, Tim graduated without having to worry about any student loans to start his career. Tim was able to spend a semester at the Copenhagen Business School—a dream semester and the opportunity of a life time that Chris wanted his brother to have. Tim has made the most of these educational opportunities because of how much he loved his brother, and how much Chris loved Tim.

When Tim was unpacking in his apartment in Copenhagen, the first thing he took out of his suitcase was the picture of Chris and Tim at Crested Butte, and the second thing he put in a place of honor in his apartment was one of Chris' Green Berets!!! Tim loved his big brother as no other!

The other thing Chris asked me to do was to take Tim to Thermopylae, the resting place for the greatest warriors the world has ever seen. It is a pilgrimage that someday, I will take with all of Chris' brothers that are available because it was where Chris, and all of ODA 316's warrior spirit was first created. It will be the trip of a lifetime, and I know that Chris and all the Spartans will be looking down and smiling on us as we walk where the 300 Spartans with their lambdas on their shields, once stood and defended the freedoms we now have.

Tim loved his brother as only a brother can. And while Chris could be obnoxious, cruel and down right mean to his "little brother," NO ONE better even look crossed-eyed at Tim, because they would feel the wrath of an older brother that truly loved his Tim. As a parent, I could not be luckier that I have such tremendous sons. It has been the greatest honor of my life to have Chris and Tim call me "Dad." I have done many things, been to many places and seen things that few people on earth have ever witnessed. But, nothing compares to the memories, the love, the fun and the joy I have had with my sons.

Thank you, Chris and thank you Tim, for giving your old dad his heart, and teaching me what love is truly all about. I love you both with all my heart, and I am so very, very proud of you.

5

SSgt Matt—U.S. Marine Corps

The path of the righteous man is beset on all sides by the inequities of the selfish and the tyranny of evil men. Blessed is he, who in the name of charity and goodwill, shepherds the weak through the valley of darkness, for he is the brother's keeper and the finder of lost children.

And I will strike down upon thee with great vengeance and furious anger all those who attempt to poison and destroy my brothers and you will know my name is the Lord when I lay my fingers upon thee.

—Ezekiel 25:17 and Jules from *Pulp Fiction*

Matt is our next door neighbor, and has been Chris' best friend since 1994, when he moved in. They went to elementary school, junior high and high school together. Wherever Chris was, Matt was right there with him. Part of the reason Chris stopped playing soccer, in part, was because Matt didn't play, and he would much rather spend time with Matt. They used to go to the field across the street from our houses to golf, play ball, dig trenches, set ambushes, and all the 'normal' stuff that two future military professionals would do for fun!

They both worked at a local movie house for their first jobs—one of the highlights for Chris was he and Matt worked the special showing of the video of the first Super Bowl victory the Denver Broncos had, and Chris got to meet several of the players!

When I was going through Chris' things, I found this school paper he wrote about an adventure that Matt and Chris had one weekend when they were teenagers. It describes the relation that Chris and Matt had, and part of the reason they were as close as brothers can be:

High and Low

There we stood, looking up with eyes wide and hopes high. The rock face beckoned to us daring us to conquer it. We all knew what the challenge was that was laid out in front of us. After a quick rest, we began to climb to the summit of the mountain. With over 500 feet to go, we had no idea of what we would soon face. I was in the front, the fearless leader, clearing a path and showing the way. Pat was the middleman, keeping pace but still holding up for the last. In the back was Matt, strongly holding the rear with a heart full of pride and a backpack full of supplies.

Nearly twenty-five minutes later, three tired, cut up, and amazed teenagers reached the top of Sleeping Indian Rock in the Garden of the Gods State Park. We had done it as a team and we could not believe it. The challenge was seen and defeated with a passion. We came, we saw, and we conquered and now felt on top of the world. However, there was now a new challenge that we were presented with, getting down. So, we began to travel back down holding our heads high. The thunderheads rolled in and began to throw spears of electricity down to the ground. The black monsters stared deep into our souls and we thought," you can't stop us now." Our pace picked up and it began to drizzle around us. We rapidly continued down the rock until we came to a thirteen-foot drop. The only way to get down to the bottom was to slowly scale or jump. However, it did not seem too bad when we were climbing up the rock.

I stepped forward and proudly said that I would go first. I began to descend slowly and made it with ease. I told Matt to throw me the pack. I caught it and slung it over my shoulder. Next, Matt began his climb down. As I looked up at him climbing down, I saw a flash of light before my eyes and it was not the lightning. I saw it again and then again and then I looked deep inside myself and found my instinct. Then I took a step back with my right foot and braced it against a tree stump waiting for something to happen not yet knowing what. At four hundred feet up with around seven feet of the face to go, the thunder crashed and

Matt slipped. He began to fall towards the ledge on which I stood. At the rate he was falling with a backward momentum, he would surely knock both of us off. Matt's foot hit the ledge and at that instant, I lunged at him with all of my force, tackling him and pinning him to the rock. We then got up and the rain had stopped. He looked at me with shocked eyes and a heart beating franticly in his chest. He moved his lips to speak but I interrupted him and said, "Shhh...listen." Pat had now joined us and we could all hear the wind rush over the rocks and whip past us. It was absolutely beautiful. Matt turned and said, "I can't believe what just happened." "What's that," Pat exclaimed. "Chris just tackled me, and he saved my life." I then spoke up and said, "A perfect display of adrenaline and an even better display of friendship." Until this day and for the rest of our lives, Matt and I will remember exactly the events of that day second by thrilling second.

When they were in high school, they both decided that they were going to enlist in the military after graduation. Chris had known from a young child that he wanted to go into the Army and join SF, but Matt and five of their other friends all decided to join the U.S. Marine Corps. For those of you that don't know, there is a "friendly competition" between the Marines and the Army, and Chris and Matt played that to the hilt! They both had fun at each other's expense when it came to their "career choice"!

After they finished Basic Training, Chris was assigned to Ft. Bragg, and Matt was assigned to a Marine camp in South Carolina, so they got to see each other quite often. One of the first trips they made together was up to Washington D.C. to see the monuments. They had a great day, and at the end of the day, there were two places that they wanted to see before heading south—the Spy Museum and the Iwo Jima Memorial. Chris insisted that they go to the Spy Museum first, as they both used to "dream" about covert missions and "secret squirrel stuff," and they had a ball! But, they spent so much time at the Spy Museum, they didn't have time to get to the Iwo Jima Memorial. Matt was convinced Chris did it on purpose, and I think he might have as well, knowing Chris and how much fun he used to have making fun of Marines. But, the last email Chris sent was to his brother, Matt, and in it he told Matt that when he got back from Afghanistan, he would take

Matt to the Iwo Jima Memorial first thing. Another promise he was not able to fulfill.

OUR book was made possible because of Matt. It was Matt that convinced me that the world NEEDED to know who Chris was. It was Matt that gave the first interviews with the local Denver news media. It was Matt that took care of business when I had to take care of Tim. It is Matt that feels the pain of not having Chris here to share his ups and downs, laughs and tears. And it is Matt that loved my son as much as I do!!!

Matt is now a Marine recruiter, and like everything Matt does, he is one of the best! He is so good at his job, he could even convince ME to join the Corps!!!…NOT!!!

But, I will say something here for all of you to read, and it is something I have never said before, but I say it to you…Semper Fidelis, my brother—I will always be faithful to you, just as you were always faithful to our warrior, our hero! I love you, Matt, as my son, my brother, my colleague, and Chris' best friend.

I am so proud of you, and all you are doing with your life. Matt also told me something that jumps into my mind on those days when I miss Chris more than usual. On those days for Matt, all he has to do is think about Chris' smile, his laugh, his actions, his talking and his movie line for everything, and his heart instantly goes from tears to joy! Well, Matt—you're right—it really does work!!!

Thank you for sharing your life with Chris—it made his life so much more full, so much more exciting, so much more ALIVE!

6

Formal Military Training

In the warrior's code there's no surrender. Though his body says "stop," the spirit cries "NEVER!"

—"Burning Heart" by Survivor

In this chapter, I will share some of my favorite stories about Chris during his "formal" military education. Chris shared as many moments of his training with me as he could. Whenever something good, or even something that was not so good, happened in training, I knew I would be getting a phone call. Chris would call as soon as he finished a test or training exercise, and the vast majority of the time, there was always so much joy and excitement in his voice! It filled my heart to know how much my son was learning, and how he was truly becoming a professional. That is something that any father would be proud of, but it was especially true for me because I was able to live vicariously through Chris' training with him, and it is one of the things I miss the most—our phone calls about what he was learning, what he was doing, and how much he loved doing his job, and becoming the professional soldier and warrior that Chris was. Here are some of my favorite stories about Chris during his formal military education:

Basic Training—Ft. Benning, GA
October 2001-March 2002

Chris was scheduled to leave for Basic Training on 10 September 2001. But a few too many beers with his friends at a farewell party on 8 September 2001, and Chris' one way ticket to Basic on Monday was cancelled by the Douglas County Sheriff. Chris and I watched the second plane hit the World Trade Center on 11 September 2001, and we spent the rest of the day watching as the world changed forever. Chris felt terrible about his DUI, and watching the Global War on Terror start in front of our eyes, he couldn't wait to be able to do something about it. However, because of the huge influx of recruits after 11 Sep, and having to take care of his DUWI before he could head to Basic, it took until 25 October 2001 for him to arrive at Ft. Benning, Georgia—the home of the infantry!

However, when Chris first got to Benning, he was placed in a holding company, and didn't formally start his basic training until after Thanksgiving, 2001. Other than a letter to tell us he got there OK, I didn't hear from him until he called to say he was getting leave for Christmas. When he got home on leave, we got to talk about his training. He was like a kid in a candy store! He loved Basic Training!?!?! Few people can say that! At the end of his leave, there was a storm heading into the deep south, and there was a chance of snow. Chris was excited about the prospect of a couple of extra days of leave, but I told him that he had to get back, in fact, I used some of my frequent flyer miles to have him fly back a day EARLY. He was so mad at me—no one else was going to be there. He would have to stay in a hotel on post because the barracks would not open until the following day, and why did he have to go back early? Well when he woke up that next morning, he looked out the window of the hotel at Benning and saw snow! It pretty much closed the area, and Chris was the ONLY person that actually reported in on time. His Drill Sergeant commended Chris in front of his entire training platoon for doing what was necessary to report on time. "I hate it when you are right, DAD?!?!" And like I always told him when he said that to me, "even a broken watch is right twice a day!"

But while Chris was home over Christmas leave, we had some great talks about not only the training, but the lack of physical preparation for the vast majority of the other recruits. We had started preparing Chris for the demands of Basic Training many months before he left for Benning. However, most of the rest of his training platoon did NOT do what we had done, and he was actually mad at the rest of the recruits, because their lack of conditioning was limiting HIS training!

One evening while Chris was home on Christmas leave, I went down to the basement to lift weights, and I saw Chris over on the computer. I asked what he was working on, and he told me to wait until he was finished, and we would work on it together. This is what Chris was working on and we finished it after he graduated from Basic Training:

Pvt. Christopher Falkel
2nd Plt. Ruff Ryders A Co. 1 Bn. 19th Inf.Ft. Benning, GA

My basic training experience has been one of the best learning experiences of my life. Having recently graduated from basic and currently in advanced infantry training at Ft. Benning, GA., I now feel ready and truly part of the greatest Army on Earth. Prior to my arriving at Ft. Benning, my recruiters, SSG Snyder and 1SG Little in Littleton, CO had given me a series of activities to learn and perform that would help me learn some of the things I would learn as part of basic training. I am so very glad I took their advice and was at least introduced to many of the components of becoming a soldier, because there were many members of my training platoon that did not prepare well prior to coming to Ft. Benning, and I think they might have had a better basic training experience if they had been better prepared.

While I felt well prepared, both mentally and physically, for my basic training experience, there were many in my platoon that were not prepared at all. I may be training to be an Army of One, but, I feel my overall basic training experience would have been even better if my platoon were as well prepared. To that end, I have a few suggestions that might help the recruiters with their overall preparation of recruits to be truly ready for basic training when they arrive on post.

Personal Fitness Training
Variations of Push-ups and Sit-ups

I was amazed at all the different exercises the drill sergeants used to help us get in shape. I have always been an athlete and thought I had experienced a great deal of variations on push-ups and sit-ups, but never in my wildest dreams would I have come up with so many. I think that if recruits knew of some of these variations, and started practicing them prior to arrival at basic training, they would be able to perform them with less stress, and have the opportunity to use basic training to get in the best shape possible, rather than using basic training to just get in shape. It would be helpful if recruits learned some of the many and challenging variations of push-ups and sit-ups before coming to basic training.

Body Movement Exercises

One of the things I enjoyed the most during basic training were my chances on the obstacle course. I have always enjoyed climbing, etc., and the obstacle courses we went through were very challenging to say the least. However, many of the members of my platoon dreaded the obstacle course because, again, they had never done anything like that before. Another suggestion would be to give recruits exercises that they could use to prepare their upper body strength to meet the demands of the obstacle course, as well as having their local recruiters find obstacle courses at community recreation centers, high schools, etc. that the recruits could practice on prior to basic training.

Walking Fitness

For the six months before I went to basic training, I started walking several miles a day, back and forth to my old job. Without knowing it, I think this really helped prepare me for all the marching and walking we did at basic training. I am also glad I had taken many walks with a loaded pack, to get the feel of what that was like, because it was not a surprise, at least for me, after our first forced march. The other suggestion is that recruits start walking with boots on at least one month prior to arriving at basic training. Again, I was lucky that I wore boots at my previous job, but many of the recruits that I went through basic training with had never worn boots, and they suffered a lot more blisters and foot pain than they needed to, if they had been better prepared. A training schedule could be designed to get the recruits ready for all the marching that they will do once they arrive on post.

Running Fitness

The hardest part of my first Army Physical Fitness Test (APFT) was not the distance of running 2 miles, but, having to run it after doing my push-ups and then sit-ups. I felt I had run and trained at running enough to do well on the 2-mile run. But, it was much more difficult than I could have imagined because I had never trained to take the test. There were many members of my platoon who could barely make the 2-mile run, even after several attempts at the APFT. I suggest that a training schedule of progressive trial runs of the three tests of the APFT be started several months before starting basic training, which would prepare the recruits for not only the 2-mile run, but also the actual taking of the APFT.

The personal fitness component of basic training would be improved if a planned program of variations of push-ups and sit-ups, upper body training, walk training and run training were given to the recruits by their recruiters several months before they are sent to basic training. I was the only member of my basic training platoon that scored over 300 points on my final PFT. If more people were as prepared as I was, I think that number would be much higher.

Nutritional Training

Three meals a day

Before I went to basic training, I would have to consider my diet and daily nutrition as poor. Not that I ate a lot of junk food, but, I did not have a balanced diet, nor did I eat on a regular schedule. At basic training, we had the opportunity to eat at 0700, 1200 and 1700, and that was it. No between meal snacks, which was very difficult for many members of my platoon. And, if you did not eat enough at each meal, you were hungry until the next chance for chow. If recruits knew that they would only get three meals per day, and the types of food that were served in the mess hall, they might be better prepared.

Drinking Fluids

We were required to drink a full glass of water and a full glass of PowerAde with each meal. After that, we could drink other beverages of our choice. It was a shock to me at first because I had never taken in that many fluids with my meals before. But, once I got used to it, I never felt dehydrated on any of our training exercises. Recruits need to know that they will be drinking a lot of water, and not a lot of pop, and again, this is something they could practice before arriving on post.

Sleep Training

Early to Bed, Early out of Bed

I was lucky, I have always been an early riser, and so 0430 was not too bad for me to get used to. But for some of my platoon, I don't think they ever got used to it. Because of this, there were many times we did more push-ups, etc. than we should have done. If the recruits knew that they would be going to bed at 2100 and getting up at 0430-0500, they could get their biologic clocks set for this amount of sleep, and this timing of sleep, and it should make sleep and rest better for everyone.

Sleep Deprivation

There had been a few times in my life that I had stayed up all night, but before basic training, I knew I could get more sleep the next day, or at least take a nap if I was tired. Part of being a soldier is learning how to function under sleep deprivation conditions. I am glad I had practiced learning how to function in a sleep deprivation environment. It sure helped after pulling fireguard duty all night. Again, if recruits knew about the amount of sleep and the amount of activities they would be required to do after little or no sleep, they would be better prepared for the requirements of basic training.

I feel very strongly that these types of training would greatly help future recruits get the most out of their basic training experience. As an Army of One, I think I could help many of my future comrades in arms be better prepared for their introduction to the U.S. Army. Therefore, I am volunteering to prepare a document that outlines in great deal what the demands of basic training are, and how to best prepare for them before going to boot camp. I will get assistance from my father, who is an exercise physiologist and physical therapist (and retired USAR Major) in designing these training programs. I would like to work on this while on my hometown recruiting in April, 2002.

That was my son! Chris always had no tolerance for mediocrity. I don't know if the Army ever did anything with his suggestions, but I hope they have.

The one story I remember the most from Chris' Basic Training experience was when his platoon had their first attempt at qualification with the M-16. Chris was an excellent marksman, and we have discussed his weapons training before heading to Basic in a previous chapter. But the day of their first qualification testing, it was very cold, and there was a freezing rain in Northern Georgia. Chris told me that his hands were so cold, all he could think about was firing all the rounds in his magazine and getting out of the weather and getting warm. So, he rushed his shots, and only qualified at the Marksman level—not the Expert qualification level he expected of himself. He was as mad at himself as I had ever heard! He wrote me a letter that night, and promised he would NEVER waste another round again. As a Special Forces weapons sergeant, he NEVER wasted another round!

But, that too, was Chris. He was as hard on himself as he was on others, maybe even harder on his own level of perfection.

Chris was called "Columbine" as his nickname during Basic Training. The shootings at Columbine High School occurred while Chris was in high school. In fact, if we lived 500 meters farther northwest, Chris and Tim would have gone to Columbine High School. Chris took that nickname without complaining, but he always used to say that Columbine would have never happened if he had gone to that school, because the shooters would have been so afraid of Chris!

Advanced Infantry Training—Ft. Benning, March 2002

When Chris went through Basic Training, the last couple of weeks were called Advanced Infantry Training or AIT. AIT was designed to teach the infantry soldier the basics of infantry tactics and develop more "functional" skill with various weapon systems and within a squad or platoon size element. My favorite story about Chris' AIT was during a graded ambush mission. Chris really loved his drill sergeant. He was a Ranger before becoming a drill sergeant, and he took Chris under his wing because he could see that this young recruit had something special about him.

When Chris got to a particular place in the Georgia woods, he saw the opportunity to get into a superior firing position, so he climbed a tree and waited for the "enemy" patrol to come strolling down the path. One by one, he "killed" each member of the patrol, and they had no idea where the fire was coming from! Then later, after lunch, on another patrol, Chris saw the chance to be camouflaged and so he concealed his location, and again, waited. This time, his drill sergeant was in the patrol, and when his drill sergeant was in the "kill zone," Chris jumped up and captured all members of the patrol. He scared the living daylights out of his drill sergeant because not only he didn't see Chris, but didn't expect anyone would be in that location. "Don't you EVER do that to me again, FALKEL! Now, in combat that would be awesome, but don't you EVER do that to ME again!!!"

It made Chris' day!

Jump School—Ft. Benning, April 2002

Right after graduation from AIT, Chris was to head over to Jump School at Ft. Benning. My mom and I went to see Chris graduate, and it was such a proud moment for me! When a soldier graduates from Infantry School, he is presented with his blue, infantry braid that goes around his right shoulder. Chris' drill sergeant allowed me to put Chris Infantry Braid on his right shoulder. While I was preparing to place the braid on his shoulder, it was the first time I actually got to talk to him since arriving at Benning for his graduation ceremony. I no sooner placed the braid on Chris shoulder when he said, "Guess what, Dad? I'm going to Special Forces Selection right after jump school!!!" I don't know who was smiling more! We only got to talk about it for a few minutes before the graduation ceremony concluded, and he had to get his gear over to the Jump School area at Ft. Benning. However, he had the entire weekend for leave, so we got to talk about it at length that weekend.

But he couldn't wait for Jump School! Jump School is basically 3 weeks long, with the first two weeks consisting of preparing to actually jump out of a perfectly good aircraft. The last week consists of 5 actual jumps. When they were in the stick waiting for his first jump, Chris had a smile from ear to ear!!! The jumpmaster came by and asked him what he was smiling about, seeing how several other people were literally getting sick waiting for the door to open. Chris told the jumpmaster, "I have been waiting my whole life for this!" so the jumpmaster told him, "Well, Airborne, you get to be first out the door on your next jump!" Sure enough, for his second jump, Chris was the first one in the stick. And while the view was better, he didn't like having the rest of the stick pushing him from behind! But the jump went off without a hitch, and he completed all five jumps and earned his wings.

As fate would have it, Chris jumped in 2003 and 2004 on his birthday, 24 Sep, as well as every other chance he had to jump. He was anxiously waiting getting in Military Freefall School, and had he made it home from Deh Afghan, he was scheduled to go to freefall school in the spring of 2006.

Special Operations Preparation and Conditioning—Ft. Bragg, NC, Spring, 2002

When Chris first got to Ft. Bragg in early April 2002, he was enrolled in a relatively new program called SOPC—Special Operations Preparation and Conditioning course. It turns out that the Captain that was the detachment commander of the SOPC program was CPT Joe Martin. It was MAJ Joe Martin that helped me design the first draft of the cover of OUR book, and it is LTC Joe Martin that is helping me with all aspects of not only OUR book, but with my More Than A Name Foundation. CPT Joe Martin wrote the book, *Get Selected for Special Forces*, which has helped countless soldiers to become ready for the demands of Special Forces Assessment and Selection—SFAS. I owe Joe so very much for all he has done to help me, and, as it turned out, Chris. Chris was in the fourth SOPC group that went through the program. SSG Jerry went through the SOPC program with Chris, and both Jerry and Chris told me that 75 soldiers started the fourth SOPC course, and only 25 made it to SFAS. Of those 25 that started SFAS, 23 were actually Selected and made it through SFAS!

Thank you, LTC Joe, for helping prepare Chris for what he cared more about than anything else—Special Forces. Thank you for all you have done for making OUR book a reality. All of the proceeds from Joe's book, *Get Selected for Special Forces*, go to the Special Operations Warrior Foundation, and he was the inspiration for me to do the same with all the proceeds from OUR book going to the SOWF. The Special Operations Warrior Foundation provides scholarships and assistance to the children of our Special Operators that are killed in either combat or training accidents. If Chris had any children, SOWF would have provided them with the funding so they could go to college. There is more information and a link to the SOWF in the last chapter of OUR book.

Special Forces Assessment and Selection— Ft. Bragg, NC, May/June 2002

Here is a paragraph from LTC Joe's book, *Get Selected for Special Forces* that describes SFAS:

SFAS is the primary testing and evaluating phase of the Special Forces Qualification Course to evaluate if you have what it takes to successfully complete the other requirements of SFQC and be successful on a Special Forces Team—(ODA). The course varies its events to prevent people from knowing exactly what to expect. Regardless ("Disregardless" as Chris would always say!), you will be expected to pass various academic exams, psychological exams, a standard Army Physical Training test (push-ups, sit-ups, timed 2 mile run), a swim test, several road marches with a ruck weighing roughly 55 pounds and several day and night land navigation events.

There are three stories about SFAS that define Chris as well as any of the dozens of stories he told me about his time in Selection. The first was the swim test. Chris was never a strong swimmer—he was a survival swimmer. He could swim from the end of the water slide to the side of the pool. Tim is a phenomenal swimmer, and loves the water, but not Chris. Well, one morning while Chris was in SFAS, I was out mowing and the whole time, I was wondering what Chris was up to that day. Then, all of a sudden, I got this horrible feeling like I forgot, or lost something—we never worked on teaching Chris how to swim with his BDU's and boots on! No worries, I would tell him the next time we talked to go to a local pool, and give him some pointers on how to survive the swim test.

As with so many things that happened between Chris and me over the course of his entire life, when I got done mowing, and I was washing up my mower, Chris called. "Guess what, Dad? " I had heard that question many times before, but this time, there was a dejection in Chris' voice. "I failed the damn swim test!" In the SFAS swim test, you jump in the pool, swim one length, turn around without touching the sides OR the bottom of the pool, and swim back to the other end. There is no time limit, no stroke limit—you just can't touch the sides or bottom. Well, when Chris made the turn, his foot touched the bottom of the 3 1/2 foot end of the pool, and he was a "no-go!" Needless to say, he was not a happy camper!!! We talked about it—he had the chance to take the swim test again, but Chris hated incompetence, and failure was

NOT part of is vocabulary. He had the chance to take the test at the end of the week. He went to the pool every night after training, to practice and improve his chances of passing.

It was a Friday when Chris took his re-test. I had absolutely no fear or concern about his passing, but while I was mowing, I went through in my mind what I would tell him if he did not pass. A second failure meant he was done with SFAS for this cycle, and I was not sure if Chris would try again, or get so frustrated that he would "take the long walk to the 82nd (many people that fail SFAS go to the 82nd Airborne Division which is also located at Ft. Bragg)." I had finished mowing, and just finished washing my mower when the phone rang. "Well, Dad, I guess you can return the birthday present I am sure you got me, because I will NOT need those inflatable water wings any more—I PASSED!!!" It was not the happiest I had ever heard Chris on the phone, but it was pretty close!

The second story was during log training. The exercises or activities that the cadre give out at SFAS are not just to provide training opportunities, but to evaluate how men work together, particularly when they are tired, hungry, fatigued, etc. That is one of the purposes of log training—where several men lift a log over their head, and move it from "point A to point B" with point B being at a variety of great distances from point A! Well, one morning, Chris was on a log with 3 other guys, and the person in front of him was a Captain. In SFAS, there is "no rank" but some people tend to forget that. That was the case of this particular Captain. He didn't think it was his responsibility to carry his share of the load. And as a result, there was more on Chris. Chris let the CPT in front of him know, in no uncertain terms, that he had better take his share of the load, or "you will be wearing this log!" Even the cadre noticed the CPT not shouldering his share of the load, and offered the CPT a donut. The cadre at SFAS when Chris went through would always have a box of donuts, and if you "dropped on request—DOR," you got a donut as you walked out of SFAS! Well, the next day, the CPT chose a jelly donut on his way out!!!

The third story about SFAS that I will always remember was the Star Course. One of the last evaluations during SFAS was a land navigation course where you had at least a 60 pound ruck sack and you carried it over approximately 50 miles where you had to reach 5 checkpoints. You had 50 hours to complete the course, but if you did not get through all five points, you were a no-go. Soldiers also had to do this by themselves; no help from anyone else was the regulation. Well, as soon as Chris started the Star Course, it started pouring rain, so his 60+ pound ruck sack soon became significantly heavier due to the rain. At 26 hours, Chris had completed four of the five points, and he knew exactly where the 5th point was. So, he stopped for a nap. After he woke up about 3 hours later, he made himself a cup of coffee! He grabbed some berries from a bush for breakfast, and completed the Star Course in just over 32 hours! When he called me to tell me he had passed the Star Course evaluation, I could hear the pride in his voice, and I could see the smile on his face! And, the thing Chris remembered the most about that part of SFAS, was how good the coffee tasted!

But, it wasn't until our last road trip back "home" after Chris' Christmas leave that he told me something that touched my heart like nothing else he had ever told me. He said that when he was in SFAS, and when things were getting difficult, all he had to do was think about all that I had gone through in my life, and when he thought about what I had accomplished, and all that I had done for him, it inspired him to work that much harder. When he told me that, I pulled the truck over on the shoulder of the interstate, got out of the truck and walked around and hugged him as I had never hugged him before! I will never again have a tribute like that…

That was my Chris!

Special Forces Qualification Course– 18 Bravo Weapons Sergeant Course– July 2002-January 2004

Chris spent the next 18 months at Ft. Bragg learning what it takes to be a Special Forces soldier. Again, I have hundreds of stories that Chris told me but I will only relate some of my favorite ones that speak most to Chris' character—and he DEFINITELY was a character!!!

Chris was in Phase II, which focuses on small unit tactics, when there was a huge ice storm in Fayetteville. Chris and another soldier were being evaluated in a graded ambush scenario. The other soldier had no idea where they were, but Chris was sure of not only where they were, but where they needed to be for optimal positioning for the ambush. "How can you be so sure, Chris?" was the question of his classmate. Chris took out his knife, chipped away at the road to show the yellow line, and told his classmate to "follow me!" They not only got to the ambush on time, they were there before the cadre!

During the 18 Bravo course, one of the requirements "in the olde days" was to have several weapons totally disassembled in a box. The candidate would be blindfolded and they had to assemble all the weapons within a certain time period. So, when the cadre told the class about this, Chris volunteered to go through the test. 16 minutes later, he had all five weapons completely assembled!

The final phase that Chris went through was SERE or Survival, Escape, Resistance and Evasion school, where the last days of SERE the students are placed in a prisoner of war scenario. During SERE the two students that get extra attention and are the focus of the "education" are normally the most senior student and then the youngest—commonly called the "SF baby." Of course, Chris was the SF baby, and so the cadre used him to try to get the senior student to "break"—Chris would not allow that. There were several situations where Chris used his ability to be a "wise-guy" to have more "personal time" with the cadre! But, after returning from some "special fun" with the cadre, he saw a bowl of rice behind one of the buildings. After the cadre left, Chris snuck out the window, grabbed the rice, and shared it with the rest of the prisoners. Chris could have hid the rice, but he knew what was right, and that was what Chris was all about!

Special Forces Schools

Between Gereshk and Deh Afghan, Big Ron and Big Al made sure that Chris got to go to the best schools, and they made sure that Chris got into two of the most difficult schools in all of Special Forces: Special Forces Advanced Reconnaissance, Target Analysis and Exploitation Techniques Course (SFARTAETC) and Special Forces Target Interdiction Course (SOTIC). In SFARTAETC, they spent a significant amount of time in the "shoot house" working on close quarters combat. In one of the drills, the students would clear a series of rooms, and within each room there were "targets" that either had a weapon, or were unarmed targets. Points are awarded for shooting "armed" targets, and subtracted for shooting unarmed targets. Well when Chris went into one room, there was a poster of Osama Bin Laden, but he was unarmed. Chris put a bullet right between his eyes! When the exercise was over, the cadre commented that Chris shot an unarmed target, but Chris being Chris said," Well, I don't care—you owe me $25 million dollars, because he is wanted dead or alive!" "Damn you, Chris!" was all the cadre could say! A couple of years later when Scott went through SFARTAETC, the cadre were still telling that story!

But Chris' favorite school was his last one—SOTIC! He started SOTIC in January 2005, and finished that March. As soon as he was done, he flew out to Utah to ski with me, and it was the best week of our lives! In addition to all the fun we had skiing, we got to talk about all kinds of things, and one of the things Chris was most proud of was how well he did in SOTIC!!! He wanted to be a sniper since he was probably 12 years old, when I first let him shoot a real weapon. The final exam in SOTIC was to design a mission to take out a target after an insertion into the area. The class was supposed to "jump" into the area, but there was bad weather and equipment problems with the aircraft, so the class was "infilled" via a deuce and a half truck. Chris, being Chris told the cadre and the rest of the class they could still "jump" into the target area, and he promptly did a PLF off the back of the truck!

He used the light on his Suunto watch to draw up his attack plan, and he drew the plan in three dimensions!

Again, as soon as Chris and his spotter took off to acquire their target, it started raining. In the final exam at SOTIC, the sniper team could get as close to the target as they wanted. But, if they were spotted by the cadre, they were a no-go. Well at about 600 meters from the target, Chris thought he had a good shot at the target, and he was tired and wet and wanted to take the shot. His spotter tried to convince Chris to get closer so the shot would be "easier," but Chris had all the confidence in the world in his and his spotter's abilities, and so he took the shot. One dead target later, Chris passed SOTIC!

Chris took his military education very seriously, being the professional he was and needed to be! Chris loved to have fun. He loved to party. He loved being a "wise-ass," and he was VERY good at it!!! But, he also understood the value of training from all he learned from the WARRIORS of ODA 316, and so he got the most out of all of his military education because he knew it would make a difference for his team, his brothers!

The Battles of Mari Ghar—
7-9 August 2005

This chapter consists of first-hand accounts, as well as, three previously reported articles on the events that occurred in southeastern Afghanistan between 1000 local time on 7 August 2005 until 1605 on 9 August 2005. It is a story of bravery, courage, valor, sacrifice and "it will live in the annals of Special Forces history" as one of the fiercest battles of the Global War on Terrorism. A map of the Battle of Mari Ghar can be found at the end of the Photo Memorial in this book. Additional information about the Battle of Mari Ghar can be found in an article by Sean Naylor, "The Battle of Mari Ghar": Army Times Volume 66, number 49, pps. 14-19, 26 Jun 2006.

The men, the warriors, the Spartans of ODA 316 that fought the Battles of Mari Ghar are not mentioned by name in this chapter for security reasons, as most are still on active-duty. However, the warriors that Chris called his brothers will be introduced in subsequent chapters. These are the men that make Special Forces truly Special, and they are the warriors that are now MY family!

7 August 2005

Chris got off the phone with me about 0730 local time in Deh Afghan. After breakfast and a team meeting, the boys loaded up their vehicles for an armed reconnaissance of a route through the rugged mountain valleys of south-eastern Afghanistan. There had been reports that a high level Taliban commander was supposed to be in the area, and they were going looking for him and anyone else that might think about seeing what this team was all about.

Chris loaded up the vehicles with all the ammunition he had in the firebase. Starting in Asadabad, it was standard operating procedure (SOP) for ODA 316 to carry about three times the basic load of ammunition than any other ODA. Someone asked him why he was putting so much on the vehicles, as they were only going to be gone for a day, but he insisted that they carry as much ammo as he could put on the vehicles. I know why—because Chris just knew they would need it!

They were going to be driving through an area of Afghanistan that this team had never evaluated. The goal was to drive into their "backyard," get the Taliban to show themselves, and then take them out. There were three modified Humvees called Ground Mobility Vehicles (GMV) that the team used, and two Ford Ranger pickup trucks that carried the 16 members of the Afghan National Army (ANA) that left that Sunday morning. Again, the numbers 3 and 16 in OUR lives!

7 August—Contact Number 1— 1855 local time

The first contact with the Taliban occurred as the sun was setting just as the boys were getting ready to set up camp for the night. The Taliban hit with sporadic small-arms fire, and the boys let them have it with their big .50 caliber turret guns and the smaller M240 that is mounted on the rear of the GMV. Chris was the .50 cal gunner in vehicle three, and his teammates told me that he had THAT smile on his face during the entire contact! Chris loved his big gun, but just as he had weapons hid all around our house in case he needed them, he had multiple weapons mounted on the top of his vehicle—just in case he needed them. He even had an old school Vietnam tomahawk that was resurrected by 5th SFG (A) from the old Indian scout tomahawk of the Revolutionary War. That was the last gift I gave him when we were skiing in Utah, and I remember like it was yesterday—"Don't worry Dad, I will put THIS to good use!!!" Chris was always ready for any challenge, and these battles would be no exception. The contact only lasted about 15 minutes, and the enemy lost their taste for battle and the hills went quiet.

At this time, the team had to make a decision—do we keep going and try to drive the Taliban back out of the hills, or do we turn around and head back to the firebase. The motto of 1st Battalion 3rd Special

Forces Group (Airborne) is: "Pressure-Pursue-Punish!," and so that is exactly what they would do! The team drove up further into the Hazarbuz valley until they came upon a camp of nomads called "Kuchi." It was highly likely that these Kuchi would tell the Taliban of the approaching Americans. The Kuchi encampment was situated so that they had a clear view of any approaching vehicles, and as the boys came up the valley, the Kuchi broke camp and headed out of the valley in the opposite direction of patrol. The team had never seen so many Kuchi, and all their animals move out of a camp so quickly, and that was the first sign that something "big" was about to happen…

8 August—Contact Number 2— 0754 local time

As the patrol continued heading north-west, a small squad of approximately 10-15 Taliban opened up with small-arms fire at the two ANA pickup trucks at the front of the American patrol. The Standard Operating Procedures (SOP) for an ambush like this would be for the vehicles to keep moving to get out of the "kill zone" but, the ANA stopped their vehicles, and dismounted to run to positions of more cover from the attack. With the three GMVs now stopped, the Taliban started to target the three American vehicles that were about 150 meters behind the pickup trucks. The boys hit the Taliban with everything they had, including LAW and AT-4 rockets, along with the 60 mm mortar that was the "brain storm" of SGM Big Ron when ODA 316 was in Gereshk. The use of the 60 mm mortar had proven to be an effective weapon given the type of terrain in this mountainous region of Afghanistan. The dirt roads tend to be at the bottom of step valley walls, which provided the Taliban with a superior firing position aiming down on the road. The 60mm mortar could neutralize some of this positional superiority in that the rounds could be lobbed up into the rocky cover, and that would drive the Taliban out into the open where the .50 cal and the M240 could pick the enemy off. These two weapon systems can lay down an incredible amount of firepower, over significant distances. And when they are in the hands of skilled gunners, like Chris and the other gunners on the team, they can greatly suppress enemy fire so the team can position itself to get the upper hand in the contact.

The senior 18C went to round up the ANA to get them back into their vehicles so the patrol could move on. They were not returning much fire against the Taliban, so he had to "encourage" them to get back into the fight and go back to their trucks. But as the 18C was getting the ANA back into the fight, the rest of the boys kept up the pressure, and the Taliban started to turn and run from their ambush locations. Our troops have very sophisticated communications capabilities, and the boys were informed that the Taliban were on the move. They were able to intercept Taliban comms throughout the contacts, and so they had some early warning about what the Taliban were about to do next.

ODA 316 was able to utilize the effectiveness of the 60mm mortars to help drive the Taliban out from their position of cover. The Taliban thought that the mortar rounds that were landing on them "from above" were close air support (CAS) from Coalition aircraft. When a mortar round would land, the Taliban would run out from behind the rocks, and then Chris and the other gunners could target the enemy once they were out in the open. The second contact lasted almost 45 minutes, but after handling the enemy so effectively, the boys were confident in their abilities, and decided to push on farther into the heart of enemy territory.

8 August—Contact Number 3— 1031 local time

By this time, the Taliban were able to retreat and form eight to ten ambush positions in the rocks and trees just west of Kuchkay. The Taliban continued to use small-arms fire on the boys, but they miscalculated the intensity of fire power that the Americans could and would lay down on their positions. The boys were hitting their marks, killing a significant number of Taliban during this contact. Total time of this contact was again about 45 minutes.

8 August—Contact Number 4— 1133 local time

After the 3rd contact, the patrol kept moving, rolling through Kuchkay. The terrain on the east side of Kuchkay was much more closed in, restricting the movement of the vehicles to a very narrow space. For the first three contacts, the boys were given a "heads-up" about areas of potential ambushes and possible contacts, so they were ready and waiting. But, as they got just east of Kuchkay, they ran into an organized ambush that they did not expect. There were about 30 Taliban held up in an orchard. As with the first contact, the initial fire from the Taliban was at the ANA pickup trucks, and as happened before, the ANA abandoned their vehicles to run and hide. This allowed the Taliban to now concentrate their firepower on the 3 GMVs.

This contact was the most intense one yet. All six ODA 316 machine gunners were laying down a tremendous amount of suppressive fire, while the other team members were shooting at the Taliban in the orchard. But within minutes, there were several A-10 "Warthog" aircraft on station, laying down even more amounts of fire on the orchard. The A-10s made several gun runs until they told the boys that they were "Winchester," which means they were out of ammunition. The A-10 is an amazing aircraft that has the capability of putting out a phenomenal amount of firepower from either small rockets or canon fire rounds from the nose mounted Gatling guns. The A-10 pilots are some of the unsung heroes of the Global War on Terror in that they risk their lives in their relatively slow moving aircraft, flying right into the mouth of the battle, to support our boys on the ground. But you will ALWAYS have my admiration, gratitude and respect for your skills, abilities and professionalism. THANK YOU for all you did for my family, and all you continue to do for our troops!!!

After only 15 minutes, the Taliban guns went silent. The boys intercepted Taliban radio comms from a commander wanting to know if there were any Taliban fighters "out there?" There was no response to his question. So again, they got the ANA back in their vehicles, and made the decision to push forward toward the village of Marah. There were several small villages along the route, but they were basically empty. The boys decided to push east to Marah because the only other route they could have taken was to go north up towards Deh Chopan. However, they knew that terrain and the size of Deh Chopan, and they made the decision that it would be better to continue towards Marah, where they anticipated their next contact with the Taliban.

After this fourth contact, the boys stopped for lunch. It was the last time that several of the team saw Chris alive, as he was the gunner in vehicle #3, which was the rear vehicle in the patrol. To a man, they ALL told me that they had NEVER seen Chris happier! This was what Special Forces was all about, and he was doing what he wanted to do since he was eight years old! He was like a "kid at Christmas" one of his teammates told me! This is what he trained so hard for. This is what he had prepared so long for. This is what he had dreamed SF would be all about. And there was nowhere else on earth Chris would have rather been on this day, 8 August 2005, than with his brothers taking it to the enemy as hard as they possibly could.

I miss my son more than mere words can possibly describe, and I will never get over the pain of not being there for him in the next battle, which would be his last. But, I am so grateful that he had the experience of his life in the first four contacts. I just wish I could have been there to share his joy and his accomplishments with Chris.

The patrol continued southeast and drove through several small villages. Discussions at the higher headquarters in Kandahar involved the possibility of putting a Quick Reaction Force (QRF) in at Marah, as intel indicated that the next battle would almost surely take place there. The previous four battles had been monitored not only by the Coalition and Joint Task Force (CJTF) 76 located at Bagram Air Force Base, but also by Task Force Rock that was formed by the 2nd Battalion, 503rd Infantry Regiment of the 82nd Airborne Division based out of Qalat. The team leader kept suggesting that the QRF be inserted into Marah, and then the boys would drive the Taliban to the QRF.

However, after moving another 10 km towards Marah, orders came down from CJTF-76 for the patrol to return to Andar, where they would meet the QRF from Task Force Rock that would not only include an infantry unit, but several helicopters, and four AH-64 Apache gun ships. The rationale given for this decision to meet the QRF in Andar was the fear that the Taliban might shoot down the helicopters if the QRF was inserted in the mountainous region in the vicinity of Marah.

While these discussions were taking place, and the patrol had to turn around and head back towards Andar. For the team, the major concern was that the Taliban would have more time to set up their ambush in Marah. As it turned out, this was the case, and additional time allowed a significantly larger enemy force to be set and waiting for the boys to come through the valley. And when the QRF got to Andar, there were no Taliban there to fight. So, rather than heading to Marah as the intel "on the ground" had suggested, the QRF got back on the helicopters and headed back to Qalat. Needless to say, this was extremely frustrating to everyone in the patrol!

8 August—Contact Number 5— 1916 local time

The patrol turned around and headed south again. It was getting dark, and as they got about 500 meters PAST where they had been earlier that day, the 5th contact, and largest battle to that point in time started. The Taliban had positioned themselves to the right of the road and around the road in a "horseshoe" fashion, and they were well protected by huge boulders between 100 to 300 meters from the road where the patrol was travelling. As soon as the ANA pick-up trucks entered the well established Taliban "kill zone," the Taliban fired at the ANA, hoping they would stop their vehicles, and run and hide as they had in the previous contacts. As soon as vehicle #1 got close enough to the abandoned ANA pick-ups, the Taliban started firing at them. Vehicles #2 and #3 continued along the road until they had to stop, with only about 50 meters between vehicles. The Taliban had the patrol right where they wanted them, and they unleashed a fury of small-arms, RPG and crew served weapons fire on the patrol. The Taliban also positioned themselves behind the patrol, so they were boxed in.

As soon as there was fire on the patrol from behind vehicle #3, Chris quickly swung his .50 cal gun around to engage the enemy. But somewhere in the rocks above the road was a skilled sniper, and he took the shot that took my son's life. He was shot in the helmet with an armor piercing bullet, and he died instantly. As Chris lay there in his turret, the team sergeant had to do something he had never had to do in his long and distinguished military career. He had to tell the team and command up to headquarters that Chris had been killed. He loved Chris as a brother, as well as, a son; in fact, he has a son that was just about Chris' age. But with the loss of his gunner, his brother, the team sergeant kept his cool and did what a professional does. He performed brilliantly, and were it not for his composure and calmness under intense fire, there is no doubt in my mind that the cost of that battle would have been significantly higher.

The amount of fire from the Taliban was relentless, and there continued to be precise, single rounds targeting the other gunners on all three vehicles. The six ODA 316 gunners had been so effective in the previous four contacts that the Taliban were purposely targeting these warriors. So while the gunners were engaging the enemy from the vehicles, the remaining six members of the team were firing at the enemy as they moved and maneuvered around the vehicles for a better vantage point on the hidden enemy positions.

The TC up in vehicle #2 decided he was not going to let Chris lay in his turret. He told the driver in his vehicle that he was going to run back to vehicle #3 to help get Chris down, and then ran under fire to vehicle #3 while two of our brothers covered his movement. This was one of the most courageous and selfless things I have ever heard of, and for that, I will never be able to thank him enough for what he did for my son, but I will spend the rest of my life trying. Once he got there, he had help from the driver of vehicle #3 and the team sergeant in moving Chris out of the turret, and then the 18 Zulu got gun up again.

After they got Chris down and into the vehicle, the sixth gun was manned and the fight continued. Bullets were flying everywhere, constantly hitting the vehicles, as well as well placed sniper rounds continued to pummel the gunner's turrets. In fact, one round hit the ammo canister of the other weapons sergeant's vehicle, and it caught on fire. The 18C helped get the fire out and rounded up the ANA to get them to engage the enemy.

Just as things were going from bad to worse, two A-10's arrived on station and started laying down fire on the Taliban from above. The air strikes were called in by an Air Force Terminal Attack Controller (TAC) staff sergeant that was assigned to the patrol. As soon as the Taliban took cover from one of the A-10 gun runs, the vehicles moved forward as far as they could, but unlike the previous engagements, even when the A-10's were making a run, there was Taliban firing from other positions, so it made movement of the vehicles difficult and very slow.

The A-10's kept making gun runs until they were out of ammunition, when another set of "Warthogs" as the A-10 is "affectionately" referred to, would arrive on station and start their gun runs. When they were out of ammo, a third set of A-10's arrived and continued the fight.

It took about 25 minutes of continuous, vicious fighting for the patrol to move out of the kill zone, and into the relative safety of the small village of Ragh, only 500 meters past the ambush. By now, it was starting to get dark, and from the air, an AC-130 gunship saw about 20 Taliban fighters massing for another attack. The gunship obliterated these fighters, but they commented that even though the enemy were subject to a massive amount of fire, these particular Taliban fighters did not turn and run, as most have done in the past. This was further evidence that these particular Taliban fighters were much better trained and were more determined than "normal." The team found out in the morning from a friendly mullah in Ragh that there were between 50 and 60 fighters, and while many spoke Arabic, many spoke a language he did not understand.

9 August—Contact Number 6— 1015 local time

The team spent the night in the town, although few of them got any sleep. They had called for a MEDEVAC to take Chris back to the firebase, but the requests were denied due to the terrain and the perceived risk to the aircraft. The AC-130 gun ships stayed on station all night long keeping the Taliban out of the town and keeping my family safe, at least for now. The warriors of ODA 316 took up security positions around Ragh along with the ANA and rotated so everyone could get a little sleep, as they knew there would be more ambushes coming! When ODA 316 had secured Ragh, Chris was gently loaded, covered and secured in the back of one of the GMVs, where he remained with his brothers through the night and the during the remaining fights. Chris returned to Firebase Lane with his team.

I can't imagine the pain and the sorrow the team had the night before when they all finally came to the realization that Chris was gone. For many of his brothers, it wasn't until they got to Ragh that they even had time to see Chris because of the intensity of the firefight. Several of Chris' brothers told me that it really didn't hit them until the morning of 9 August when they realized that Chris was not going to be up in "his gun." That he was not going to be joking around with them. That they were never going to see his smile or hear his laugh again. I am so sorry for your pain, my brothers. I so wish I could have been there to take it from you.

During the night, the other 3rd SFG (A) ODA at Firebase Lane moved toward ODA 316's position but it would take some time for them to link up. At approximately 1015 in the morning, the patrol was hit with the 6th contact of the battle—another ambush along the winding road that took the team to Marah. The 18C spent much of the night before talking to the ANA, convincing them that they needed to stay in the fight or push through the ambushes, and not run for cover when the bullets started flying. During this 6th contact, they did just that. They not only stayed with their vehicles, but they engaged the enemy as well, allowing the patrol to continue moving. The patrol made it through this contact without incident.

9 August—Contact Number 7— 1132 local time

No sooner had the patrol crossed the small river just before entering the village of Marah, when the 7th ambush started from an orchard next to the river. There were over 50 Taliban fighters in this orchard and they were laying down massive volumes of fire on the team again. Just about this time, the other ODA arrived, and so now there were 6 gun trucks returning tremendous amounts of fire on the orchard. In addition, more A-10's arrived to continue pounding the Taliban, and none too soon as one of the other team's vehicles was hit and set on fire. The team leader and several of his men were injured, but not seriously, and they stayed in the fight.

Vehicle #2 was hit so hard by enemy fire that the brakes and hydraulic system were disabled. So, while the A-10's continued bombing the orchard, the decision was made to move on before any more vehicles were damaged. After re-supply with the other team, the two teams slowly continued their patrol until they arrived back at their firebase at approximately 1605 local time.

Fifty-four hours of the Battles of Mari Ghar. Seven contacts. Over 65 Taliban killed. And miraculously, only one fatality. As I have told the boys, 99% of the Battles of Mari Ghar were "textbook" in terms of how the team performed, and the incredible bravery, valor, courage and professionalism that was exhibited by both teams. In a battle of this size there are always going to be things that could have, or should have been done differently. But because of the training of the team, because of the heart of the team, and because of the skills and bravery of the team, the cost was so much less than it SHOULD have been. I am so grateful to each man there for bringing everyone else home. I am so thankful for the courage and valor of each man in saving the lives of the rest of my family. And, as I have told each man on the team—looking them in the eyes, and talking directly to their heart—I am so very proud that Chris had them as his brothers and that I know that they did everything they possibly could to keep their shields up to protect their brother next to them. Because of the training, because of the professionalism, because of the love each warrior on ODA 316 had for his brother, the results of the Battle of Mari Ghar were much less costly than they might have been.

Chris used to say to his brothers, as well as to me, that he wanted "to go out in a blaze of glory," and that you did, my son. You faced the enemy with a smile on your face and a warrior's heart. As hard as it was for the boys to tell me what happened, it made me so very, VERY proud of each and every one of them for the professionals, the warriors, the Special Forces that they truly are. My only regret, of the entire battle, was that I was not there. It is really the only regret I have for my entire life. It is a pain that I will never recover from. But it is not a pain for losing Chris, because even if I were there, it probably would not have mattered. No, my pain is because I was not there for his brothers. I was not there to help them when they needed it the most. For I would gladly give my life for each and every one of them, just as Chris did. Chris gave his life trying to save the lives of the men he loved the most. So, all I can do now is to love them as I loved my son. I will try to make it up to them and their families for the rest of my life, because they WERE there for my son. They WERE there for each other. And they need to know that they are indeed heroes for what they did, and how they did it!!!

8

7-22 August 2005

So live your life that the fear of death can never enter your heart. Show respect to all people, bow to none. Sing your death song and die like a hero going home.

—Tecumseh

The mind is an amazing thing—not that I have any "first hand" experience with a mind, but that is what I have been told! Some things that the mind sees stays with it forever. Some things that it experiences, it can never remember. And some times, when you least expect it, it can bring you back to a time, no matter how long ago, or how minute a detail, that you never thought you would ever experience again.

That is what my poor mind had to endure for the two week period from 7-22 August 2005. There are some things I remember like they were yesterday and I will never EVER forget even the smallest detail of that experience. Yet, there are others that I can't remember no matter how hard I try—and some of those things are experiences I should never have forgotten. I will do my best to recall the events of this two week period that changed the life of OUR family forever.

Much of OUR book has been written sitting on my stationary cycle in my weight room at the house. But, right after Chris called me the night before ODA 316 went wheels up for Deh Afghan, it was incredibly difficult, if not impossible, for me to go down to the weight room to train. EVERY time I would start lifting, or start riding, my mind would INSTANTLY start to think about what I would do if Chris was killed. I don't know why I had those feelings; I had NEVER had them before. But the feeling was so strong; I actually stopped lifting and riding so that I would not have those feelings! I look back now, and think it was preparing me for what was about to happen on 9 August 2005.

Saturday Night 6 August in Colorado/ Sunday Morning 7 August in Deh Afghan

For some reason, I was not feeling very well on Saturday night, 6 August 2005, and so I went to bed early. I usually get up at 0330 during the summer to get ready to go out to Fox Hollow to mow greens, so I had gone to bed about 2100. I was barely asleep when Dianne came upstairs to tell me that Chris was on the home phone. He NEVER called on the home phone. In fact, as soon as Chris got out of Basic Training, and he was able to have his cell phone again, my cell phone was NEVER turned off. Even when I was in meetings, or giving a lecture anywhere in the world—I would apologize before hand, and explain that my son was in the Army, and that if he called, I WAS taking the call! So, my cell phone was on the night stand next to the bed, but Chris had called on the house phone. I asked Dianne which phone, and she said the hard-line down stairs. One of the things I don't remember was flying down those stairs, but she told me later she had NEVER seen me move that fast!

We had an amazing talk! It was the first and only phone call I had received from Deh Afghan. Chris was very apologetic about that, telling me that they had been very busy, and the reception at their firebase was not very good. I asked him how busy, and Chris, being Chris, had a riddle for me: He told me, "Core temperature, Dad—Core temperature!" I laughed and said, "OK—I'll play along" and for the next few minutes while Chris was talking, I was trying to figure out what he meant by "core temperature." It didn't take me long to figure out what he meant—the abbreviation for core temperature is Tre—for rectal temperature. I knew that Deh Afghan could be a pain in the ass, but that is not what he meant for me to figure out—no, Tre was his way of telling me he was in a "Target rich environment!" We talked about the team, and how the new guys were doing. Of the men that were on ODA 316 during the Deh Afghan rotation, most were with Chris in 2004 in Gereshk, and they were: Tony, Scott, Dan, Big Al, and Chuck. The four other members of ODA 316 were new: CPT Brandon was team leader, SFC Cliff was another weapons sergeant, SGT Jon was the junior engineer sergeant, and SGT James was the junior communication sergeant. We talked about all kinds of things that night. Chris asked me to send him a CARE package—he wanted the new Madden 2006 Football video game which came out on 9 August 2006; he wanted some Bronco t-shirts for him and a friend from the Q course—SSG Jerry that was on another team in the area; he wanted some peanut brittle, and he wanted another American flag. That was all he "needed" but if there was anything else I wanted to throw in the box, that was fine as well!!!

Then, the last 10 minutes, we talked about our conversation the night before ODA 316 went wheels up for Deh Afghan just before Father's Day in June 2005. That phone call is one I will NEVER EVER forget. He told me he was sorry that he would probably not be able to call me on Father's Day because they would be somewhere between Bragg and Afghanistan, but that he would call or at least email when he got to his firebase. Then, he said, "Now Dad, there are some things we HAVE to talk about. I know you don't want to hear these things, but we HAVE to talk about them. Just in case something happens—and I don't think it will—but, just in case, this is what I want you to do...," and we talked for almost two hours about what he wanted me to do if "something happened." He wanted to be buried at Arlington National Cemetery. We have a National Cemetery about 15 km from our home, but he wanted to be with his brothers at Arlington. He wanted to be buried with his left arm on his chest, so the Spartans waiting on the other side could see his lambda. He wanted Tim to get some ink, he wanted to get some ink for Scott, and he wanted me to get a lambda on my left arm. He wanted me to get Mom a good quilting machine. And there were several other things he asked me to do that I have done, but they are between Chris and me.

We talked about what happened to me earlier that Saturday morning. I needed to stop at the bank on my way to see my first patient for physical therapy treatment when I stopped at an intersection where there were all these anti-war protestors with signs. It bothered me that these clowns were so uneducated, but maybe they would get run over by a car as they jumped out into traffic trying to force their message on the drivers waiting for the light. But, when I saw them getting their young, 8-10 year old children into the protest and having them run out into traffic, it made my blood boil. I went to the bank, and I SHOULD have kept going away from that intersection to get to my patient's house, but I couldn't let those fools hurt their children, so I drove back. And, as fate would have it, I was the first truck at the red-light. This idiot looked at the Veteran's license plate I had on my truck and so he comes up to my window to get in MY face about the illegal war … BIG MISTAKE ON HIS PART! I started his "education" with … "You have NO idea who you are messing with, do you!?!?" I then proceeded to inform this "oxygen thief" as Chris would have called him, how wrong he was and that I was about to provide him an education he would never forget.

Those of you that know me know I am not the smallest guy. And I tend to get just slightly animated when I have a message to send!!! There was a fear in this moron's eyes that just fueled my "education!" But, just as I was getting to my 'good points', a local Douglas County sheriff showed up, and pulled me aside. He told me that while he understood my points and that he was also a Veteran, if I hit this fool; I would have to be arrested. If HE hit the clown, it would be in 'self-defense' and so I got in the truck while the officer arrested the protestors for obstructing traffic and for some other violation.

Chris was SOOOO mad at me—"You SHOULD have cleaned his clock, Dad!!! But I am proud of you. I wish I could have seen the look on his face when you got out of the Tundra!!! Must have been 'classic'!!!" he told me, and we had a good laugh about "my day!"

We continued our conversation about what he had been doing, the weather, what else he wanted me to send, etc. Small talk, but GREAT talk!

Finally, the last few minutes of our talk on that Saturday night in Colorado and Sunday morning in Deh Afghan were spent reviewing what I was to do for him if something happened. At about 0630 local time in Afghanistan, he told me he had to get some breakfast and then get to a briefing as they were going out on a mission, and he had a few more things to do to get ready. He told me that he loved me, and he thanked me for all I had done with him over all the years. His last words were, "I love you, Dad" and there was something dramatically different about the way he said that this last time. From the time Chris was a young boy, we would always end our talks by telling each other that we loved one another. But this time, the last time, there was something so very different in Chris' voice as he told me he loved me.

One of the things I have learned and I knew Chris learned this as well, is the meaning of the word "love" from the men, the warriors, the Spartans of ODA 316. I have never been around a group of men that so freely told their brothers they love them, and how deeply they meant those words. Chris had learned about love from his brothers, and there was something very special in the way he said his last words to me, "I love you, Dad."

Monday 8 August in Colorado

Tim was going to start his sophomore year at the University of Hawai'i on 21 August, so we were going to fly out to Honolulu on 9 August 2005 to move him out of his apartment and find him a new place to live. So, on 8 August, we did the errands we needed to do to get him ready for our trip. In the course of our running around town, I got the things that Chris wanted me to send him, all but the Madden game, which I could pick up first thing Tuesday morning, 9 August, at Wal-Mart. The game was supposed to be available at 0500 local time and Tim and I didn't need to leave for our flight until about 0900 for our 1145 flight to Honolulu.

Tuesday 9 August, 2005 in Colorado

I got up early, drove out to the Wal-Mart at 0445 and got Chris the Madden 2006 football game. I picked up a couple of DVD's for him as well, and headed home to box up his CARE package. I arrived at the post office when it first opened, and then headed home to wake Tim up and load the truck. I had told Tim we were leaving for the airport at 0900, and he told me he would be ready. About 0830 he jumped in the shower, and while he was drying his hair, I walked out to put our gear in the back of my Tundra pick-up truck. We live on the end of a cul-de-sac, and so by 0840 everyone on the street that went to work that day had left by then, and so it was very unusual for any other vehicles to come down our street at that hour.

I was half way down the driveway when I saw a white Suburban with government license plates coming down the street. My eyes instantly went from the plates to the driver, and I saw a man in Army Class A uniform. My eyes then saw as big as a billboard the Special Forces Long Tab and Unit patch on his left shoulder, and I froze at that point in the driveway. I dropped my luggage and watched as the Suburban drove around the cul-de-sac and parked in front of our house. Two soldiers got out, the driver put on his Green Beret, and they started up the driveway toward me.

The only thing I could say was, "Who else was killed?" The SF Warrant Officer said to me, "Mr. Falkel, can we go inside?" Again, I demanded in a much louder voice, "WHO ELSE IS KILLED???" and he told me, "No one else, sir. Can we go inside?"

I couldn't move. My legs would not function. I just stood there, for what seemed an eternity. Finally, the Warrant Officer took my left arm, and the chaplain took my right arm and helped me into the house. We sat down in the living room, and the young Warrant started to talk. "Wait, I told him, let me get Tim." And I yelled up to Tim and told him to get down stairs NOW! He later told me he knew something was wrong because he had never heard me talk like I did ever before. Tim came running down the stairs, his hair still wet from his shower, and when he saw who was in the living room with me, he looked at me with a look I will never be able to get out of my mind. I introduced Tim to the officers, and the Warrant started to talk again. "Wait!" I told him. "I know how difficult this must be for you, and my wife just got to work. Let me go get her so you only have to say this once. Is that OK with you?" He said, "of course ," and so I raced to the library about 3 km from our house.

The library opens at 0900 sharp, not a nanosecond before, and so when I got to the library about 0855, there were about 15 people waiting outside the front doors for the library to open. I ran up to the front door, and saw Dianne right near the front check-out desk. I started banging on the door to get her attention. She saw me, looked at her watch, and I could see by the expression on her face that it was NOT 0900 yet, and so she was NOT going to open the door. I keep banging on the glass door—I am surprised I did not break the glass I was hitting it so hard—and still she would not open the door. I could see her mouth the words, "What is so important???" And without any hesitation, I yelled at the top of my lungs, "Chris is DEAD!"

I want to apologize to the people waiting for the library to open that morning of 9 August for my outburst. Dianne's supervisor came to the door, opened it, and I went inside. Dianne asked again, "What..." and I walked over to the counter and collapsed while I told her that Chris was killed. I told her that two soldiers from 10th SFG (A) down at Fort Carson in Colorado Springs, CO were at the house, and we needed to go to the house NOW! I asked her if she wanted me to drive, and she said no, she wanted her car back at the house, so I got in the truck and headed to the house. While I was driving, I called the people I needed to call to start the phone tree going so that I didn't have to personally call everyone in my family. I called one of my oldest and dearest friends, Dr. Tom Baechle first. When he saw on his caller ID it was me, he answered the phone with the great joy that he normally had when he saw that I was calling. It was the first time I broke down when I told him that Chris was dead and could he make all the calls to our brothers and sisters in the strength and conditioning profession. He of course said yes, but I could tell how much it affected him. The next call was my supervisor at work. I had taken 10 days leave to take Tim to Hawai'i, and I told her that I had no idea how long it would take for the memorials, the funeral, etc. She told me not to worry, to take as much time as I needed, and she would take care of my patients for me. The last person I called on my way back to the house was my brother, Mic. Mic is a dentist in Monterey, CA, and he was already at work. I told him to go to our mother's house who lived about 10 km from his office and be with Grandma when he told her. Grandma loved Chris so very much, and I knew it would be so hard on her. She had to be there 3 years earlier when my brother and sister-in-law lost their new born son, Jay Harmon Falkel, and that almost killed her—I was worried that learning about Chris would be divesting to her—and it was.

I waited for Dianne in the driveway, and we went into the house together. I introduced her to the officers, and we sat down and heard what they had to say. They told us there had been an intense fire fight, and that they did not have all the details as the battle was still going on. They did not know exactly what happened, but that Chris was killed by small arms fire, as opposed to an Improvised Explosive Device (IED). I told them that I wanted to hear directly from his teammates what happened, and so they didn't have to worry about that. We then talked about what would happen next. As they started to lay out the details of what would be happening, it hit me—Tim and I needed to cancel our flight! I let Tim and Dianne continue talking to the officers while I called United Airlines and explained the situation. Again, it wasn't until I said the words, "my oldest son was just killed in Afghanistan" that I lost it! The United representative was terrific. She told me not to worry, she would take care of everything, and she told me that there were seats on all the flights from Denver to Honolulu for the next several days, and that she would get Tim and me on the first plane we could take.

I went back into the living room and we started talking about where we wanted Chris to be buried. I knew Chris wanted to be laid to rest at Arlington, but in a moment of selfishness, I thought about the local National Cemetery in Colorado, so he would be close to me. Well those thoughts lasted about 16 seconds—Chris' wish was to be at Arlington, and Arlington is where he belonged. Next, they asked about any local memorials. There would be a Memorial at Ft. Bragg, but if we wanted a Memorial in Littleton, we could do that as well. Dianne wanted one at her church, so we said we would like one there as well as at "home."

I finally asked the question that barely came out of my mouth— "Who is bringing Chris home, and when will he get here?" I then asked if I could go to Kandahar to bring him home myself. They told me that they didn't know the answers to any of those questions, but they would let me know. It was then that the hole in my heart tore my chest and my soul wide open. I was not there when my son needed me the most. I may be old, but I still have a particular skill set, and I wasn't there for Chris. I don't know what was worse—the thought that I would never see my son again, or the fact that I was not there at his hour of need. I begged the Warrant Officer to see if there was anyway that I could bring my hero, my warrior, my son home.

Tim and Dianne were holding each other, pretty much in shock. After about 30-45 minutes of talking about logistics of what would be happening over the next few days, we came to a point in the conversation where we needed to get some intel from Bragg before we could make any more decisions. The tremendous soldiers were so compassionate, so professional, and I could see how difficult it was for them to have this

Casualty Assistance duty, because even though they did not know Chris personally, he was part of the community, part of the SF family, and they were hurting as well.

While we were waiting for some answers, I went out on the front porch to be with my thoughts. Our next door neighbor, Thomas, who is Tim's age and a member of the U.S. Marine Corps Reserve, drove up to his parent's house and saw me sitting on the steps. Thomas always has a smile on his face, and he came over to tell me that his older brother, Matt—Chris' best friend from home—was on his way to Colorado for the birth of Thomas' first child. As he came up the yard, he could see how upset I was and when I told him, he stood there in total disbelief. Thomas told me he would let Matt know. Then, my cell phone started ringing. I took some of the calls, others, I let roll over to my voice mail. I called two of my closest friends and within 30-45 minutes, Bob, his son SSG Cody and Dr. Tom were there sitting next to me on the front porch.

By mid morning, we had set up that the Memorial at Ft. Bragg would be 18 August, and Chris would be interred at Arlington National Cemetery on 22 August 2005. We were still waiting to see about a memorial in Littleton, that we were planning to hold a day or two before the Memorial at Ft. Bragg. I knew I needed to get Tim to Hawai'i, so we planned to fly over the next day, on 10 August, get his gear out of his apartment, temporarily store it at my sister-in-law's brother's house on the North Shore of Oahu, and then we would look for an apartment for Tim after we got back from Arlington.

The rest of the day was total chaos. People were calling to see what they could do for us. Dianne, Tim and I wandered around the house, still in shock. But at some time that afternoon, two things happened that I will always remember: first, Dianne told me that "our family will never be the same again!" Those words, of all we said to each other that day, stick in my mind like no others, because she was right—our family changed forever from that day forward. But, as I would say in my eulogy at the Memorial in Littleton, our lives became that much fuller for the tremendous family we now had—Chris' SF family.

The second thing I remember was my first call from CPT Jim. While I had never actually met CPT Jim, Chris talked about him constantly, and he was calling to tell me how sorry he was, how much he loved Chris, and to let me know he would take care of everything he could. I knew from that first phone call that Jim and I shared the same heart, and that he loved my son as much as I did. Thank you, my brother, for all you did for me that day, and EVERY day since 9 August 2005.

Later that evening, I was sitting out on the front porch when Matt arrived from the airport. I ran to meet him as he got out of the car and we held each other, needing all our strength to keep each other on our feet. We walked back to the porch, and started talking. Matt told me he couldn't believe it—in fact, he told Thomas when Thomas told Matt what had occurred, that, "That is not funny Thomas! There is NO WAY Chris is dead—he is too good to be killed!!!" We sat there for hours, talking, laughing, crying, and missing Chris as I never knew you could miss someone.

At this point in the summer of 2005, there was an anti-war protestor that was the mother of a fallen hero that was killed in Iraq. She was making a name for herself by her protests, and the news media was covering everything she did. My fear, and Matt's too, was that some reporter was going to stick a microphone in my face, and ask me what I thought about the war that took my son from me, and I would rip their throat out! So, we decided that we would NOT talk to the media. That was not going to be a problem for me because I was going wheels up the next morning with Tim, but Dianne would be here by herself, and I was concerned for her. Matt looked me in the eye and told me not to worry—that he would take care of EVERYTHING, including the media. So as bad as I felt about leaving at this critical time, I knew Matt would, indeed, take care of everything.

Wednesday 10 August 2005 in Hawai'i

Tim and I left early for our flight. The only seats available were two seats in First Class that United provided to us for the same price as our economy seats that we cancelled the day before. Somewhere over the Pacific, I started writing notes about Chris on the napkin that came with my Cran-Apple Juice with no ice! I asked the flight attendant for some more napkins and she brought me some paper. As I flew at 36,000 feet, I felt a closeness to Chris that I had never experienced before.

From that day until now, there is a feeling I have when I am wheels up that I do not experience at any other time. The VAST majority of this book has been written at over 30,000 feet because I feel Chris there as closely as at any other time with the exception of out at Fox Hollow. I have also written parts of OUR book while I was riding my stationary cycle; while ruck marching for fitness; even while sleeping. I have written down notes on napkins, "Kleenex ," magazine margins, "Rite-in-the-Rain" notebooks (over 70!), and even the back of my hand until I found some paper.

We landed in Honolulu, and the first thing Tim and I did was to go down to Waikiki beach and get in the water. The Hawaiian's call the water off Oahu the "healing waters" and they were just that on that day. Tim and I spent several hours in the water—talking about Chris. It was just what Tim and I needed to do. Up to this point I had been so busy trying to get things organized that I had not had much time to spend with Tim. He loved his big brother, and I knew this was as hard on him as it was on me. That conversation in the healing waters was one of the best that Tim and I have ever had! Thank you for taking care of your old dad that day, Tim—I love you with all my heart!!!

After we got out of the water, we started moving Tim's apartment into our relative, Dave's, truck. My cell phone rang, and it was Jimbo. He was checking to see how I was doing, and to let me know that Tony would be bringing Chris back to me. As with the rest of ODA 316, while I had never actually met them, I knew a great deal about them for all my talks with Chris. But of all his brothers, I knew the most about Tony. I was glad that T was the one that would be bringing Chris home— it was fitting. After we dropped off our first load, I checked my email, and there was an email from Tony (that I have included in his chapter). It touched my heart, and even though I had never met him, I knew from his email how much he loved Chris, and for that, I would always love him. Before Tim and I went back to the beach, I talked to Matt. I was just about to tell him about my writing notes about Chris on the plane, and that maybe we should talk to the media, when Matt told me, "We NEED to let the world know about Chris and what an amazing person, soldier, warrior, friend, brother and son he was!!!" Matt and I started crying together on the phone because we were both thinking exactly the same thing at the same time—something that happened to Chris and I more times than I can possibly remember!!! Matt told me that there were multiple news stations trying to get an interview, and he kept them away from Dianne. But there was one station, the CBS affiliate in Denver, that had a reporter that seemed to really care about Chris, and NOT just about a story, so he would talk to her and give her Chris' story.

I hate the news media! I rarely watch or listen to the news because I get so mad at the bias they have in their reporting. Case in point: One of the local Denver stations said that I was "unavailable for comment about Chris' death because I was on 'vacation' in Hawai'i!!!" Oxygen Thieves!!!

Over the next two days, I got over 300 emails, and over 400 cell phone calls from literally all over the world. Tony kept me informed every step of their journey from Afghanistan to CONUS. Jim emailed and called me several times. Markus called and emailed me several times and told me he would be coming along with several of Chris' other brothers to any memorial we had in Colorado. We decided to have a Memorial Service on 16 August at Dianne's church, and then we would fly to Fayetteville on 17 August, the day before the SF Memorial at the JFK Chapel on 18 August. And it was all scheduled—Chris would be buried with full military honors at Arlington National Cemetery on Monday, 22 August 2005.

That night, while Tim tried to sleep, I took some of the things I remembered about Chris on the flight over to Paradise, and wrote them down. Markus had asked me to put some thoughts together about Chris for "OUR boys" and for me to send out to people that did not know Chris. As I sat there on the balcony of Tim's apartment, somehow this document was put into my computer. I literally have NO memory of typing this, but it was the first of many emails I would write about my hero, my warrior, my son:

> My son, my hero
>
> Chris had always, since he was a very young boy, wanted to be a soldier. His first noises were imitations of various weapons. When he was old enough to want to start playing with guns, I wouldn't let him, in fact, he

never owned a toy gun because guns are not toys. And he would get so mad at me because I would not let him even own a squirt gun. When he graduated from the 18 Bravo course, one of his first comments to me was remembering that story. But it was then, and I think only then, that he realized what I was trying to teach him. I had always told him that when he was old enough to learn how to use a weapon correctly, I would buy him one. And for those of you who served with Chris, it was Dad who provided him with his "arsenal" as he liked to call it!

One day, when cleaning out the rafters in the garage, I found an old ruck sack of mine that Chris had taken and he had it stuffed it full of various home made weapons that he thought he might need someday, if we were ever attacked! He started making his own designs as a young child and continued perfecting them until he reached high school.

Chris' room at home had an aspen tree next to the window, and when we moved into our Colorado home, Chris got that room instead of the room on the other side of the house where he would have to jump off the roof to get to the ground. I figured he would be safer climbing up and down the tree (plus it would be more fun, and he definitely knew how to climb!).

Chris was the first kid to wear BDU's to school, EVERYDAY! He would take my old uniforms and adapt them as he needed for what ever "mission" he was planning next.....

Chris was always a great athlete, and loved hitting things. Once, at about the age of 8 or 9, we were off to a soccer game and half way there, he realized he did not have one of his soccer shoes. So we turned around, and when I ran into the house to get his shoe, I noticed all these marks on the Adidas stripes. Chris told me that each mark stood for a guy that he had taken out when tackling for the ball. In all the years he played soccer, he never once got a yellow card as a warning for a severe foul. But he played the game, as he did his life, full speed ahead and with full force.

He also loved the mountains and the outdoors. Snowboarding, camping, hiking were his passions. He was just as comfortable sleeping under the stars as he was in a five star hotel room, and I think he would much rather be outdoors under the stars. We started land navigation when he was young as a game, and even as a young child he knew where he was going, and how he was going to get there.

Even though he had a tough exterior and possessed a serious expression that would frighten even the toughest individual, Chris also had a soft interior and was very emotional, particularly with his family. One of my proudest moments was when I saw him at his AIT graduation at Ft. Benning, and he told me that after jump school, he was going to try for selection into Special Forces. I'm not sure which one of us starting crying first, but they were tears of joy and pride for both Chris and myself. He was always my "protector ," particularly after one of my many surgeries. Chris always made sure I was never walking alone while everyone else was walking so much faster and farther ahead of me.

We loved talking "shop" about SF. It was a good thing we had the same cell phone company where our plan allowed us to have unlimited minutes, because there were many, many phone calls that were hours in length. And then there were others that might last only a few seconds. When Chris wanted to talk, he could do it with the best of them, but when he didn't, you couldn't get him to say a word. As much as I will miss him, I think I will miss our "shop talks" the most. Being an old soldier, it was so great to hear what he was doing, and even better to be part of his world in some small way.

Chris loved his job, and loved the brotherhood he developed with his team, ODA 316. Whenever we would talk about the team, you could see the pride and passion he had for each guy on 316. He loved to make fun of me, and my "short term memory loss" when it came to who was an 18 Charlie and who was an Echo! But there was never any question who the Bravo was! Tony, Jim, Scott, Mark, Dan, Shawn, Chuck, Big Ron and Big Al, JT and everyone else, he loved each of you guys like a brother, as I do now. And he loved Tim, his first brother. Oh there were many, many times when he would drive Tim crazy with his sharp wit and constant teasing. But no one, and I mean NO ONE better ever do anything to his "little" brother (who was taller than Chris ever since elementary school… much to Chris' dismay!).

Chris had a thirst for knowledge, and not just about what he was interested in. He loved to learn and more importantly, loved to question, just about EVERYTHING, for he felt he truly learned best by questioning what others accepted as truth.

I was truly blessed to not only have had such a wonderful son as Chris, but to have had him as a friend and colleague. He was one of the few people who understood why I would get emotional whenever he would leave to go back to Ft. Bragg, for he too, would let me know how much he loved me and how much he would miss me as well. We will all miss you, my warrior, my son, but none more than your old dad.

I love you and you have made me so very proud of all you were, all you became, and all you meant to me and everyone else whose life you touched. You are my hero, my son, and I know you will always be with all of us who loved you so very much.

Tim and I got home on 14 August. We tried to get home for Dianne's birthday on 13 August, but there were no flights available. I have absolutely no memory of the flight back, and the rest of 14 August. With the exception of literally the minute I walked in the door back at our house in Littleton. I was no sooner in the door and there was a knock on the door. I opened the door to see the FedEx man there handing me a package. It was a book—*Gates of Fire*!!! I just stood there and lost it—It actually took me almost 30 minutes to get through the unbelievable letter that the author, Steve Pressfield, had written to us! This was the author of MY favorite book, the book that Chris and I read together when he first got to Gereshk over the internet, the ONLY book I have ever read more than once (… and I am up to 4 times, Steve but I have a long way to go to catch the number of times Jimbo has read it!!!), and HE was sharing his heart with me!

It was years later, after I actually met Steve, that he shared with me the email he got from Markus that prompted him to send me the signed book and that tremendous letter. Here is what Markus shared with Steve:

Mr. Pressfield,

It is with a heavy heart that I write to you now. One of my brothers has passed on. He has made the Great Journey. He was killed in Afghanistan on Aug 8th, during a 54 hour continuous fight against our nation's enemies. ODA 316 performed like true warriors. 69 confirmed kills by the C-130 gunship video. It is well agreed at SF Command that there is NO other team that could have made it out alive. My BROTHER'S name is CHRISTOPHER M. Falkel, 22 year old, weapons Sgt. for our team. His dying request, before passing, was to be buried in blue jeans and a tee shirt, WITH HIS LEFT (SHIELD SIDE) FOREARM ACROSS HIS CHEST. This is where Chris—aka JR.—had his Lambda tattooed. He was a man of small stature, but possessed the heart of a LION!!!

His father and brother, along with others that fought along side JR., will have a bon-fire in my back yard to honor Chris. He is being recommended for the SILVER STAR for his acts of heroism... There will be a Battalion Memorial on 18 Aug 10:00 hrs, at the Special Forces Chapel, Ft. Bragg, NC. Chris will be buried at Arlington National Cemetery on 22 Aug.

I invite you to the BN Memorial on 18 Aug to join the brothers left behind as we bid JR. our farewell. His family will be there along with many other Special Forces Warriors.

Thank You for your book of inspiration.....

Chris was a true Spartan and he will be missed but NEVER FORGOTTEN !!!

WITH IT or ON IT !!!! SFC MARKUS ODA 316

Chris' Father is a great warrior also, I KNOW he would appreciate a phone call if you can. JEFF knows and understands that we live by the Spartan code. He knows of your book. JEFF FALKEL (XXX) XXX-XXXX

Maybe now you understand how much the words you have written mean to us.

That email was sent to Steve on 13 August, and the FedEx package arrived 14 August!!! Palamo yelo, kola!

Monday, 15 August 2005 in Colorado

While we were in Honolulu, Tim and I bought some shirts for ODA 316. There were some really cool University of Hawai'i "Warrior" t-shirts, and of course, we had to get everyone an aloha shirt! I have talked about my aloha shirts earlier in OUR book, so it was so very important for me to get shirts for my new family.

At mid-afternoon, Tim and I headed out to the airport to meet the boys coming from Bragg for the Memorial. We were not exactly sure who was coming, or even what they looked like. Whenever I travel, I always wear a bright red aloha shirt so whoever is picking me up can easily spot me in the crowd; so I told the boys to look for a red aloha shirt. Right on time, I saw a group of men coming off the escalator at Denver International Airport, and I instantly knew they were my son's brothers! The first one off the escalator was CSM Buzzsaw. He had his Kansas City "Chefs" hat on, and ONLY Buzz would wear a Chiefs hat to meet Chris' dad! I instantly recognized Tony because he was the only one of Chris' teammates that I had actually seen a picture of, and I had seen so many pictures of Chris and Tony over the years. But the third person I saw had a look in his eyes that I will never forget. His look went right to my heart and touched my soul. It had to be CPT Jim, and it was. Then came Shawn, Markus, JT, CPT Tim and the chaplain. They instantly saw my red aloha shirt—after all, they ARE professionals…Ha! Ha! I hugged each one of them, and the first thing I told each of them was that I loved them! I can only imagine the looks on the faces of the other people in the airport of these enormous, inked up men hugging and crying in each other's arms!

We went from the airport to the rental car place. Shawn and Markus rented a Cadillac!! I don't know why I found that funny at the time, but I REALLY find it funny now! Tim and I then lead them to the hotel so they could check in, and then we had all the boys come to our house for a dinner that Dianne's friends had prepared. After dinner, I had to show the boys some things around the house. I showed them Chris' room and they all had to touch the SF "Long Tab and Arrowhead" that Chris had on the wall above his bed, as he had told them all that story. We went down to my weight room in the basement and I told them I wanted to give ODA 316 one of my Lakota replicas, and that I wanted one to make the journey with Chris. Shawn instantly said that my Crazy Horse shield needed to be in the ODA 316 team room back at Ft. Bragg, and my ceremonial pipe needed to go with Chris—so that was what we did.

Over the course of that evening, I sat on the back deck with Shawn for a long time—talking, laughing, crying and loving my son! I sat out on the front porch with Jimbo and JT, again sharing our hearts and our pain.

That evening at the house, I learned first hand WHY Chris loved these men as much as he did—I have been around the military most of my life, and I have NEVER been with men, warriors, Spartans like Chris' brothers! They touched my heart with their love of my son. They filled my spirit with their love for me. They showed me what Chris used to tell me all the time—"These guys put the SPECIAL in Special Forces!" But most of all, it made me so very, VERY grateful that Chris knew, experienced, and lived SF with these amazing warriors!

Tim and I escorted the boys back to their hotel late that night, and we planned to link up before the first Memorial on 16 August 2005.

Tuesday 16 August 2005 in Colorado

I let the boys sleep in a little before heading down to see them in the morning. The Memorial was going to be in the evening, so I thought I would take the boys to one of Chris' favorite places—the Coors Brewery in Golden, Colorado!!! I had gone there with Chris for the first time when Chris was home on his last Christmas leave, and it was fascinating! What I remember most was our stop at the gift shop because Chris HAD to get something for everyone on ODA 316 from the Coors factory! The only one of his brothers that he had a hard time finding "just the right gift" for was 1 LT Dan—Dan was a Guinness man, but Chris was able to find Dan a Guinness shirt somewhere!

CPT Jim and CSM Buzzsaw stayed at the hotel to work on their eulogies and correspond and coordinate with HQ back at Bragg. So, we left them at the hotel, and the rest of us headed to THE factory! Even though I had been there only 8 months earlier, it was like I was seeing the brewery for the first time! Because, this time, I was seeing it through the eyes of the men Chris loved as much as he loved me! We laughed and cried together—I will always remember that tour!

After I dropped the boys off back at the hotel, and I was driving back to the house, I decided that I would give a eulogy at the Memorial. I didn't think I could, and I still don't know how I did it, but I felt this need to write down something just in case the spirit moved me at the Memorial.

I was 90% done with my thoughts, and I had about 15 minutes before we had to leave for the church when my brother, Mic, showed up from California! I didn't know he was coming to Littleton—I thought he was just going to meet us at Arlington, but it was so good to see him. However, while I wanted to spend time with him, particularly because he had to fly back to California right after the Memorial, I needed to finish my eulogy!

When we got to the church, Dianne's friends and colleagues from the library set up a display of some of Chris' things. It was MY mission to set up the display that meant more to me than anything I had ever seen before…

All of the men on ODA 316 wanted to come back with Chris, but command would only let one person, and the team selected Tony. So, Tony not only brought my son back to me, but he brought the Green Berets of the rest of ODA 316 to be with us at all the Memorials and at Arlington as well! That act of respect, honor and love was something I never expected, and on one of the worse days of my life, this act of LOVE did more for me that you can possibly imagine. We set up a table at the back of the church for 316's Green Berets!

The Memorial Service was very special. Several ODA's from 10th Special Forces Group (Airborne) at Fort Carson in Colorado Springs came up for the service. None of them knew Chris, but they wanted to be there for their fallen brother. People that I hadn't seen in years were there for us. There were several speakers at the Memorial. The Governor of Colorado—Bill Owens—read one of the scripture readings, which was such an honor for us.

One of Chris' friends from high school read this poem:

Always With Us

Choices, choices many are they
They decide what we do each day
Where we go and the games we play
The good times and bad we'll be OK

Chances, chances that we will take
From the dares we do to the friends we make
How fast we drive and the rules we break
Not knowing the facts or the heartache
Changes, changes are beginning to grow
As we watch the sun set and the rivers flow
Chris we all wished that you did not go
I know we will see you again, I know

When you look up into the sky
A tear will fall from your eye
We will hear his voice whisper "Don't cry"
For in our hearts he will never die

We'll all pull through no matter the cost
You will be here through sun, rain and frost
From the winters first snow to the springs first moss
The memories of you will never be lost

Chris you will be remembered dear
All will feel love and none will feel fear
We will all think of you as if you were near
Your life may be gone but your spirit's still here

This poem was originally written for a high school classmate of Chris' that was killed in a car accident. The poem was originally written by Chris! His friend just changed the name in the last stanza to "Chris!" Chris had many talents, and writing poetry was one of them. There is no real good place to share this other poem that Chris wrote many years before we all heard his eulogy poem but, it seems appropriate to place it here in OUR book:

Life

I love life
Life is something we all should love
Some people waste their life

Life gives you freedom
It gives you a chance
To some, life is long
To others, it is very short

—By Chris Falkel, Age 13

There were several other speakers at the Memorial. Another one of Chris' friends read another Bible passage. The priest had some very thoughtful words.

But then it was time for us. Markus got up first, and shared his love for Chris! He didn't have a script—he spoke directly from his heart. When he was done, I have no idea how I did this, but I went up to the alter and hugged him. It might not have been proper protocol, but it was Chris moving through me—thanking his brother for loving him, and now me.

Then, it was Tony's turn. I have included the magnificent words he spoke in his Chapter in OUR book. But, everyone in that church KNEW how much Tony loved his little brother! Again, Chris had me get up and give Tony a hug for both of us.

The third eulogy came from CPT Jim. Jim wrote two eulogies. This was the one he gave at both the Memorial in Littleton and again at the JFK Chapel at Ft. Bragg:

> *Although extraordinary valor was displayed by the entire corps of Spartans, yet bravest of all was declared Dienekes. It is said that on the eve of battle, he was told by a native of Trachis that the Persian archers were so numerous that, when they fired their volleys, the mass of arrows blocked out the sun. Dienekes, however, quite undaunted by this prospect, remarked with a laugh, "Good. Then we'll have our battle in the shade."*

> *Chris was a warrior and he was my friend.*

> *I was not there the day Chris fought so bravely and died. I want to make that very clear. The men who fought with Chris that day are still in Afghanistan*

preparing to do battle with the enemy again, minus one, Tony, who is here with us today and was given the great honor of bringing Chris home.

However, I loved Chris dearly and he loved me as well. And I believe I can shed some light on a part of Chris that you did not know.

I was Chris' first commander on ODA 316. I need to tell you briefly about ODA 316—they were and still are—a great band of warriors. You will not find a better fighting force in any army, anywhere in the world. Aggressive, tenacious, smart, dedicated, courageous, brave, and loyal. Through this rare mixture of warrior ethics and personalities grew two things: an overwhelming need and urge to kill the enemies of our nation, and a great love for one another.

This was the situation a young Chris Falkel found himself thrust upon. ODA 316 had already been deployed to Afghanistan and was full of veterans who had proven themselves under fire. Men before him had come and tried to join this group and failed.

Chris excelled. I want to make one thing perfectly clear: Chris was not accepted because he was a good guy, or for his great sense of humor, he was accepted because he was a warrior.

The history of war is the history of warriors; few in number mighty in influence. Chris was a warrior. He knew no fear.

He took part in incredible Air Assault raids deep into enemy territory, he drove hundreds of kilometers into infamous Taliban strongholds, he cleared tunnels and caves, and ultimately fought in a great battle that will go down in the annuals of Special Forces history. This is how Chris fought.

Chris was a warrior.

I have heard it said that this country's greatest treasure is its children. I disagree. A country's greatest treasure is its warriors. In today's world, true warriors are the rarest breed of all. And this country is less one warrior today.

Chris lived for his country, freedom, his beautiful family, and Special Forces.

He died for his team—the men fighting with him on 8 August 2005. He died for the values and ideals that the team stood for and that is the bottom line.

Chris made the ultimate sacrifice.

But know this: Chris died doing what he loved the most, with the men he loved most, and men who loved him dearly. And I swear when you see him again, he will tell you just that.

Chris, the Spartan Honor Guard is awaiting your arrival. They are three hundred in number, dressed in scarlet and gold with the "lambda" displayed proudly on their shields... just as you display it—tattooed on your left forearm.

And lastly to our brothers who still even today find themselves on the field of battle, they will honor Chris through their relentless pursuit and destruction of our enemies. This I know for certain. It is all they know.

Chris, leading you was the greatest honor and privilege of my life.

Chris was a warrior and he was my friend.

WITH IT OR ON IT.

(The second eulogy Jimbo wrote is presented in his Chapter in OUR book. He wrote it on the plane flying to Denver, with tears in his eyes ...)

As with Markus and Tony, I got up and hugged Jimbo. But this time, it was different. It was at that moment, and that moment alone, that I decided if Chris' brothers could find the courage, the strength, and the love to get up and talk about Chris, there was NO WAY that I was not going to!!!

So, this is what I had to say about my warrior, my hero, my son:

Because we are honoring an SF warrior, I need to become more stealthy.

Thanks for the shades, Thomas, they have come in handy this week.

There is a hole in my heart that all of you are needed to fill...

My dear wife said last week that our family will never be the same, and she was right, it has grown more than I can imagine.

Chris would always get "pissed" off when I would brag about him...but too bad, buddy, I'm just getting started!

First I would like to recognize some very special, Special Forces:

CPT Jim
CPT Tim
WO1 Shawn
CSM Buzzsaw
SFC Markus
SFC Tony
SSG JT

I started Chris' education in the military, but these are warriors gave him his Ph.D.

I also want to introduce SSG Cody Armstrong and the rest of the 10th SFG that are here today to honor their fallen brother. Thank you, my brothers for your service to our country, and your love of my son.

Chris wanted to be SF since he was 8 years old.

For Chris, it wasn't a job or an adventure, it was a way of life.

He wasn't Always Faithful, he was always ready.

No way Chris would Aim High, that would be a waste of a round.

And he wasn't an army of one, but one with his SF brothers.

One of my dearest friends told me a story about her five year old son last week, setting up his Army men in a neat orderly row on the floor. When asked if he wanted to be a computer genius like his dad, or a police man or fireman, his response was, "No, I want to be an ARMY man!"

Chris always wanted to be in SF, in fact when he played army, there were squads in superior positions, some set for ambushes, etc. and he would use the whole room to simulate the battlefield.

When we lived in Ohio, he would hide my tools in the large field next to our house in strategic locations in case of an attack.

Only Chris—

Would beg me to put in a tether ball pole in the backyard so he could beat all the other kids in elementary school.

Would put hash marks on his soccer boots for the number of guys he took out while winning the ball.

Would beat the high school sprint star while running in his, or rather my, combat boots.

Would get my car stuck in the mud up to the doors trying to get a friend to McDonald's before it closed.

Would want a sniper rifle for a high school graduation gift.

Would put an air horn in his golf bag to get his brother during his back swing...don't worry Sonny, I wouldn't let him do it!

Had eyes that told you everything about him, from happiness to anger and every emotion in between. For being the tough, badass he was, he wasn't afraid to cry... another skill I passed on to him.

Chris loved to write poetry

Hated the water

Loved wearing hats—particularly Bronco hats

He was competitive at EVERYTHING

He always had a movie line for every situation

He had a very dry wit, and he loved to laugh

The world is a safer and better place for having him in it.

I know he is with his grandfather, another warrior, as well as the other great warriors that have fallen before him. Chris is waiting there for us now. But I am going to miss you, my son until I can stand by your side and tell you I love you again.

Chris had two expressions that he said to me constantly:

The first was, "Short term memory, Dad, Short term memory!!!" And the other was his dislike for officers, right CPT Jim???

But, he would always tell me, "I will NEVER call you sir, because I get to call you DAD!"

HOKAHEY, CANTI SAKAPI … CATO HNAKE

After my eulogy, the Memorial was over. Dianne, Tim and I were escorted out by my two closest friends from Colorado. Dianne and Tim headed out of the church to meet people, but when we got to the back of the church where we had put ODA 316's Green Berets, I stopped in my tracks, and knew that is where I needed to stand.

Good thing I did—someone came up to me as he was leaving the church, and said, Wow, these are cool!!! Are they souvenirs of the Memorial?" Needless to say, he was very quickly educated!

After we left the church, I have no memory of what happened later that night. My next memory was heading to the airport to fly "home."

17 August 2005—Littleton to Fayetteville

Dianne, Tim and I flew out to Fayetteville early that morning. The gate agent recognized our name from all the media coverage, and he was so gracious and respectful. He was not able to upgrade our tickets, but did give us coupons for the Executive Lounge, and he sent us on our way with his heartfelt sympathy.

I had my Crazy Horse shield, and my ceremonial pipe, and those were my carry-on luggage. I don't remember this, but Tim and Dianne told me later that I got some very strange looks walking through three different airports between Denver and Fayetteville, but NO ONE was going to take these sacred things from me until they got where they NEEDED to be.

As we flew east, I wrote down more stories for OUR book, and it was on that flight that I came up with the title. I wanted to share how Chris became a warrior, and wanted to tell anyone who would read OUR book about the men, the warriors, the family that Chris had and I now have. So, it was determined somewhere over our great country that we would call this book, The Making of OUR Warrior!

Jimbo and his amazing father met us at the airport in Fayetteville. I clearly remember hugging Jim for what seemed like an eternity, but I have no other memories of the rest of that day. As hard as I try, there is nothing there. It was almost like that day never happened ...

18 August 2005 Ft. Bragg, NC

Up to this day, I had probably only slept a total of 10 hours since the Suburban pulled up in front of our house. But, for some reason, I slept like a baby the night of 17 August. The Memorial Service at the JFK Chapel on Ft. Bragg was early the morning of 18 August. We met in the reception area before going into the chapel, and that is where I met so many of Chris' SF family for the first time.

CPT Jim and MSG Tony spoke at this Memorial. LTC (P) had told us that we were NOT to cry at the Memorial, and that was an order! And, I made it all the way until that last part of the ceremony—when they played a recording of "The Ballad of the Green Beret." I lost it as soon as I heard the drums that start the song.

But the most moving part of that ceremony for me was when CSM Buzzsaw performed "The Last Roll Call." He called out, "SSG Christopher Falkel. SSG Christopher Falkel. SSG Christopher Falkel ," and all I could hear was Buzz yelling at Chris for some antic, for making fun of the "Chefs ," or to tell him he needed to take his Coors Light hat off in formation! To this day, I have NO idea how you were able to get through that Last Roll Call, my brother! I have given many speeches about Chris that have pulled at my heart, but ONLY you could have done The Last Roll Call with the class and professionalism of Chris' CSM! Chris loved you CSM, and hearing you say those words with such class and dignity lets me know how much you love Chris!

After the Memorial, there was another reception and that is where I met even more of Chris' family. With each person that came up to me, hugged me and shared a tear with me, it made my heart smile that so many people loved my son. He touched so many, many people's lives, and it was actually a very proud moment for me at a time when my heart was torn apart.

Later that night, we were supposed to have our bonfire at Markus' house, but it was pouring rain. So, we moved the "bonfire" into his garage. I know I was there, and I remember talking to Scott's step-father-in-law, and being with my brother, Dr. Tony Abbott, but that is about it for my memories of that night. I do remember worrying that I had not seen Tim in quite a while. But when I found out he was on the back porch, talking to Markus, it made me happy that one of Chris' big brothers was now Tim's big brother.

We stayed in Fayetteville until Saturday, when we drove up to Washington DC. There was a service at the funeral home on Sunday night, and then Chris was to be interred at Arlington National Cemetery on Monday, 22 August 2005. There are very few things I remember about those 4 days …

21 August 2005—Arlington, VA

I don't remember much before we drove over to the funeral home. When we first got there, my nephew and I got to talk for a few minutes. Mark was leaving for Basic Training in a couple of days, and so I told him how proud I was of him, how much I loved him, and I gave him a set of Chris' BDU's. I remember the confusion initially with CPT Chandler's family, but LTC (P) took command, and everything worked out fine. I remember walking into the room, and seeing the American flag covering Chris' casket. That is a memory I have actually tried to forget, but it will be there forever. I just stood in the door to that room, completely numb. But, Shawn was there to hold me up with his strength.

Believe it or not, I have no memory of Jimbo, JT or ANYONE other than Shawn and LTC (P) being there at the funeral home. Which is so very, very strange to me. I do remember seeing my "little sister"—Chris' godmother, and the rest of her family. I had not seen her beautiful children in several years, so it was good to see them. But I remember thinking I was not going to get to spend any time with them, and that made me incredibly sad.

After what seemed like an eternity, no one got up to talk to the "crowd" that was gathered, so I felt like I needed to get up and say something. I know I was standing there. I know I was looking out at the people that I loved. I know my mouth was moving for some time. But I have no memory of what I said, how long I talked, or what their reaction was to my speaking.

The only vivid memory I have of that night at the funeral home was lifting the cover of the casket with LTC (P), and seeing my son lying there. LTC (P) was so concerned for me, but I told him I HAD to see Chris one more time. So, we folded back the American flag, and lifted the cover together. LTC (P) stood there with me for several minutes to be sure I was OK, and then he left us alone. I leaned forward and kissed his head as I had done thousands of times from 1831 EDT on 24 September 1982 until that night. As I put my hand on his head, I knew then what I had anticipated was the cause of death. When ODA 316 came back in February, 2006 and I finally got to talk to Chris' teammates, they confirmed what I felt that night—that Chris had been killed by a sniper's bullet. He died instantly, and for that, I am eternally grateful that my son, my warrior did not suffer, for that would have been a burden that I could not have handled.

I placed my ceremonial pipe on his chest, and made sure his left forearm was facing forward, like he had asked me to do. I put several other things in his coffin for his journey—things that Chris knows and he is all that needs to know what I gave him. For he gave me so much! He gave me my heart. He gave me his love. He gave me my new family— OUR 316 family. He gave his life so others would have theirs. He gave me my memories of his laugh, his eyes, his wit, his emotions, and most of all, his love. No man ever loved his son more. And no son ever loved his dad as my Chris loved me.

We spent a good amount of time together. And the only reason I left was for the rest of my family, as I knew they would be worried about me being in there. I would have stayed with him there all night until we left for Arlington National Cemetery if they would have let me. There is no word for "good-bye" in Lakota, so it was so hard for me to leave Chris there. Tony had been with him all the way from Mari Ghar, and now, I had to leave him alone. It almost killed me. As I closed the casket, and returned the flag to the place of honor it held, I had never felt so alone in my life. It is a father's job to protect his children, and I was not able to be there when Chris needed me the most. It is a father's job to be there for their children, and I had to leave Chris there alone that night. It is a father's job to give all he has for his children, and I had nothing else to give my son. It broke my heart, and even to this day, it is still broken.

I have said it before in OUR book, and I will say it again—I only have one regret in my entire life. I have done more, seen more, been more places, and had more done to me than most people can even imagine. But the only regret I have in my entire life, is that I was not there on 8 August 2005 with my son, and his brothers. I may be old, I may have had 42 different surgeries, I may have beaten 3 different types of cancer—but I still have a particular skill set that I could have used on 8 August 2005. I realize that my being there would probably not have changed a thing. But, I wasn't there, and even with all the pain I have been through with all that I have done to myself, the pain of not being there when Chris needed me the most is a pain that will never go away. I tried to tell Chris I was sorry, but I guess it will have to wait at least a little longer…

After I left Chris, LTC (P) asked me if I would spend some time talking to CPT Jeremy Chandler's father. I told him of course, but I had no idea who CPT Chandler was. On 10 August, 2005, CPT Jeremy Chandler was killed in action in Afghanistan, not far from where Chris was killed. So, after we got back to the hotel, LTC (P) and I met with Jeremy's dad, and then he and I talked into the early morning hours. We instantly formed a bond that will last for all of time, until we can be with our sons again. Jeremy is interred next to Chris, on his left where Chris' shield can protect CPT Chandler for all of eternity. Jeremy's dad sat in front of me at the Memorialization for our warriors in May 2006, and we needed to be there for each other again to get through that ceremony. You will always have a special place in my heart, LTC (P), and I know our boys are there for each other just as I am always here for you!

22 August 2005 at Arlington National Cemetery

That Monday was a beautiful sunny day in our Nation's capital. We were supposed to meet the Army's Casualty Assistance officer at 1000 to head over to the National Cemetery. The CAO was a wonderful SFC who treated my family with the utmost respect, and did everything she possibly could to make our stay at Arlington as comfortable as possible, and for that, I thank you, Sergeant, with all my heart. When I got downstairs to wait for the limo to take us to the Cemetery, I saw so many of my family and friends that I did not know were going to be there for me. It touched my heart more than I can possibly express. The person that had the most impact on me that day was my "little sister's" brother, a New York City Police Officer, in his dress uniform. I had known Todd for many years, but since that day, Todd has become my brother as well! I kept looking at him, in his uniform, and it actually gave me a strength I didn't think I would have on this day. Todd spent five days searching through the rubble of the World Trade Center trying to find survivors—non-stop! Anyone that had that much strength and love for his fellow officers has my respect and admiration. Over these past three years, Todd and I have shared so much—a love for Chris, our family and our country. Todd, I don't think I have ever told you this, but seeing you that morning was the best thing that could have happened to me, for if you weren't there, I don't think I could have gotten through that day.

We arrived at Arlington, and went into a building to meet family and friends, as well as take care of some official paperwork. I was shocked to see so many of my friends that I hadn't seen in years, and did not expect to see on that day. Thank you for being there for me—it meant and still means so much to me that you would come all that way to be by my side! Before we left for Section 60, I had to meet with an administrator to determine what would be on Chris' stone. When I sat down at the table, and looked at the form, I went blank. I knew what had to be on a stone at a National Cemetery, I just didn't want to see the words as they applied to my son. The one thing that had to be changed was removing the Bronze Star Award, and adding the Silver Star on Chris stone. I remember the administrator asking me, "Are you sure he was awarded the Silver Star?" and the look on my face 'convinced' him. Plus, LTC (P) was standing there next to me, and if I didn't convince him, LTC (P) sure did!!!

After the paperwork was done, we drove over to Section 60, where the heroes from the Global War on Terrorism are all at their eternal rest. The limo pulled up behind the hearse, and we started to gather. The ranking officer at Chris' funeral was a Brigadier General, and he was so very professional. I remember him asking me if he could escort Dianne out to the site. "You are the General, sir! Of course you can escort Dianne!" I told him. For some reason, that was very funny to me. I was standing there next to Tim and the rest of my family was behind us. Tim and I were talking when they opened the door to the hearse, and my heart stopped. Again, I knew it was going to happen, but when it did, it almost killed me again. But just as the honor guard was beginning to turn to walk toward the grave site, my brother-in-law came up and told me there was an eagle over head! Sure enough, as the casket was being moved down the row of granite stones, a huge eagle was soaring about 10 feet above the row where Chris was going to be laid to rest. The eagle soared down the entire row until he got to the tree line at the end of the row, and then he flapped his wings for the first time to gain elevation and soared out of sight. It was a very special thing for me, and fortunately, most of our family that was up near the front of the line got to see our amazing brother soaring over my Chris.

The graveside ceremony was very professionally done—unfortunately, they have had lots of practice over the past few years. BG gave me the American flag that covered Chris' coffin. The Assistant Secretary of Defense came up to me, gave me one of his coins, and told me that the only reason Secretary of Defense Rumsfeld was not there was because he was out of the country. I was fine until they fired off the 21 gun salute, and my heart stopped again. After the ceremony was over, CW2 Shawn, MSG Tony and I stood there by Chris' grave for quite a while. MAJ Jim went back to be with the rest of the family. SSG JT was by Tim's side as he had been since JT got off the escalator in the Denver Airport. I can never thank you enough, my brother JT, for being there for Tim. I marvel at your love for your brother's brother!!!

However, after our time with Chris was over, Shawn, Tony and I turned around, and everyone was gone! I had expected there would be some form of reception where I could get to talk to all my friends and family who had travelled so far to be there, but they were ALL gone! Tim and I were driving back to Ft. Bragg with the boys to get Chris' truck and personal things, so Dianne went with my brother and his wife to the airport to fly back to Colorado. So, for my family that travelled to be there with me on the day that I needed you the most, I thank you from the bottom of my heart. I am so sorry I didn't get to talk to you, or be with you when you came so far to be with me, but know that your mere presence was the strength I needed on the second worse day of my life. I can never thank you enough for being there for me, and for Chris—but I will spend the rest of my life trying.

It was a long drive back to Fayetteville, NC. It should take about five and a half hours, but that trip that day seemed to take forever. When we finally made it back, Tim and I went to Chris' apartment, and we started packing Chris' gear that we wanted to take back to Colorado. We spent that evening together talking, laughing, and remembering all we could about Chris. I tried to sleep, but couldn't. I used to "work" with Chris on developing sleep deprivation tolerance, and all my "work" over all those years actually did pay off, because I probably got about 10 hours sleep total from 9 August until 22 August—that last night in Chris' apartment. I was there in 2004 when Chris moved in. We struggled to get his couch through the front door. Chris made sure I got to sleep in his bed the first night while he tried out the comfy floor! We had cereal for his first meal in his first apartment—Cheerios!

Now, I was there on the last night, with my other son.

The next day, Jimbo, Tony, Shawn, Markus and his infant son Gabe came over early in the morning to help us load the truck. We then went to breakfast at the International House of Pancakes, and while the boys were eating, I held Gabe. I don't remember ANYTHING that was said at that breakfast—all I could do was look into Gabe's beautiful eyes, and think about holding Chris when he was that age. All I could think about was that Chris would never have the chance to hold his son as I got to hold Chris that first day of his amazing life. All I could think of was how I would miss watching Chris grow into even more of a man than he was when he crossed over. All I could think of was how I couldn't wait to be with my warrior again, and I was actually angry for the first and only time since he was killed, that I would have to wait to be with him again.

Tim and I thanked Jimbo, Shawn, Markus and Tony for everything, and then we were on our way. 26 hours later, we were in Littleton. We unloaded Chris' truck, took a shower, loaded up my Tundra, and drove 16 more hours to get to Santa Barbara so we could put the Tundra on a boat to send it over to Hawai'i for Tim. The boys and I used to love our road trips. We would take at least one long road trip a year, just the three of us. They were very special times for all three of us, so this 42 hour road trip just wasn't the same. It was a good time for Tim and I to talk, and we had some tremendous talks over those 42 hours. But, it just wasn't the same without Chris.

My life will never be the same again without Chris…

9

Falcons

When the eagle or falcon's mighty wing feathers become heavy with oil and dirt, and his beak and talons become calcified and brittle, he retires to a hiding place in a cave or rock out of reach of predators and experiences a period of renewal.

With his great beak, he pulls out his mighty wing feathers one by one. Then he extracts each claw. Finally, he begins to smash his beak against the rocks until it too, is gone.

Left defenseless, this peerless, unique bird waits patiently until beak, talons and feathers have re-grown, emerging in his renewed condition—stronger than ever!

—Unknown

Falcons have always held a special place in my heart and in my life. My dad sent me out on my vision quest when I was very young, and a small falcon came to me and told me he would always be there for me, he would always watch over me, and my life would soar like he does with such grace and beauty. He left me with some of his feathers, and I have given those to the people who have blessed my life and have kept me under their wings. They are some of the treasures of my life, and for me to be able to share them with my loved ones has truly been a great honor for me. So, to all of you that have received one of my special feathers, I say again, I love you with all my heart.

When we moved to Colorado in 1990, there were more falcons "living" there than I have ever seen before, and it was a sign to me that our family belonged here. In fact, the "mascot" for our town is the falcon. One of my first memories of showing Chris and Tim the magnificence of a falcon came shortly after we moved into our house. We went over to the school to play soccer, which was pretty much a daily occurrence. But on this day, it was very windy. After playing for several minutes, we looked up, and saw this huge falcon hovering right over the field! It was basically "standing still" getting lift from the wind. It was only about 20 feet above the ground, so we could see clearly every thing he did. Then, almost as suddenly as he appeared, he dove straight down to the edge of the field, and grabbed a field mouse in his talons! Well, the boys went nuts, as did Dad!!! This was the beginning of some truly amazing falcon stories for me and OUR family. They have given my life meaning, they have helped me find my path when I was lost, and their strength and their spirit lift mine and help my heart to soar again.

Since Chris has crossed over, OUR family has had an amazing number of falcon sightings, many more than anyone can ever recall! We would like to share some of them with you…

This is an email to one of OUR friends, Ruth, about one of the first falcon sightings after Chris left us:

> I don't know if Tony ever told you about my experience on Sunday, 28 August. That was the day that Tony was in Buffalo Wild Wings, and at about the same time, you were lighting the candles for Chris. Well, at approximately 0930 Pacific Daylight Time, (…or 1230 in Fayetteville), I was in California with Tim. We were going to drop off my truck in Long Beach to send it over to Hawai'i for him. On that Sunday morning, Tim and the friends we were staying with wanted to go surfing. So, at about 0930, Tim was out in the water, and I needed to go for a walk. Something was compelling me to walk down the beach rather than watch Tim in the water. After a few minutes, a small peregrine falcon started circling over head, and I instantly knew it was Chris. I don't know if you knew this or not, but our name, Falkel, actually means "little falcon" in Lakota. I have seen

falcons all over the world, and when Tony gets back, he will share with you my vision when I was very young about a falcon. But, the amazing thing about this story is that at EXACTLY the same time—1230 EDT/0930 PDT—all 3 of us had the same feeling—that Chris was talking to us through the falcon and letting us know that he was OK and that we would be OK too! Tony had that feeling at the same time I did—only we were 3,000 miles apart!

When I told our friends, they told me that it was very unusual to see a falcon at that location down near the ocean. They had seen them up in the canyon, but never down by the water. I smiled behind my tears, because I knew!

This is an email I sent out to my family on 8 November, 2005—the third month anniversary of Chris' crossing over.

8 November

Today has been a very good, very difficult, very rewarding and very devastating day for me. It was 3 months ago that my son, my warrior was taken from all of us. Believe it or not, that fact did not occur to me when I was working out at the golf course this morning. We are done mowing, but we still have to blow leaves off the greens and fairways so the golfers don't have that as an excuse why they can't put the ball in the little hole!

I had blown the leaves off my favorite green, the one we have numbered 16. It is a short par 3 hole, with a small stream passing to one side, and some beautiful trees surrounding the green. Two of my most memorable moments in golf have occurred at number 16. The first was Chris missing a hole-in-one there by less than 1 inch (from the black tees, I might add)! He was so excited and so mad at the same time that it didn't go in! The second was one time when Tim had just placed his golf bag on the collar, and before he could get his putter out of the bag, the sprinkler head popped up and absolutely soaked him!

Anyway, I had finished blowing the leaves off 16 and then went around the course to complete the rest of my day's work. There was little or no wind this morning, and therefore no need to go back and recheck any of the greens I had already cleaned up. But, a force pulled me back to 16. And sure enough, there were enough leaves on the green that I thought I should re-do it. I had no sooner finished blowing off the leaves when I turned around to walk back to my cart and a beautiful peregrine falcon slowly and majestically landed about 10 meters away from me. One of the reasons I love working at the golf course is I feel so close to nature while I am out there. I get to see beautiful sunrises almost every day, and the number and variety of animals that share the course with me at that time of the morning is phenomenal. But, it has always been a time when I felt closest to Chris, first when he was going through Selection, then the Q course, and even when he was deployed to Afghanistan last year, and particularly this year. While I am out there, I always sing to myself "The Ballad of the Green Beret" (…and not because of "Caddy Shack!").

I was actually not surprised to see this falcon this particular morning. When I was a young boy, I went on a vision quest, and a small falcon came and talked to me. He gave me guidance, he gave me hope, and he gave me some of his feathers so I could have his strength, power, speed and wisdom in my life. Those feathers were and are some of my most prized possessions, and there are only a very few people who have one. Each of you will be reading this, and know that the strength and power of that feather is even more powerful and tremendous today.

I got to talk to this falcon for several minutes, all by ourselves. Normally, there would have been a number of people traveling through this part of the course, but for some reason, I was there alone with this magnificent creature. Almost immediately, I knew who it was; it was my son. He knew he needed to see me this morning and to prepare me for what was to happen later today. He wanted me to know, first hand, that he is fine, and he is happy, but most importantly, he wants me to be the same, and he knew I was not and have not been. At times, I feel like I am recovering, but then at other times…

But Chris felt he needed to come to me today, to kick me in the butt, and help me get better, as only my protector could. He was always there for me, after my many surgeries, to do whatever he could to help me help myself. And, he knew that he needed to come to me today, and he was right.

For today, I received the final death certificate. I still have not heard all the details of what happened, when and how, and I will wait until my brothers come back from Afghanistan to hear it directly from them. But, the Lakota in me knows a lot, and reading the death certificate today confirmed what I have felt ever since the guys from 10th SFG drove up in front of my house on 9 August, and then when I got to spend some time alone with Chris at the funeral home. Chris wanted me to know he is not in pain, but it hurts him to see me in pain. So, he asked me to help him by helping myself. I have always tried to do whatever I can for my children, and so, Chris, I will try to do this for you, and for me.

But today, I also received a most wonderful and glorious gift from my brother Jim. I will forever hold your words in my heart, and they have done much to help heal it and me. I am so grateful for all the love and support, compassion and caring, friendship and fortitude that all the people who are reading this letter have given me, Dianne and Tim. I will forever be in your debt, and will always hold you in my heart. It is truly amazing to me that losing one son has resulted in my family growing exponentially.

Then, before he flew off, the falcon told me what I have known ever since 8 August—that Chris is and always will be with me and all of us. He died for us, so we could be safe and live our life's as he was able to live his. He told me that he died as a warrior, and that he couldn't have asked for anything better. He misses us, but that last thing he said was how wonderful it will be when I can be with him again. And although I miss him more with every day, I do know I will get to hold my warrior, my hero, my son again.

It is no coincidence that on the 3rd month anniversary on a par 3, hole number 16 that Chris choose to come to me there and then; for the numbers 316 are intertwined in both Chris' and my lives.

So, my dear family, know that I am better, I am getting stronger, and I am so very grateful for all the amazing memories I have of having Chris with me as long as I did. I truly feel today was meant to be, and I thank you, my son, for loving your old man as much as you do.

Cato hnake, canti sakapi!…And I love each of you, too! Jeff

Here is another email written about a falcon at the same area of the golf course. It is truly a miracle that a falcon could have been responsible for my going from the depths of despair to shear joy, but my brother was there for me when I needed him the most, just as he told me he would be so many, many years ago…

We were aerating the golf course, and I mean the entire golf course. In the morning we punched holes in the fairway, and then in the afternoon, I would take a riding mower, and munch the plugs up. However, the aeration plugs in the rough throughout the golf course were left alone. The machine I was using had a problem with the steering on fairway #1, and so I helped the mechanics fix the hydraulics, and my hands got full of hydraulic fluid. I cleaned them off as best I could, and then headed over to fairway #18. From there, I went to #15 and finally #17.

When I got to #17, I had a strange sensation. I looked at my right hand and my eagle ring that Jimbo had given Chris, and then Tony returned to me was gone! I have only known that level of despair one other time, and that was when the Suburban pulled up in front of our house 9 August 2005. Where do I even begin to look??? I tried to retrace my path, but between munching the plugs on the fairway, and the large plug holes all throughout the rough around the rest of the golf course, I was so worried that my ring was gone.

It was getting dark, so I came in early the next morning, and using a metal detector, I went all over the last five holes that I had worked around—nothing. With each minute, I became more and more depressed. I spent almost the entire day looking for my ring, but no luck. When I got home that night, I emailed Jimbo, in tears, for I felt so depressed that I had lost something that was so special to Jim, Chris and me.

The next morning was Saturday, and I mowed greens 14-18, again looking around each of the greens when I finished mowing. I spent another hour with the metal detector, but to no avail. While I was mowing the greens, there was another worker mowing the step cut around each fairway and green.

After looking and looking, I decided to go home. But, as I was driving out of the golf course, something told me to go look one more time. I parked the truck, and as I walked through the parking lot, I heard the falcons that live in the trees over by #16 screeching like I had never heard them before. They were telling me something, but I just didn't know what it was. So, I walked over toward #16, but had to walk around the back of green #15 because there were golfers in #15 fairway. As I got closer to the green, the falcons became louder and louder. I looked at the back of the green and see something shiny. I don't run after my knee replacements, but I ran up to the silver object, and it was my ring!!! It must have been pulled up by the step cut mower, and believe it or not, there was absolutely no damage to the ring at all! I almost collapsed with shear exuberance! What was lost was now found!

But, were it not for my brothers talking to me, I would have kept driving out of the golf course, and would never have found what means so very much to me and meant even more to Jim and Chris!!!

Another falcon story that has an amazing ending occurred on another part of Fox Hollow golf course:

Good Evening my brothers!

Well, today was the last day of the season for me out at the golf course. The grass has stopped growing, the leaves are all down and there is not much to do, particularly with the snow coming this week. Plus, there are several full time employees that need the work.

I was driving our water and trash truck today, and as I was heading up the hill from the first tee up towards the first green, a big falcon came down, and was flying about 3-5 meters above the ground, almost following the cart path I was driving on. It was fascinating to see him flying so low, and basically going where I was about to drive. As I got up around the green and was heading over to pick-up the trash at the second tee, he dove down very rapidly, and grabbed a small snake that was just off the side of the cart path!!! It was amazing!

I HATE snakes!!! They are probably the only thing I REALLY don't care for! In fact, I missed most of the Indiana Jones movies because of all the snakes in the movies, and I really can't even look at them on the movie screen. When Chris was about 4, I was weeding our flower garden, and so he was "helping me" messing around in the drainage ditch about 2 meters from me. Where we lived in Ohio, there were ALOT of bull snakes... very big, not dangerous, but still VERY BIG!!! So, Chris and I were having a good old time, talking and laughing when all of a sudden, he started screaming—I was sure it was a snake, and so I leaped over the flower bed, grabbed Chris, and was looking to rip the head off this damn snake that dared scare my son...well, it wasn't a snake—Chris had stuck his shovel in a wasp's nest!!! I knocked the wasps off him, but he was bitten 8 times. But, being the moron I can be, I was so concerned about him, and looking for a snake, that I didn't realize I was still standing in the wasp's nest. Got over 200 bites, and my ankle got really swollen. I just thought it was from the wasps...WRONG!!! I had broken my ankle, and didn't even know it for several months when it just didn't feel right, and finally got an x-ray! Oh well...I STILL hate snakes!

Someday, I hope to get all of you out here to play golf with me out at our course. It is so beautiful, right up against the foothills, with amazing sunrises and sunsets, a significant number of different animals, and of course, our brothers, the falcons! It is a place of peace, reflection and contemplation. It is also a place that Chris and I spent so much time, working on many of the skills he possessed that made him the warrior he was—and for that, and all the wonderful memories I have, it is one of my favorite places on earth. Someplace I want to share with all of you!

My memories of Chris are yours as well, just as yours, are mine. Thank you, my brothers, for all you did with Chris to make him the man, the hero and the warrior he was. For that, and all you do for me now, I will always love you, just as Chris did!

molon labe

P.S. As an amazing post-script to this email, I use Mozilla as my firewall protection on my computer. After composing this email, I sent it out to all my brothers, but for some reason, and NO ONE I know in the IT industry can figure this out, as soon as I sent this email out on 27 November 2006, the icon on my computer that says Mozilla now says "Snake Eater" and it has remained as "Snake Eater" ever since!!! In Vietnam, members of 5th Special Forces Group (Airborne) were known as "snake eaters," and this email only went out to members of the United States Army Special Forces...you figure it out!!!

But, falcons have also talked to the rest of OUR family as well, and have been there to let us all know that Chris, and we, would be all right.

When Scott got back from Deh Afghan, one of the things we both wanted to do was play golf together. Chris was teaching Scott how to play golf, and it was right and fitting that Scott and I play golf while I was still "home." Even though I work at a golf course, I don't play very much. And Scott was just learning the game, and had not hit a golf ball in over 8 months, so, needless to say, we were significantly over par!!!

On the last hole, we both hit our drives right down the middle of the fairway—the first time all day! And both golf balls were only about 5 meters from each other. As we walked over to take our second shot, this beautiful falcon came swooping down, and flew down the fairway, only about 3 meters above our heads! We both looked at the falcon, looked at each other, and then we hugged each other and cried on each other's shoulders! We BOTH knew Chris was looking down on us, and so glad that we have each other!!!

Scott had another falcon experience not too long ago. When Scott was in SFARTAETC, he got a piece of glass in one of his eyes during a breaching training exercise. The medics wanted Scott to stop training, but if he didn't continue, he would have to be re-cycled. He needed to finish the course before his next trip downrange. Well, Chris had taught Scott how to shoot with "both eyes" and so, Scott was able to continue in the course, even though he had to sight with only one eye!

Right after he graduated from SFARTEATC, as soon as he stepped outside the building, he saw a falcon circling over head—letting Scott know how proud Chris would have been for him completing the course!!!

The third falcon story with Scott was during the Special Operations Warrior Foundation marathon in 2007. Scott wanted to run the marathon for Chris, and to raise money for the SOWF. It was a very warm day in Florida, and as the race progressed, and it got hotter and hotter, it became more and more difficult for Scott to keep his pace. He told me after the race, that at about mile 20, when he was getting dehydrated and depleted, he looked up and saw a falcon soaring over head. It told Scott that Chris was with him, and he would give Scott the strength to finish the race. And he did, even though the vast majority of people that started the marathon never finished!

When Markus and Shawn were in Yemen, Markus would see a huge falcon almost every morning on his way "to work." One morning, the falcon left one of his feathers for Markus, who in turn, sent it to me. While he and Shawn were in Yemen, they felt Chris watching over them through the beautiful falcon they saw every day.

This next falcon story still sends chills up my spine when ever I think about it. This email was sent to me by Chief on 6 Dec 2006 at 1831 (6:31 PM):

Jeff,

Good morning to you! This is just a quick note. I had to write about something I saw a few weeks ago. Actually as I sit here and write it was Friday the 10 of Nov, the day after I meet the Gov and Director TN DHS, and a day before Veterans Day. I was driving home and saw something that seared a moment in time into my memory.

There are a couple of highways around here one of which is HWY 31 commonly referred to as the Nashville HWY. As in a lot of places one sign post will have a half dozen signs on it. So I am driving and as I approach a sign post, I see what appears at a distance to be a sign for 316. In the same way clouds sometime take on shapes - a huge bird of prey was standing on the sign below HWY 31 and the curve of color difference between his wings and chest strongly suggested the number 6!

The bird looked right at me as I drove past. Crystal clear in my mind forever will be 316 with this huge Falcon as the six. In that instant I remembered last year you writing about a Falcon on the golf course. Not the recent one about the real snake eater.

I am one of the most optimistic guys in the world. I had just had some very successful business meetings and yet because of the approach of Veterans Day I was feeling a little down. I do not know anything about birds of prey but I am convinced that was a Falcon. There to remind me of my brothers in arms and to let it be known that everything is OK. I guess I miss being in the fight more than I realized.

I trust my description makes sense. I will take this opportunity to wish you a Merry Christmas, God Bless.

Take Care, Brian

When Tim and I were driving "home" on 16 December 2006, I saw a falcon sitting on the Halstead Road sign of Exit 249 on I-70 in Kansas!!!

The last few months of Tara's pregnancy with the twins, Tony was downrange in Iraq. One morning just after they found out they were having twins, she was out on their deck, and she saw two falcons soaring over the lake behind their condo. The falcons soared over their condo for several minutes, and until Tony came back for the birth of their twins, Tara saw those falcons almost everyday!

Then, on Memorial Day, 2008, Tony was going up to Arlington, and as he was loading the kids in their vehicle, he found a falcon feather on the ground next to their car. He had every intention of leaving the feather at Chris' stone, but when he got to Section 60, it occurred to him that he should give the feather to me, seeing how I gave one of my falcon feathers to him when he brought Chris home.

I have that feather in my vehicle, and it goes every where I go. Thank you, my brother for sharing that wonderful gift with me, just as your loving my son and me is one of the most wonderful gifts I have ever received!!!

This email was sent originally on 16 June, 2006 JUST to ODA 316, but I want to share it now with all of you...

My brothers!

I have been shown such an amazing outpouring of love, caring and support over the past 10 months, and I am truly grateful for all that I have received. But, the men getting this are truly SPECIAL Special Forces, and for you alone I will share something that happened to me this morning.

I was mowing my favorite green, number 16, just as the sun was coming up, with some of the most beautiful colors I have ever seen (...and I see ALOT of really beautiful sunrises!), and I was thinking about all of you, and how lucky your family and I am that we have you and we have each other. I was seeing each of your faces, and particularly the faces of your children and teammates as you talked to them, and how they light up because you are in their lives. I was then thinking about how lucky I am that all of you had such a HUGE impact and influence on Chris. He loved all of you with all his heart, and he loved telling me about each of you, and what you taught him, showed him, shared with him and all that you did for him. I miss him so very much, but one of the things I miss the most was listening to him talk about all of you. But now, I get to talk about each of you and I am so lucky you are such a HUGE part of my life now.

The rays of the sun were coming through the trees around #16, the clouds were orange and red, and I just had to stop for a moment to marvel in the beauty I was witnessing. Then, out of the corner of my "good eye," I saw something that truly made this marvelous morning even more magical, and it was something I have NEVER seen before in my life... over the top of the tree at the far end of the green was a falcon teaching it's youngster how to soar!!! As you all know, our last name, Falkel, means little falcon in Lakota, and I have seen thousands of falcons all over the world. But I have never, ever seen a parent falcon teaching a really "little" falcon how to perform their miracle of flight. I just stood there with shivers (and by the time I get to green #16, I am sweating VERY profusely!!!), tears and a smile as big as Chris'!!!

They were only above me for a few minutes, but it is a scene that will be with me for the rest of my life. I couldn't wait to get home to share this with you, because only you, my brothers, can understand how much this meant to me.

This was a just what I needed going into this very different Father's day for me. Last year, ODA 316 was in route down range, and Chris was so upset that he couldn't wish me a happy Father's day until they arrived in-country. While I may have lost Chris, I have gained so much more, and that is all of you, your families, and your love. I give you all my most heart felt thanks and gratitude for all you have done for Chris, to have helped him become the man, the warrior and hero he was. That was always my wish as a dad; to have sons that loved life, were capable of loving others with all their heart, and were able to do something great with their lives. I truly have gotten my wish, and all of you contributed more than you will ever know to making my wish and dream come true.

I also want to thank you, from the bottom of my heart, for sharing your families with me. They are all such special people, and they approach life and love because of the marvelous fathers and men you are.

So, thank you and I love you. Give my best to your families, and I will see most of you very soon when I get to Fayetteville on 15 July.

Molon labe Jeff

Here is a falcon experience I had while I was finishing writing OUR book in the fall of 2008:

Yesterday, when I was mowing green number 3, a poem started rattling around in my head, based on the title—More Than A Name! I always carry a small "Rite-in-the-Rain" notebook just in case the one synapse that STILL functions just happens to work (I have written in over 70 Rite-in-the-Rain notebooks since that flight to Hawai'i with Tim on 10 August)—Well, while I was on green number 3, and then the rest of the morning, I started writing down lines to my poem. I'm sure that if anyone else out at the golf course saw me, they must have thought I was crazier than "normal" because just about every 3-5 passes, I would stop, pull out my notebook and write something down! The worst part was when I thought of something in the middle of the green, and then by the time I got to the edge where I could stop, I would FORGET what popped into my head—like I said "a mind is a terrible thing!!!"

Then, later in the day when I went downstairs to the weight room to lift and ride, I keep having more lines pop into my head, so I would stop and write them down. But, once I got on my stationary cycle, the thoughts started flowing like crazy, and I went through about 16 pages of notes with ideas, sayings, words, thoughts, etc. It was pretty cool, and made the 45 minutes on the erg go as fast as I have ever ridden!!!

So, when I got out to the golf course this morning, I was scheduled to mow the greens on the Meadow, where green #16 is located. When I arrived at #16, the sun was up and it was a magnificent sunrise—the nicest one I have seen in several weeks!!! I no sooner started mowing and 3 falcons came flying out of the tree next to #16 and they dove right into the river that runs along the cart path leading to #16, where all three grabbed a fish!!! Normally, falcons are not active early in the morning like that—they tend to wait until the sun is a little higher so they get more lift while they are soaring. But, because they needed to talk to me, they were up at it, and I could almost have reached out and touched them—they flew that close to me!!! Of course, I had to stop to watch, and then it hit me, almost as fast as they hit the fish—we could possibly get some funds for OUR More Than A Name Foundation if I turned my poem into a song!!! I have as much musical talent as a blade of grass, but I know at least two of our family that are very musically inclined, and more than likely the second book from the More Than A Name Foundation will be written by a Gold Star Father who is a minister from Nashville—the home of country music!!! Plus LTC (P) and Chief are in Nashville and they may have connections as well. This all happened so fast, but the more I mowed, the more of a vision it became!!! It could be just the answer to many of the questions I have had over the past couple of days about the More Than A Name Foundation!!! I will be talking with several people over the next day or so to get more intel, but this just feels right!

When 3 falcons at green #16 talk—I listen!!! I am almost done with "the song" and will finish it up hopefully as soon as I finish OUR book. Once I get to the musicians in the family, we will see what happens, and I will keep everyone posted!

When I was in college, my roommates and I used to listen to John Denver all the time. And one of my favorite John Denver songs was "The Eagle and the Hawk." We would listen to that song just before we would go into competition, and as soon as the song was over, we would almost rip the door off the hinges—we were so psyched up!

When ODA 316 came back from Deh Afghan and I got Chris' iPod back, I looked through his music list, and found "The Eagle and the Hawk"! It was the only John Denver song on Chris' playlist, but I know he heard that song hundreds of times growing up around our weight room. Even though Chris used to give me shit about listening to John Denver, I know that this song spoke to his soul and helped explain OUR relationship to our falcons. I know Chris is soaring above OUR family, and my spirit soars when ever I see one of OUR magnificent falcons, because I know Chris is looking after his old Dad!

The words of that song, particularly the last two lines of the first stanza, are even more powerful to me and OUR family now:

I am the eagle, I live in high country
In rocky cathedrals that reach to the sky
I am the hawk and there's blood on my feathers
But time is still turning they soon will be dry
And all of those who see me, all who believe in me
Share in the freedom I feel when I fly

Come dance with the west wind and
touch on the mountain tops
Sail o'er the canyons and up to the stars
And reach for the heavens and hope for the future
And all that we can be and not what we are

—Words and music by John Denver and Mike Taylor

On 8 August, 2006—one year after Chris left us, our town initiated a Veteran's Monument, and in part, it will be dedicated to Chris. This is a project that Dianne is very involved with, and when the Monument is completed, it will be approximately 20 meters from the front door of the library where she works.

This is the speech I gave that night, dedicated to my falcon, my son, my hero:

> *In 480 B.C., the forces of the Persian Empire, under King Xerxes, numbering, according to Herodotus, two million men, bridged the Hellespont and marched in their myriads to invade and enslave Greece. In a desperate delaying action, a picked force of three hundred Spartans was dispatched to the pass of Thermopylae, where the confines between the mountains and the sea were so narrow that the Persian multitudes and their cavalry would be at least partially neutralized. Here, it was hoped, an elite force willing to sacrifice their lives could keep back, at least for a few days, the invading millions.*
>
> *Three hundred Spartans, lead by the Spartan King, Leonidas, held off the invaders for seven days, until,*

their weapons smashed and broken from the slaughter, they fought with bare hands and teeth (as recorded by Herodotus) before being at last overwhelmed.

Prior to the battle, King Xerxes demanded that Leonidas and the Spartans lay down their arms. Leonidas responded with two simple words, "molon labe," which means, "Come and get them!"

The Spartans died to the last man, but the standard of valor they set by their sacrifice inspired the Greeks to rally and, in that fall and spring, defeat the Persians at Salamis and preserve the beginnings of Western democracy and freedom from perishing in the cradle.

—From *Gates of Fire* by Steve Pressfield

It is fitting that we are here in the library tonight, to honor those veterans who have so bravely, and valiantly and without regard to their own safety, stood up and did what needed to be done. This is what one of our greatest warriors, someone who is and was a Spartan did for his team and his country, and that was SSG Christopher Falkel. Those words in my Introduction, were from one of Chris' two favorite books, Gates of Fire by my friend and brother, Mr. Steven Pressfield. Chris' other favorite book was The Ultimate Sniper Manual, but no one here tonight has a high enough security clearance, so I will not be telling those stories.

When Chris first arrived in Afghanistan in February, 2004, he was given Gates of Fire by one of his 18 Delta's (SF medics) and told that he needed to read the book, "Because it defined who WE were on this ODA (Operational Detachment – Alpha)."

About a week after Chris arrived in Gereshk, he called me and told me to do something for him. I was prepared to do anything for him, and all he asked was that I go out and get a copy of Gates of Fire, because, as Chris put it—"it is all about US!!!" And he was right! Then, when he got over the shock that I could figure out email, we "read" Gates of Fire together over the internet. We would read a section and then "talk" about it. I had never read a book that touched my soul before, neither had Chris, and it was an experience I will cherish forever.

Chris was born to be a warrior. In fact, even at the moment of his birth, when most kids come out screaming and crying at the top of their lungs, Chris demonstrated his stealthy ability to me by making no noise what-so-ever, and with his big eyes looking all around the delivery room—he was probably looking for some superior position to mount his attack on life!

As a child, he loved to play "army," wearing my old uniforms and hiding my tools in the field around our house in case of attack. Last fall, when I was cleaning out our garage, I found an old ruck sack of mine up in the rafters. Inside there were all these home-made weapons that Chris had "invented." One year ago today, it was Chris' creativity with his weapons that allowed his ODA to survive five brutal ambushes and attacks before he died during the fifth attack. His teammates all told me when they returned in February that were it not for Chris' professionalism, his understanding of what needed to be brought and his insight to be prepared for whatever might be encountered, the toll from 8 August would have been significantly higher for his ODA.

Chris was never allowed to have a toy gun as a child growing up, because, "guns are not toys, Chris" was my standard line that I must have said to him over 1,000 times. At his graduation from Robin Sage, which is the forth phase of the Q Course in the Selection of Special Forces operatives, Chris graduated as an 18 Bravo—a weapons sergeant. After the ceremony, we were sitting in his car (something he loved almost as much as he loved his new truck that he got after graduation from the Q course), and he said to me, "not bad for someone who was never allowed to have a toy gun!!!" But it was at that moment, when he realized what he had said, and what I had done, that he finally got IT about guns. After a laugh and some tears, he uttered one of his most famous and most frequent lines to me, "… I HATE it when you are right, Dad!!!!" I had told him, even as a young child, that when he was READY to learn, I would not only teach him, but I would BUY him every weapon he ever needed, and, as his teammates can attest—he had A LOT of weapons that are now in his brothers' possession. Chris was

VERY good with each weapon he used. In fact, he told me in an email from Gereshk that one of the first times he shot with his ODA, someone challenged him to see "how good he really was!" They had heard that this new kid was supposed to be "not bad with a weapon" but they needed to see for themselves. Well, one of Chris' favorite things was having a movie line for each and EVERY situation, and he told me later that he would put on a "show" until he heard one of his favorite lines of all time from Top Gun "...this kid is GOOD!" It wasn't too long before more than one of his teammates was saying that!

Fourteen or fifteen years ago, Chris and I might have been right here where we are all sitting today. But we were probably working on land navigation skills, or trying to sneak up on the antelope that used to roam here. We used to come down here in the late afternoon, but Chris' first run in with the Douglas County Sheriff (the first of way too MANY!) was here when we were "kicked" off the open space that used to be much more prevalent around here. So, we would come down and have fun at night, which was another skill he possessed. We used to go to the golf course I work at part-time, Fox Hollow in Lakewood, to work on distance estimation, and accurate pacing for land nav. We would get up in the foothills and play "hide and seek," and he always found me. I remember one time skiing up at Keystone, and while we were on the chair lift heading up the hill, we saw a "bunch of Army guys" learning how to ski. Well, this was just too good an opportunity to miss, so we "snuck" up on them, without them knowing it of course, and had a great day following them around the mountain.

Chris was a great athlete. His tackles in soccer were feared and revered. His speed and quickness was cat-like, and his strength and power were unmatched for someone his size. When he first arrived in Gereshk to his ODA, several of his teammates questioned to themselves how this "little guy" could do what needed to be done. And then, they trained with him, and had a very difficult time keeping up! In fact, it was his strength, power and smallness that were utilized on multiple occasions to get into places that the larger members of his ODA could not! Chris wrote poetry and was an artist. He could imitate almost anyone, and loved laughing as much as making fun of some unsuspecting soul! And EVERYONE was fair game for that!!!

Chris was a professional. One of the first memories of one of his teammates of Chris was seeing him drive around the firebase before sun-up—and after he had only been there a VERY short period of time—cleaning up the mortar pit and getting ready for what might be coming at any time. No one needed to tell him to do this, it is just what needed to be done, and he did it. But he had some amazing examples to learn from what it takes to be a professional, what it takes to be SF. His first captain, 18 Alpha, shared the Spartans with Chris, and told stories of the great warriors of the past who are with him now. 18 Alpha gave him a ring, and told him that to fly like an eagle, you have to soar above everyone else, and like his 18 Alpha who right now is taking it to the enemy in the big sand box, Chris did fly like an eagle. His team sergeants, both in Gereshk and Deh Afghan, showed Chris what it took to be a leader, what it took to do everything and anything for his teammates, and he learned from their example of what is so Special about Special Forces. His 18 Charlie and 18 Echo took him under his wing and were the big brothers that Chris never had. They shared their families with Chris, and made him one of them. His 18 Deltas looked over him and gave him their confidence and abilities, their compassion and their intensity, their love of life, and their ability to make it a truly special life. One of his 18 Delta's is now an 180A, and he shared with Chris more than just his professionalism, he shared his heritage with Chris and he loved him as only another Lakota can. His 18 Foxtrot and 18 Zulu gave him their sense of humor, their keen eye, and their attention to detail. Chris also had the best Sergeant Major (SGM) and Battalion Commander (BC) in all of Special Forces, and these two men created an environment where one of the best ODA's in all of SF had the opportunity to do what needed to be done because they always knew that the SGM and BC had their backs! These were the MEN that Chris went to battle with, partied with, lived with and died for. They all have lambdas on their arms, they all share a brotherhood that only they can truly comprehend, and they would gladly have given their lives for each other, just as Chris did for them.

Although extraordinary valor was displayed by the entire corps of Spartans, yet the bravest of all was declared the Spartan, Dienekes. It is said that on the eve of battle, he was told by a native of Trachis that the Persian archers were so numerous that, when they fired their volleys, the mass of arrows would block out the sun. Dienekes however, quite undaunted by this prospect, remarked with a laugh, "Good, then we'll have our battle in the shade!"*

These are the kinds of men that make up our Special Forces. These are the kind of warriors that will do whatever, whenever and wherever. These are the brothers who lived and loved with Chris, and they are all MY family now.

I want to thank everyone here tonight, and I look forward to seeing the monument to the bravery, valor, selflessness and courage of the veterans we will honor with this memorial. Because of their commitment, their pride and their love of us and our country, we can gather here today. It is right and fitting that we do this, and it should be done in every town of every state of our great nation, to honor those that have and continue to make our country the nation it is today.

Those of us who knew Chris are the lucky ones, because he touched each of us in so many, MANY ways. Every day I am home, I go out to Fox Hollow to mow. I get to see amazing sunrises and get to marvel the beauty of our state and nation. My eyesight is not what it used to be, and I have Dr. Wilson to thank for trying to fix what ails this old warrior. But in the early morning, when I first walk across the dew on the greens I mow, I swear I see two sets of footprints.

Hokahey, canti sakapi—cato hnake!

Falcons have been, are and will ALWAYS be such an integral part of OUR lives. Where ever I go, and when ever I see one of my brothers, my heart soars on their wings, I see my path through their eyes, and my spirit is lifted to heights I never imagined possible. Chris flies with OUR falcons now, and just as they are always near, Chris looks down on me, and straight into my heart.

*From Gates of Fire, Steven Presfield

10

Operational Detachment Alpha (ODA) 316

This is my shield.
I bear it before me in battle.
But it is not mine alone.
It protects my brother on my left.
It protects my city.
I will NEVER let my brother out of its shadow.
Nor my city out of its shelter.
I will die with my shield before me, facing the enemy.

—"Alexandros" in Steven Pressfield's *Gates of Fire*

In late 2002, CPT Jim and six other Special Forces warriors stood up what has become one of the greatest ODA in the history of SF—ODA 316. They didn't even have a team sergeant when 316 was first stood up. And of those original seven men, Chris went to war his first trip downrange with 6 of those warriors!!!

ODA 316 are what Special Forces are and SHOULD be all about! They are the consummate "quiet professionals." They are warriors that use their superior training, superior mentality, and superior knowledge to go directly for the throat of the enemies of our great country. They could be violent beyond belief, and then the next second, show compassion that is hard to comprehend. They trained hard, and partied hard. They would not accept anyone who was not a warrior into their team, and there were many SF operators that could not meet the standards of ODA 316!!! Every man who has worn the ODA 316 logo on their chest and on their hat, has known what it takes to be not only a warrior, but a Spartan!

This was the band of brothers that Chris joined. These were the men he grew to love more than any others on the face of the earth. These were the warriors for whom he gladly gave his life for, trying to save their lives in one of the greatest battles in the history of Special Forces.

MAJ Jim, along with 1LT Dan, MSG Tony and SFC Scott, molded ODA 316 into a finely tuned, tremendously lethal group of "pipehitters" that would go deep into enemy territory and would take the fight to the enemy like they had never seen before! ODA 316 trained, and trained and trained—even though they had to use rubber weapons when they were first stood up because there was not enough funding for actual weapons! They learned each other's strengths and weaknesses, and how to become a team. They complemented each other, and made sure that every man on the team knew not only his job, but the job of the man next to him.

And when they thought they finally knew what they were doing, they trained even harder!

The men on ODA 316 become warriors—they became Spartans. CPT Jim was given a book by his commander when he was a platoon leader in Hawai'i called *Gates of Fire*, by Steven Pressfield. Steve's book spoke directly to Jimbo's heart. It put into words how he wanted to lead his men. It explained his approach to leading HIS men. So, he shared passages from his favorite book with the warriors of his ODA 316 and most of the boys have read *Gates of Fire* at least once! When Chris arrived in Gereshk, he did not have a chance to get a copy of Gates of Fire before he went wheels up, so Markus let Chris read his copy. Several days after Chris started reading Gates of Fire, he emailed me and told me to get a copy NOW—and told me why he was reading it. Through the wonders of modern technology, Chris and I read Gates of Fire "together" through emails over the internet! It was an experience I will always cherish, not just because I read my favorite book of all time with my son, but because of what Steve Pressfield has meant to ODA 316, and now to me! Palamo yelo, kola!!! Your words have had such an influence on so many, many people, and the warriors that mean the most to me!

So, ODA 316 became known as the Spartans!

ODA 316's first deployment was to Asadabad, Afghanistan. In the first 90 days downrange, they only took one day off!!! The other 89 days were spent "outside the wire" on combat missions or training behind the firebase. They attacked and drove the Taliban back at every contact. One of the things I enjoy most about being with ODA 316 is hearing their stories of their time together and their battles, and the bond that was forged by all while they grew together as a team, and also as brothers. I can see each of them, in the situations they found themselves in, and I can experience the love that they have for each other that was created by what they did and how they felt about each other.

ODA 316 was a truly special group of Special Forces warriors, and it was destiny that Chris became one of these warriors, one of these Spartans.

When Chris finished SERE school, he was assigned to ODA 316 by CSM Buzzsaw. ODA 316 was already downrange in Gereshk, Afghanistan when Chris arrived, and as Markus and Buzz will tell in their chapters, Chris had to earn his way onto ODA 316. Several other Special Forces operators tried, but they did not meet the standards that made ODA 316 the team that it had become. But Chris had to prove himself to become a member of ODA 316. As his brothers will tell, he did, and I am so glad Chris had the chance to learn what Special Forces was really all about from the warriors on ODA 316.

These men, my brothers, have given me so much in the past three years. But the greatest gift they have given me was letting Chris experience SF with them! As I told Chris at his graduation from Robin Sage when he was assigned to 3rd SFG (A), he was destined to be in 3rd SFG (A). And I believe with all my heart, that he was destined to be a member of ODA 316. The BEST days of his life were spent with the men of ODA 316! He learned about life from them. He learned to be a warrior from them. He learned about love from them. And he became the man I always knew he would be because of them! I thank God, and the wrathful god of war, all the Spartans and all the Lakota after them that Chris was a member of one of the GREATEST ODA's of all time! They made Special Forces SPECIAL for my son, and for that, and all they have done for me, I will never be able to thank them and love them enough, but I will spend the rest of my life trying. One day while ODA 316 was in Gereshk, Chris emailed me to tell me about their lambda patches. Markus and Tony went up to Kandahar, and had patches made that had the Greek lower case "L" on the patch, just like the symbols the 300 Spartans had on their shields as they were from the Lakedaemon region of Sparta. When Chris first got to Gereshk, he was the only one without a lambda patch that they wore on their left shoulder of their uniforms. He told me in his email that these patches had to be earned, and he WAS going to earn his patch, I could count on it!!! I could feel his excitement and knowing how once Chris set his mind on something, NOTHING was going to deter him from his mission! It was not long after that Chris called me and asked me to guess what was on HIS left shoulder!!! I can never remember Chris being more proud of anything in his life.

That is, until he got his lambda on his left arm. Another tradition of ODA 316 was to get a lambda tattoo on your left forearm. The left arm was the shield arm for the Spartan warriors, and it was their shield that protected the Spartan next to them. It was not for their own safety, but for the safety and love of the warrior next to them. Chris was absolutely beaming when he called me to tell me had gotten some more ink, but not just any ink—his lambda!!!

When Chris was in Gereshk, he was involved in several operations with ODA 316, and for his courage and bravery, he was nominated for a Bronze Star. His award was downgraded to an Army Commendation Medal, but what was so amazing to me about Chris' and his teammate's narratives were that two of the dates that are mentioned in all of the narratives are mine, and my dad's birthdays!!!

As I said, Chris was destined to be a member of ODA 316!

Here is the narrative for Chris' award from Gereshk:

Narrative recommendation for award of the Bronze Star to Sgt Christopher M. Falkel, Alpha Company, 1st Battalion, 3rd Special Forces Group (Airborne), Fort Bragg, North Carolina, 28310

Sergeant Christopher M. Falkel distinguished himself by exemplifying spirited bravery as the Junior Weapons Sergeant for Operational Detachment Alpha (ODA) 316, Combined Joint Special Operations Task Force-Afghanistan in support of Operation ENDURING FREEDOM from

15 February 2004 to 01 July 2004. SGT Falkel distinguished himself in over thirty combat operations in the Helmand Province of Afghanistan while deployed to Fire Base Gereshk. SGT Falkel's calmness under fire and tactical competence were imperative to the detachment's survival. On six separate occasions, SGT Falkel was involved in missions to capture local terrorist facilitators. On 16 February 2004, SGT Falkel took part in a Sensitive Site Exploitation (SSE) in the town of Musa Qalay, Afghanistan. The Operation was a joint USSF and Other Government Agencies (OGA) operation with the mission of capturing a local terrorist network leader. SGT Falkel was instrumental in the planning, execution and ultimately the capture of several local terrorist facilitators. On 8 May 2004, SGT Falkel participated in a Joint NAVSOF and TF 31 air assault raid into enemy held territory. SGT Falkel was the detachment "tunnel rat" for the entire operation. SGT Falkel cleared over one dozen tunnels and caves complexes. On 10 May 2004, SGT Falkel took part in another aerial interdiction raid to capture a major terrorist facilitator in the Zabol Province of Afghanistan. SGT Falkel was personally responsible for the capture of two mid level terrorist facilitators during this action. SGT Falkel was personally responsible for the security of an A-Camp located in Gereshk, Afghanistan. The A-Camp was the focal point of all operations in the entire Helmand Province. SGT Falkel was able to show his skills in a joint capacity that involved working with Afghanistan Security Forces (ASF), the Afghanistan National Army (ANA), the United Arab Emirates (UAE) TF-2 (Special Forces), the New Zealand Special Air Service (SAS) and NAVSOF forces. SGT Falkel's flexibility, adaptability, and knowledge of the enemy's tactics allowed the detachment to improve its mission capability. SGT Falkel has performed his duties flawlessly under fire and always shown bravery and aggression in engaging a determined enemy. SGT Falkel willfully and voluntarily chose to serve in Operation ENDURING FREEDOM supporting his fellow soldiers, the legitimate Government of Afghanistan and the United States of America in the global war on terror. The distinctive accomplishments of Sergeant Falkel reflect great credit upon himself, the Combined Joint Special Operations Task Force-Afghanistan and the United States Army.

Chris was able to do these things BECAUSE of his team, and FOR his team, and so I wanted to present his narrative for Gereshk, and his Silver Star narrative from Mari Ghar here, in this chapter about HIS team,

ODA 316. I have included the narratives for valor, courage, bravery and professionalism of his brothers in their chapters following this one. Chris was who he was in large part because of the warriors he loved.

On 8 August, 2005, SSG Chris Falkel was killed in action. He was awarded the Silver Star for his heroic acts, his valor and his bravery. I miss my son more than I can possibly describe, but at the same time, I could not be more proud of what he did, how he did it, and why he did what he did to save the lives of his teammates. Here is the narrative for his Silver Star:

Narrative Recommendation For Award Of The Silver Star To SSG Christopher M. Falkel, Alpha Company, 1st Battalion, 3rd Special Forces Group (Airborne), Fort Bragg, North Carolina 28310

Staff Sergeant Christopher M. Falkel distinguished himself by exemplifying spirited bravery as the Weapons Sergeant for Operational Detachment Alpha (ODA) 316, Combined Joint Special Operations Task Force-Afghanistan in support of Operation ENDURING FREEDOM from 7 August 2005 to 8 August 2005. SSG Falkel distinguished himself in five fierce enemy engagements with a well trained, emplaced aggressive enemy during a time span of thirty four hours while operating as the 50 cal. machine gunner on the last vehicle of our element, while conducting operations in the Zabol Province of Afghanistan while deployed to A-Camp Lane. SSG Falkel's calmness under fire and tactical competence were imperative to the detachment's survival. During our unit's first engagement in the Buka Ghar Valley, SSG Falkel was instrumental in helping fix and engage enemy positions that had the entire element pinned down. His continuous engagement without concern for his own well being allowed our heavily suppressed elements to get to positions of better cover and his relentless punishment to the enemy while fully exposed later caused them to retreat. During our second contact in the Buka Ghar Valley, SSG Falkel once again was instrumental in accurately putting down heavy volumes of fire on well emplaced machine gun positions so other members of our unit could move up to pinned down Afghanistan National Army (ANA) elements that were part of our patrol and help consolidate, assess, and get control of their situation. We continued to receive heavy volumes of machine gun fire and RPGs from numerous positions. He played a crucial role in the final elimination and forced withdrawal of the enemy by providing cover for the ODA's mortar team while they engaged the extremely fortified machine gun positions. If it wasn't for the cover fire and marking of these positions by SSG Falkel, our element would have been seriously devastated by the well emplaced, heavily armed and numerically superior forces. Our element continued to pursue the enemy during their retreat when they sent ahead for reinforcements to set up what was to be the third ambush. During our pursuit, we received Anti Coalition Member (ACM) communications stating that they were targeting the last vehicle because it was very strong. This information didn't faze SSG Falkel, as he still insisted that we must go forward and finish the enemy off. Upon the third ACM ambush, SSG Falkel immediately located and fired upon the well emplaced and trained enemy force without care for his own life while being engaged himself by a flanking element. His bravery allowed our ANA element to maneuver on the larger ACM element, later causing these same elements to maneuver to a location they thought would give them a tactical advantage. This only led them to a better vantage point for SSG Falkel, who was able to eliminate them during their maneuver to what would have been a position devastating to our ANA element. The remaining ACM elements broke contact again, only to reform and gather more experienced and trained fighters further down our route. The fourth ACM contact opened up on our lead element with concentrated fire, but SSG Falkel quickly and effectively responded as he had done in the previous contacts, knowing that he would draw fire upon himself. Immediately to the flank of our vehicle the major portion of the ambush opened up with an extraordinary amount of heavy machine gun fire.

SSG Falkel, while fully exposed, quickly and effectively spun his turret and machine gun in the direction of fire and began to engage. The whole time rounds were impacting all around our vehicle and him. He continued to engage without care for his own welfare or safety, his only care being that of his fellow team members. He continued to suppress the well concealed enemy until aircraft came on station.

SSG Falkel was able to spot and lay down effective fire so the aircraft knew where to fire to completely eliminate the enemy threat. Once again, we intercepted ACM communications that again said they were reorganizing at a location that they had success with in the past. SSG Falkel demanded that we continue on and finish the enemy. As we entered Cakyan Ghar Valley, the enemy opened up with what was to be SSG Falkel's fifth and final encounter with this highly trained, numerically superior, and well equipped ACM force that we had been dealing with and pursuing for the past thirty hours. They opened up on our lead element as before with extraordinary volumes of machine gun, RPG and AK-47 fire. SSG Falkel rapidly spun his turret and gun while informing the rear gunner of our vehicle where the fire was coming from, and began to engage without care for his own life. His only concerns were for the care of his fellow team mates and trying to eliminate, or draw some of the fire from those machine gun positions that had our lead element pinned down. No sooner had SSG Falkel begun to engage the well emplaced enemy positions, when the rear gunner of our vehicle saw him slumped over his 50 cal. machine gun still orientated towards, and covering down on the ACM elements that were heavily engaging his team mates. It was later discovered that he had taken a single shot to the head. It is my belief that SSG Falkel was targeted by an ACM sniper due to his effectiveness during the four earlier enemy ambushes that accrued in the 34 hours prior. SSG Falkel willfully and voluntarily chose to serve in Operation ENDURING FREEDOM supporting his fellow soldiers, the legitimate Government of Afghanistan, and the United States of America in the global war on terror. The distinctive accomplishments of Staff Sergeant Falkel reflect great credit upon himself, the Combined Joint Special Operations Task Force-Afghanistan and the United States Army.

Chris carried two pieces of paper with him during every battle while he was on ODA 316. The first was a letter from WO1 Markus that Chris received when he first got to Gereshk. The second was the citation from Private First Class Jack G. Hanson, who was awarded the Medal of Honor for his heroic acts during the Korean War. Here is PFC Hanson's Medal of Honor citation:

Private First Class Jack G. Hanson, Infantry, United States Army, a machine gunner with the 1st Platoon, Company F 31st Infantry Regiment, distinguished himself by conspicuous gallantry and intrepidity at the risk of his life above and beyond the call of duty in action against an armed enemy of the United Nations near Pachi-dong, Korea on 7 June 1951. The company, in defensive positions on two strategic hills separated by a wide saddle, was ruthlessly attacked at approximately 0300 hours, the brunt of which centered on the approach to the divide within range of Private Hanson's machinegun. In the initial phase of the action, four riflemen were wounded and evacuated and the numerically superior enemy, advancing under cover of darkness, infiltrated and posed an imminent threat to the security of the command post and weapons platoon. Upon orders to move to key terrain above and to the right of Private Hanson's position, he voluntarily remained to provide protective fire for the withdrawal. Subsequent to the retiring elements fighting a rearguard action to the new location, it was learned that Private Hanson's assistant gunner and three riflemen had been wounded and had crawled to safety, and that he was maintaining a lone-man defense. After the 1st Platoon reorganized, counterattacked, and resecured its original position at approximately 0530 hours, PFC Hanson's body was found lying in front of his emplacement, his machinegun ammunition expended, his empty pistol in his right hand, and a machete with blood on the blade in his left hand, and approximately 22 enemy dead lay in the wake of his action. Private Hanson's consummate valor, inspirational conduct, and willing self-sacrifice enabled the company to contain the enemy and regain the commanding ground and reflect lasting glory on himself and the noble traditions of the military service.

Mounted on top of Chris' vehicle next to his turret was his M-4, his .45 caliber pistol, as well as a replica of a Vietnam SF Tomahawk that I had given him on our last ski trip together to Utah. Finding PFC Hanson's citation in Chris' possessions did not surprise me in the least, in fact, it made me so very proud of my son, because, like PFC Hanson, Chris was prepared to fight with all that he had for his brothers.

The men and the families of ODA 316 truly know what "love" means, because they KNOW how precious life really is! The Warriors of ODA 316 use a lot of "four letter words" in their normal, day-to-day conversations, but the four letter word they use the most, is L-O-V-E!!!

Here is what 316 and Love mean to me:

- As strong as the men on 316 are, their love is even stronger
- As tough as the men on 316 are, we still cry when ever we see each other
- We share EVERY THING and every emotion
- The last thing we always say to each other is, "I love you!" just as Chris used to say that to me
- They would give every thing to and for each other, including laying down their life for their brothers
- They share laughter, anger, faith, courage, joy, and pain, but the greatest emotion we share is love
- They taught each other how to love, just as they taught Chris what love was truly all about—what family is all about—what being a brother truly means
- There is a bond between the warriors on 316 that is like no other I have experienced in my entire life
- They are warriors, brothers, heroes and "Spartans ," and the 300 Spartans who stood so bravely in Thermopylae would bow in homage to the "Spartans" of 316!
- I love hearing OUR family talk about Chris. I love hearing the joy in their voice when they remember what he did, or said, or how he acted. I love to see in their eyes how much Chris meant to them, their families and their lives. And I love how much they love me now.

So, without further ado, the next chapters are a brief introduction to the men, the warriors, the heroes, the "Spartans" that Chris called his brothers—the men of ODA 316. There is an old adage in the military that "rank has it's privileges ," and so, we will present Chris' brothers by rank. The order of the chapters in NO WAY indicates how Chris or I feel about these men, for we BOTH love ALL of them with ALL we are, and always will. But there had to be an order established, and by rank made the most sense to me.

I love each of these men like no others I have ever known. I would have given everything I own to have had the honor and privilege of fighting next to these men. They are the men my son loved more than any others. They are the men that taught my son to be the man, the warrior, the hero he became and was. I love each of you, and THANK YOU from the bottom of my heart for sharing your family, your love and your life with Chris and now, with me!!!

Photo Memorial

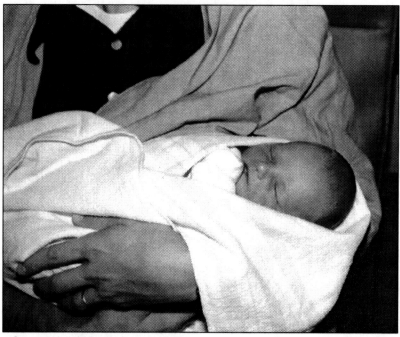

Above: The first picture of Chris, 24 September 1982. I did not think I could ever be more proud, but over the course of his amazing life, I had so many other moments that made me even more proud of my son.

Left: I have always enjoyed mowing the lawn, and my favorite part-time job is mowing greens at Fox Hollow Golf Course in Lakewood, Colorado. Some of my best memories are of Chris mowing with me!

Left: From an early age, Chris and Dad trained together to the mutual benefit of both of us!

Below: I used to throw Chris up in the air and he would catch a branch of a tree in the front yard and do pull-ups!

Right: I used to do push-ups with Chris or Tim on my back, so Chris figured he would see what was so much fun about exercising USING his little brother.

Above: This is one of my favorite pictures of Tim with his Big Brother. I love the expression on Tim's face that says it all.

Left: One of Chris first Halloween costumes—"an Army guy" complete with my dog-tags and full-on camo paint that Chris applied himself!

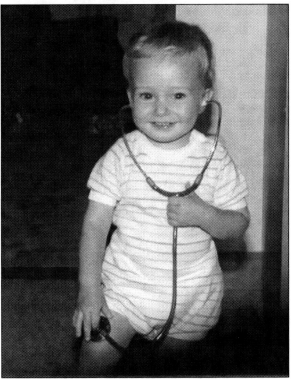

Above: At a very early age, it became obvious that Chris would never become a medic!!!

Above: Chris' first day of skiing at the Galloping Goose in Winter Park, Colorado at the age of 7.

Below: Chris and Tim used to love coming to the weight room with Dad, and the "rides" there were ALMOST as much fun as those at Disney World?!?

Above: Chris and Tim used to love in-line skating with Dad, and even more so with each other!

Above: This was Chris' favorite photo of himself, taken during his Basic Training at Ft. Benning, Georgia in 2002.

Above: Right after the graduation ceremony from Basic Training, Chris says to me, "Guess what Dad—I signed up to go to Special Forces selection!!!" Even though we had not talked about that prior to his graduation, I KNEW he was, and so I told him, "I knew you wouldn't need this infantry cord for long!"

Above: This was Dad giving Chris his first salute after his Basic Training graduation ceremony.

Above: Chris and Dad at his graduation from Robin Sage, during the Special Forces Qualification Course, 21 May 2003. Tim graduated high school at EXACTLY the same time on the same day back in Colorado—there was NOT a lot of discussion which graduation ceremony I was going to!!!

Left: Chris going through his pre-jump check before one of his first jumps at Ft. Bragg, North Carolina.

Below: Chris jumped on his birthday, 24 September, three of the four years he was in the Army. This is a birthday jump above the "Sicily" landing zone at Ft. Bragg, North Carolina.

Above: Another one of my favorite pictures of Chris with "his" Ruby—Scott and Chrissa's precious daughter! He loved her just as if she were his own daughter, just as Grandpa does now!

Above: Chris with Sean, 1 LT Dan's son, probably teaching him the fine art of "beverage selection." Chris loved kids, and there is no doubt in my mind that he would have been an amazing father.

Right: THE Lambda patch on one of the Spartan Warriors of ODA 316 in Gereshk, Afghanistan. I will ALWAYS remember the joy in Chris' voice when he had earned his Lambda patch!

Below: The ODA 316 party when MAJ Jim gave Chris his eagle ring. I have seen that look on Chris face several times, and this is one of my most prized pictures because of what it meant to Chris, Jim and to me.

Bottom: Chris with his M240 when he first got to Gereshk, Afghanistan. As he learned and proved himself, he eventually became a .50 caliber gunner—HIS weapon!

Right: I gave Chris and Tim tickets to the Denver Bronco vs. Indianapolis Colt NFL game on 2 January 2005. Chris made this sign, and it actually was seen on national television when the camera panned the "nose bleed" section of Invesco Field at Mile High Stadium. I am so glad that Tim got to go with Chris, because it was the last time they were together.

Below: Tim and Chris on our last ski trip all together at Crested Butte, Colorado over Christmas leave, 2004. That was a very special ski trip for all of us!

Left: Chris in Deh Afghan, Afghanistan only a few days before the Battle of Mari Ghar in August, 2005.

Below: Chris in his "Captain Morgan" pose after he and MSG Tony "blew up the shitter!"

Above: The last picture of Chris, taken on 8 August 2005 between battles 4 and 5.

Above: Chris' stone at Arlington National Cemetery. MAJ Jim took me there the first time after Chris was interred while we were waiting for ODA 316 to return from Deh Afghan, Afghanistan in late January, 2006. It still tears my heart out every time I go to be with Chris and all our brothers at that sacred place.

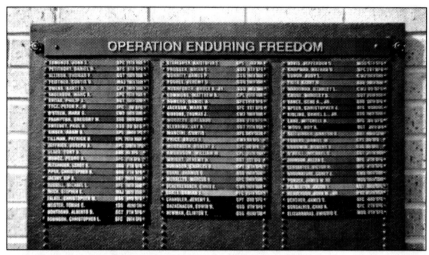

Above: The Memorial Wall for Operation Enduring Freedom at the United States Army Special Operations Command at Ft. Bragg, North Carolina. Chris' name is the fourth from the bottom on the left column. Unfortunately, there are way too many names on this Wall, and even more now than in 2006 when Chris' name was placed there.

Above: The Memorial Stone behind 1st Battalion 3rd Special Forces Group (Airborne) Headquarters at Ft. Bragg, North Carolina.

Above: One of the USASOC tributes to SSG Christopher M. Falkel of 3rd Special Forces Group (Airborne).

Above: This is the range dedicated to Chris in southeastern Afghanistan. He would be as proud of that as I am.

Above: One of Chris' brothers at Arlington National Cemetery on his first trip there after he returned from Deh Afghan, Afghanistan.

Left: Two more of Chris' brothers at Arlington National Cemetery in May 2006.

Above: T, Grandpa Jeff and Christopher Matthew on his birthday—the day the hole in my heart started to heal!

Left: Tim and his brother while on leave in "paradise" in 2008—thank you for loving my son as much as I do!!!

The Battles of Mari Ghar— 7-9 August 2005

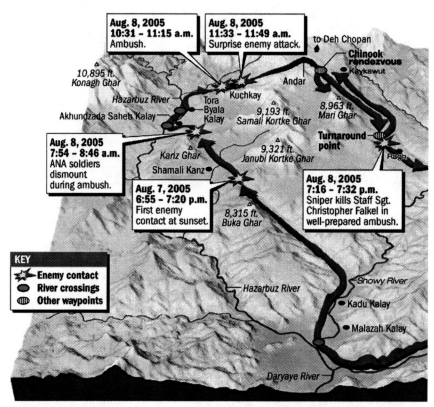

Credit: Army Times and U.S. Geological Survey, Department of the Interior/ USGS, U.S. Geological Survey/image by John Bretschneider

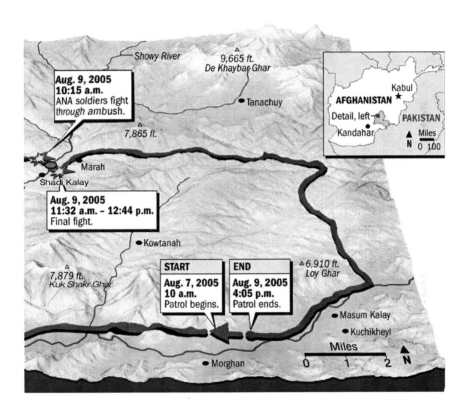

Showy River

9,665 ft.
De Khaybar Ghar

**Aug. 9, 2005
10:15 a.m.**
ANA soldiers fight
through ambush.

Tanachuy

7,865 ft.

Marah
Shadi Kalay

**Aug. 9, 2005
11:32 a.m. – 12:44 p.m.**
Final fight.

Kowtanah

7,879 ft.
Kuk Shakr Ghar

**START
Aug. 7, 2005
10 a.m.**
Patrol begins.

**END
Aug. 9, 2005
4:05 p.m.**
Patrol ends.

6,910 ft.
Loy Ghar

Masum Kalay
Kuchikheyl

Morghan

Miles
0   1   2   N

AFGHANISTAN ★

Kabul

Detail, left

Kandahar

PAKISTAN

Miles
0   100
N

11

LTC (P)

Here is where the spirit of Patriots reside
In troubled times and triumph both

Soaring high so as to ever remind us
Of vigorous Duty for freedom and justice

With heaven's light shining through and down
The price of heroes sacrifice clearly evident.

—Timothy M. Slemp

LTC (P) was the Battalion Commander of 1st BN of 3rd Special Forces Group (Airborne) when Chris first went to Gereshk in 2004. His physical stature is only dwarfed by the measure of this great man. He was a warrior's Commander! He loved his men, and his men loved him. He spent over 20 years in Special Forces before he retired in 2006.

And as with all of the men, the warriors, the brothers that Chris had in Special Forces, I knew about LTC (P) before I ever had the honor and privilege of meeting him on 18 August 2008 at the JFK Chapel for the Ft. Bragg Memorial Service for Chris. My favorite story about LTC (P) was one that Chris told me about in one of his phone calls from Gereshk. While LTC (P) was the Battalion Commander and was based up in Kandahar, he would go out to the firebases where his men were stationed every chance he could. And he loved being with his men—particularly ODA 316! Well, on one trip to see ODA 316, they were getting ready to roll out the wire on a recon mission when LTC (P) arrived at their firebase. He asked CPT Jim if he could ride along, and of course, he was more than welcome to roll with the boys! Before they mounted their vehicles, LTC (P) asked Chris if he could ride up in the .50 cal turret. Chris, very politely—or at least that is what he told me—said to

LTC (P), "with all due respect sir, this is MY gun…" and before he could finish his sentence, LTC (P) gave Chris a "Roger that" and sat somewhere else on the mission! That was my son, and that was ALSO LTC (P)!!!

When we got to the JFK Chapel on the morning of 18 August 2005 for the Memorial Service, one of the first people that came up to me was LTC (P). I didn't even need to see his name tag on his ACU's—I recognized him by his presence in the room. LTC (P) is one of, if not THE most intelligent and articulate men I have ever known. In fact, there have been several times that Jim and I have gone into see LTC (P) in his office when he was the Deputy Executive Officer for 3rd SFG (A), and when we walked out after a terrific meeting, we both shook our heads at the vocabulary that LTC (P) has!!! So, when LTC (P) came up to me and hugged me, I knew I was in the arms of a warrior that loved my son as much as I did! We moved away from the rest of the people that were gathering in the chapel for the service, and LTC (P) told me what I already knew—Chris was going to be awarded the Silver Star for his bravery, valor and courage during the battle of Mari Ghar. I remember thanking him, and he quickly corrected me in that he and a grateful country needed to thank me for all I did for Chris, and all that Chris did for his team and his country.

After we talked, he gathered CPT Jim and SFC Tony together and told us that while there is a time for tears, this Memorial was NOT the time! We were to act as professional soldiers and save the tears for another time. It was EXACTLY what he needed to say, and what I needed to hear! And, believe it or not, I made it all the way through the service until the very end when they played a recording of the Ballad of the Green Beret, and then I lost it. But again, CW2 Shawn was there behind me, and his strength got me through my moment of weakness.

When we got up to Arlington on Sunday night for the service, LTC (P) was there before we arrived, and he was taking control of the environment as only he could. I was not aware of this, but two days after Chris was killed, Captain Jeremy Chandler of ODA 334 was killed in another location in Afghanistan, and his internment was to be the day after Chris' on Tuesday 23 August 2005. So, LTC (P) needed to coordinate the rooms, getting the families to the right area, and being there for not only our family, but for CPT Chandler's family as well.

But, it wasn't until LTC (P) asked me if he could ask a favor that I noticed LTC (P) had on his aloha shirt that Tim and I had brought back from Hawai'i for all the boys! He had made the "command" decision that everyone was to wear their aloha shirts as the "uniform of the day" and it filled my heart to see LTC (P) wearing his aloha shirt!

The favor that LTC (P) had to ask was if I would talk to CPT Chandler's father later that night after the service was over. I told him I would be honored to talk to him, but I was sorry that I did not know who CPT Chandler was. It was then that LTC (P) told me of what happened to CPT Chandler, and the first thing I did was go over to the room where CPT Chandler's family was, and hug his dad and tell him how much I looked forward to talking to him later that night. LTC (P) arranged our meeting at the hotel, and the two of us talked into the early hours of the morning about our sons. CPT Chandler is resting next to Chris, on his left, and his dad and I have a bond that only we can possibly share—again, because of the love of LTC (P) for his men and their families.

After the service was over, I asked LTC (P) if I could see Chris. He had a closed casket for the rest of the family, but I needed to see my son one more time. Because of the nature of the fatal shot, LTC (P) needed to make sure I could see Chris—all the more evidence of his love for Chris and for me, but he made the command decision again that only I could be there when he opened the casket. He stayed with me for a few minutes and then asked if I wanted some time alone with Chris. I thanked him from the bottom of my heart, and he left to be with the rest of the family.

I wish I had had a commander like LTC (P), but I am even more grateful that Chris and ODA 316 did! Whenever I would go "home" to Ft. Bragg, I would stop by to see LTC (P), and no matter how busy he was, and "busy" is a huge understatement—he would always make time to see me, and make me feel like I was the most important person in the room. On the last visit Jimbo and I had with LTC (P) before he retired, half way through our visit, he jumped up from his chair, walked over to his wall, and took down a framed picture he had on his wall. He gave it to me, and told me that he wanted me to have it as a token of his love and appreciation for everything I had done for all HIS men. LTC

(P) was so proud of this gift because he had created it all by himself using PowerPoint and it was the first time he had done anything like that! It was a picture of "Bronze Bruce"—the statue that stands in the Memorial Square at the United States Army Special Operation Command (USASOC)—and behind Bronze Bruce is a picture of a woodland area like out at Camp MacKall where most of Special Forces training takes place. Then, over the pictures are the following:

What America Gives and Takes from the World

When in England for a big conference, Secretary of State Colin Powell was asked by the Archbishop of Canterbury if the United States' plans for Iraq were just another example of empire building by President George W. Bush.

He answered by saying that, "Over the years, the United States has sent many of its fine young men and women into great peril to fight for freedom beyond our borders. The only amount of land we have ever asked for in return is enough to bury those that did not return.

The picture, signed and dated by LTC (P) hangs on the wall in our house next to my portrait of Chris and the falcon in the place of highest honor because of all that LTC (P) meant to Chris, and all that he means to me.

LTC (P) retired from U.S Special Forces in 2006, and he and Chief have started a security company that has and WILL do great things to keep our country and other countries safe from terrorism. When I think of honor, commitment, selfless sacrifice, valor, dedication, and love—I think of LTC (P)!!! My life, Chris' life and the lives of all the warriors who were fortunate enough to have LTC (P) as their commander, are that much more complete and full because of having LTC (P) in our lives! I love you, sir, and I thank you for loving me as you did my son and his team. I can never thank you enough for all you have done for Special Forces, ODA 316, and all of our family, but I will spend the rest of my life trying.

12

MAJ Jim

I AM my brother's keeper…

The first time I met Jim was in the Denver International Airport terminal on 15 August 2005. Jim, Tony, Markus, Shawn, JT, Buzz and Tim had just arrived for the first Memorial in Littleton, and we had gone out to the airport to meet their plane, and escort them to their hotel.

And, while I had never met any of the "boys," there were three that I instantly knew who they were when I first saw them on the escalator: I knew Buzz because he had his Kansas City Chief's hat on, and I have NEVER seen anyone come off the escalator in Denver wearing a Kansas City Chief's hat—PARTICULARLY in Denver! I recognized Tony because of everything Chris had told me about him, and I had seen a couple of pictures of Chris and Tony doing what ONLY Chris and Tony would do!!!

But, there was something in Jim's eyes that instantly touched my soul. There was something about that look that I will never, EVER forget! His eyes looked right into my heart and I knew in a nanosecond that this man, this hero, this warrior, this Spartan—was MAJ Jim!!!

Chris used to talk about all the boys on ODA 316 constantly. And so I knew a great deal about each and every one of them before we ever actually got to meet. But, there was always something different in Chris' voice when he talked about MAJ Jim. There was always a different look on his face when he told me about HIS Captain—HIS team leader. As I have said before, Chris HATED officers—but I knew as only a father can know, that Chris truly loved, respected and honored one officer—and that was MAJ Jim!!!

That was what I saw in MAJ Jim's eyes when he got off the escalator. It was the same look I had seen in Chris' eyes so many, MANY times when he talked about MAJ Jim. MAJ Jim's eyes are just as revealing as Chris' were. Those of us that know MAJ Jim, those of us that love MAJ Jim, and even those that fear MAJ Jim—KNOW what he is thinking and feeling by looking into his eyes!

MAJ Jim is one of, if not, the most amazing men I have ever known. In addition to his "ink," MAJ Jim wears his heart on his sleeve like no other. If MAJ Jim loves you, his love is unconditional and will last for all eternity. But if you are an enemy of our country, MAJ Jim will hunt you down like no one I have ever known either!!! MAJ Jim is a WARRIOR—he defines to me what a WARRIOR is, can be, needs to be and should be! He is a myriad of people—son, brother, father, husband, leader, comedian, mentor, student, professor, soldier, hero, killer, Spartan—in a word: WARRIOR.

My memory of the first few hours after we got the news about Chris is very confused, and while I remember many things—some of them I will NEVER forget - there are some that I don't see as clearly. And one of them is who contacted me first from "home"—Ft. Bragg—but I am pretty sure it was MAJ Jim. MAJ Jim was Chris' first team leader on ODA 316, and MAJ Jim was the Captain that was assigned to "stand-up" or start ODA 316. When Chris was in Gereshk on his first trip to Afghanistan, MAJ Jim was his team leader. I knew that if there was something on the news about Afghanistan that might involve Chris, I KNEW I would hear from Chris because MAJ Jim wanted all his team's families to know that ODA 316 was OK MAJ Jim has done this throughout his military career—having his men contact their families, and when it was necessary, MAJ Jim would contact his men's families personally. He would call or send a letter to tell the family how much their son meant to him. He would let the families know, as only MAJ Jim could, that their son was so important to the team, to the mission, and how proud MAJ Jim was of their son. Sometimes it was a condolence letter or email, but most of his reaching out and touching his men's families was to let the family know that their son, MAJ Jim's brother, was more than "OK," that they were loved, that they were a warrior, and that the families should be as proud of their son as MAJ Jim was!!! Those calls and letters mean so very much to our families, and take it from me—MAJ Jim loving our sons means to world to us. It is in a small way a measure of the man, the professional, the leader, the warrior, the Spartan that MAJ Jim is, and for that, and for ALL the families that MAJ Jim's love, kindness and concern have touched, we are ALL eternally grateful to you, my brother!!! So, I am pretty sure that the first person that contacted me was MAJ Jim. I have talked to MAJ Jim about this many times, and NEITHER of us—who's professional jobs over our entire lifetime have been to be very detail orientated—can clearly remember what we both said to each other on that first phone call.

But, the following email is the first email that MAJ Jim sent downrange to ODA 316, and it tells as much about MAJ Jim as anything I can write:

> To the Great ODA 316,
>
> For many years now, my words have sparked a fire within your soul, my words inspired you to kill the enemy, my words have made you cry, my words have made you laugh, my words have given you hope, my words have been important to you...know now that the words I have to say to you now will fall short and will do none of the things that they did in the past. But you must know. And I must know that you know.
>
> First, know beyond all other things that I am so very proud of you. I am more proud of you and more proud to be a part of ODA 316 than I ever have been before. You fought like the true warriors that I already knew you were. Now, the rest of the world knows of your bravery and courage, as I do. You have always been lions among mere men - and you have proven it beyond any possible words. Do you remember my stories of Leonidas, Dienekes, and Achilles? Do you remember the night in Asadabad when I first told you of the battle of Thermopylae and the great Spartan warriors who fought there? It was like yesterday to me, and now, you have put your names along side the list of great warriors of past and present. The great battle that I always told

192

you would come - came. And you performed superbly. I envy you. KNOW HOW VERY, VERY PROUD OF YOU I AM.

Second, know once again, how very much I love you, and how very much all of you have meant to me as a warrior, and as a man. With you by my side, I was able to be the warrior and man that I have always wanted to be. The times we spent together were the best times of my life, and I love you all in a way that I love no other people in all of the world. It is a love that I share with no one else, not my wife, my father, or my children. I love you for all your weaknesses and strengths, I love you as warriors, as brothers, as friends. KNOW HOW VERY, VERY MUCH I LOVE YOU.

Third, know with all your heart and soul that I wish I had been there, not because I think anything could have been avoided or done any differently, I know that is not the case. I just wish I could have fought next to my brave men when they needed me the most. I will NEVER get over the fact that I was not there for you when you needed me the most. EVER. KNOW HOW VERY, VERY MUCH I WISH I HAD BEEN THERE FOR YOU.

Fourth, know the hardest days are ahead. You must continue to hunt and kill. More blood must spill for what has happened. Sixteen is the last number I heard. That is not enough. We got revenge for Luke, we got revenge for Sweeney and Chief Price. And now the time has come to get revenge for one of our own. Get names, get places, and pounce in the middle of the night with your knives and start cutting throats. Don"t let it die. Remember as in Asadabad, it is going to get worse before it gets better. They think they have won, prove them wrong, go after them harder, faster and more often...FEAR NOTHING!

Fifth, know that I know you did everything you could for Chris. Know that I know nothing else could have been done. Know he is a great warrior, who has some great warriors awaiting his return to his home. Mark, Shawn and I got it. And I promise you he will be buried like the great warrior he is. I spoke with Chris' father today and of course he is deeply, deeply wounded and yet he knows Chris died doing what he wanted to do with men he wanted to do it with. We all loved Chris very much. And now you can honor his death by continuing to take it to the enemy. His father even agreed that you all needed to stay there and keep up the fight. I told Chris' father that I am sure you all would be up there to see him as soon as you could but in the mean time you got pretty good 316 boys to handle it for you so you can fight. We all loved and cared for him deeply, he looked up to us all and all of us would have traded places with him in a heartbeat...

Some of you knew that "with it or on it" was more than a catchy phrase. Now the world knows. Chris is coming home on it, but I will be here to take him off it. I swear.

I love you all deeply, and I am proud to be a part of your legacy....I hope someone lets me fly out there to see all of you soon. I will be trying very hard to make that happen.

I AM MY BROTHERS KEEPER, JIM

… that is in just a very small way, the measure of the man that Jim is!!!

He also sent this one to me after my first email to him asking him to review the letter I wrote—My hero, My son:

Sir, It is perfect. Don't change a thing. I am so sorry. I would give anything to trade places with him. We all loved him very much. He was a warrior and he was my friend. I will see you soon. We will cry. We will hug. We will recall stories of humor and bravery of your great son, who I was privileged to know...

I AM MY BROTHERS KEEPER, JIM

MAJ Jim sent emails to all of the "boys" on 9 or 10 August 2005. He shared many of them with me, and they were EXACTLY what they needed at that time! As I have said several times in OUR book, I want to share as much as I can about Chris and the men, the Warriors he called his brothers, but those particular emails from MAJ Jim and me are just for us.

However, here is one of the first emails he sent to Buzz, who was the Company Sergeant Major at the time ...

> Dear SGM,
>
> Thank you for the letter to my boys. They are hurting as we all are. Chris' father is a strong man and for that we are all lucky.
>
> Is there some way I can get over there if only for a while to help things through. I could run the intel and work as firebase commander out of that camp so the teams could have more time to train.
>
> Of course the better option is let me go over there give me one satcom radio, a few Motorola's, two trucks, one terp and ten hajji's and I PROMISE I BRING THOSE RESPONSIBLE BACK IN ONE MONTH. DEAD.
>
> ... but I bet no one wants to do that do they?
>
> I AM MY BROTHERS KEEPER, Jim

... that too, is MAJ Jim!

I could spend the rest of this book and several others talking about MAJ Jim—and we may just be doing that very soon!!! Jim and I have spent countless hours on the phone with each other since Chris crossed over. We have sent more emails to each other than almost anyone else. I have stayed more days at MAJ Jim's house sharing his family and his love than I deserve, but I cherish every minute with them!

But, some place in almost every conversation we have, we BOTH say the same thing to each other—we wish we could have been there for Chris and the rest of ODA 316. We BOTH know it would not have mattered. We BOTH know it probably would not have changed anything. But loving Chris as we BOTH do, it is so very, VERY hard for us to have not been there. It is the one true regret I have in my life. I have done many, many things in my days—and I have very, very few regrets. But for the rest of my life, I can never forgive myself for not being there for Chris when my son needed me the most. MAJ Jim feels EXACTLY the same way, and while we are "good" at consoling each other, it will never, EVER take away the pain we both feel inside because we were NOT there.

But, we also both know we will see Chris again, and once we cross over to meet him on the banks of the River with all the other Spartans and WARRIORS waiting for us, we will ask Chris to forgive us then for not being there for him on 8 August 2005.

As you have seen by now, the number "3" is one of the numbers that are woven into OUR family, and there are "3" gifts that MAJ Jim gave to Chris that have touched my heart just as I KNOW they touched Chris' heart—because as soon as MAJ Jim gave these things to Chris, the FIRST person he told was me!

The first was Chris' lambda patch! As we have said earlier in OUR book, the lambda patch that was given to the MEN of ODA 316 has a meaning that few people in the world can possibly understand. Chris was one of those people. On the second phone call home from Gereshk in 2004, Chris told me about the lambda patches that ODA 316 so proudly wore. And the gift that MAJ Jim gave ME on that phone call was hearing in Chris' voice that he wanted to EARN his lambda patch, and that he knew the ONLY way he would get one WAS to earn it! THAT was what he was going to do, and, I can still hear his voice today—it had a maturity, a confidence, and a desire that I had NEVER heard in my son's voice ever before! The third phone call from Gereshk was to tell me that Jim had given Chris his lambda patch!!! It was another phone conversation I will never forget because there was a pride in Chris' voice that I had never heard before—he was now a SPARTAN, and he only became one because he KNEW that he EARNED that honor that so very, very few men had ever earned! Again, Jimbo—your gift to Chris was one of my greatest gifts!

The second gift was when Chris was promoted to E-6 or Staff Sergeant. I was out of the country when the date was determined, and so Chris asked MAJ Jim to pin his new rank on his shoulders. Chris was very apologetic, but I told him that MAJ Jim was the one that should pin his rank on, and that it would mean so much to BOTH Chris and to MAJ Jim … and it did! But, as with so many, many things that Jim has done for me, pinning Chris' rank on was even MORE of a gift to me!

But the third gift probably means more to me than any earthly possession I have. My absolute favorite picture of Chris was taken at MAJ Jim's house when MAJ Jim gave Chris his eagle ring. I have so many pictures of Chris, and my favorites are included in OUR book. But that picture shows just how much Chris loved MAJ Jim, respected MAJ Jim, and was honored to have had MAJ Jim be such a tremendous part of his life. It was the last night MAJ Jim saw Chris, as it was the party before Chris and ODA 316 left for Deh Afghan. MAJ Jim gave Chris his eagle ring, and told him "to be an eagle, to fly high above everyone else, and to always, always go for the throat of the enemy every single time you can!" MAJ Jim knew Chris was a warrior, and a Spartan, and the last thing MAJ Jim told Chris was how much he loved Chris. Those are the things I see in that picture—the look on Chris' face I have seen before when he looked into my eyes, and the ONLY other time I have ever seen that same look, is in that picture of Chris looking into Jim's eyes when MAJ Jim gave Chris his eagle ring. I wear Chris' eagle ring now, and while material things are just that to me, the ring that MAJ Jim gave to my son is a link between the "3" of us that is ONLY between the "3" of us, and THAT is why it is so very, VERY special to me. As we discussed in the "Falcon Chapter," when I lost our eagle ring, I was absolutely crushed and devastated. I could barely type the email to MAJ Jim to tell him, but I had to. MAJ Jim was in Iraq at the time, and he responded almost instantly to the most difficult email I had ever written. He told me not to worry, that when he returned we would replace it in a very special way, and I could tell from MAJ Jim's email that he was more worried about my heart than he was about his own safety in the heart of Baghdad and the violence that he saw on a daily basis! So, when our brothers helped me find "our" eagle ring, my heart soared higher than any of our brothers have ever soared before! Mere words can not possibly convey how important "our" eagle ring is to me—because it was so important to Chris and to MAJ Jim.

Earlier in OUR book, I shared the eulogy that MAJ Jim gave for Chris at the Memorials in Littleton and again at Arlington. There is one more, however, that MAJ Jim wrote that I want to share with everyone, because it helps define MAJ Jim and his love that much more...

This was the Memorial that MAJ Jim wrote on the plane as he flew to Denver—It has never been seen by anyone else until now ... As MAJ Jim told me in an email, " these were my initial thoughts about what I would say in my eulogy that I wrote on the plane to Denver sitting by myself with tears pouring down my face..."

ΤΟ ΧΗΡΙΣ Α ΩΑΡΡΙΟΡ ΑΝΔ ΜΨ ΦΡΙΕΝΔ

Although extraordinary valor was displayed by the entire corps of Spartans, yet bravest of all was declared Dienekes. It is said that on the eve of battle, he was told by a native of Trachis that the Persian archers were so numerous that, when they fired their volleys, the mass of arrows blocked out the sun. Dienekes, however, quite undaunted by this prospect, remarked with a laugh, "Good. Then we'll have our battle in the shade."

I have done many difficult things in my life. None of them more difficult than what I will do today. I am overwhelmed and humbled. For those of you who know me, you know I have always worn my heart on my sleeve, and I have always let tears flow freely from eyes. Bear with me today, and do not let those tears make you uncomfortable, for we are all family.

Chris was a warrior and he was my friend.

In order to tell you what I want to tell you about Chris, I must first tell you a little bit about ODA 316. I know the life of a warrior. I have lived it my entire adult life. I fought with the 5th Special Forces Group during the first attack on Iraq. I have been a team leader in 3rd Group for three years, most of that time in combat or training for combat. So I know a little bit about the warrior culture and all that it entails. ODA 316 is unique. Unique in that we lived the warrior ethos that you hear so much about every single day. It was not something we just lived at work or downrange. We trained together, we laughed together, we cried together, we fought together, and oh yes, we partied together. But it was deeper than even that. Our families were all close. We spent as much time together away from work as we did at work. We were and are a true extended family.

That is the situation Chris found himself put in. A situation that others before him had tried and failed. Others had tried to make it on our team and were unable to adjust to the seriousness of how we viewed our mission, and the closeness and loyalty that we demanded. This was not a group of men who freely opened their hearts or team door for just anyone. I have never been a part of a more dangerous, intense or loving group of men. There were no weak links. No chinks in the armor. I told you that to try and set the stage for Chris' arrival on 316.

I do not tell this story often because no one ever believes it, but there are many people in this room that can vouch for its truthfulness. We were told that Chris was in Kandahar and made the combat patrol from Gereshk to pick him up. As we were getting settled, an old, mean warrior who just happened to be my great battalion commander LTC(P) called myself and my Team sergeant into the TOC and asked us how long it would take us to be ready to go on a mission. And of course we gave the same answer we always gave. We are ready right now, sir. He said good, you are going after Osama Bin Laden. After a quick initial planning session with LTC(P) and some of the staff, Ron and I laughed all the way back to the tent. We were laughing for a lot of reasons, none of them which can be repeated here. Here we go, the perfect mission. A mission worthy of our team. When we got back to the tent we sat the men down and told them what we were going to do. Welcome to the team Chris. As I looked at my assembled warriors,

I got the same looks of excitement and anticipation that I always got. And Chris did not flinch. After a quick brief to get the ball rolling, I had my very first conversation with Chris, alone just he and I sitting on top of my GMV. I will summarize it for you.

"Welcome to the team. You have no idea how lucky you are to have come to this detachment. You are among warriors and you now have no choice but to become one. I am asking you to go on this mission as we need every gun possible. But you have not gone through our team training, you do not know our SOP's and this is as dangerous a mission as there is. This conversation stays between us. No one else will ever know of this, but I need to know if you want to go on this mission. I promise you it will be the last time I ever give you a choice." Chris did not hesitate. "Sir, I have been told by SGM Buzz about the team. I am honored to be here and have been told by him about the great standards that ODA 316 has. There is no other place in the world I would rather be, and yes I want to go more than anything." This marked two major events in my relationship with Chris. First, I knew we had another warrior, and second it was the last time I ever expected him to call me sir. But Mark can tell you the rest of the "Sir" stories. Chris then zeroed his weapon, received his team gear, got loaded down with bullets, rockets, hand grenades, PDM's, claymores, radios, chemlites, and of course the infamous 'Dan medical kit.' Osama Bin Laden got lucky that day; powers above my battalion commander did not let us launch.

I could spend the next two hours telling you about what a great man Chris was, about his wonderful sense of humor, about how my wife thought he was so cute, about how Mark, Tony, and Scott took him under their wings, about how Dan taught him to give IV's and how unfortunately I was his first victim (and I got the pictures to prove it), I could tell you about great air assault raids deep into enemy territory where I had to send Chris into a small cave by himself armed with only his 9mm. Oh, by the way he did five of those air assault raids. I could tell you about how dearly my children loved him, especially my seven year old son Tristen, who is here today, and was humbled by the thrashing Chris gave him in Play Station football. I could tell you about the t-shirt he gave my dad with his favorite saying on it, one that I cannot repeat here. I could tell you about how close he was to Chrissa, Dilly, and Ruth, and how he was a part of their family. I could tell you about him asking Chuck where he was going...I could tell you about him always being the first one at the team parties, and about how many times he spent the night, which in most cases was a requirement at most 316 gatherings, I could tell you about how his face lit up when he spoke of his dad, but I won't. I could tell you about the beer holster he carried at those crazy nights. I could tell you about the last team party we had together where I had bought him a ring with an eagle on it, and told him to always be an eagle, to always soar. And I could tell you how just last week he was a lion among men laying down his life for his comrades. But I won't.

We did not love Chris because he was a good, and kind young man. That came later. We loved Chris because he was a warrior and believed in the Spartan symbol that we all have tattooed on our bodies. A symbol that we all would die for, and yes that is what Chris died for.

I don't know a lot of things right now, as I am still searching for answers, but I do know this: To all of you here and especially our brothers who are still down range and will continue to fight; We all loved Chris, he loved us and he died doing what he wanted more than anything in the world to do, with the men he wanted to be doing it with.

In honor of the foundations on which the great 316 was built, there will be an honor guard awaiting his entrance into that place that great warriors go. The honor guard will consist of 300 Spartans. There will be others there. I speak to Dienekes, Hektor and Achilles in my dreams or visions whichever you wish to call them, and I have been assured that the greatest warriors of all eternity will be there to greet him as well. The Green Berets that will be there are far too numerous to count, but Bruce, Dan, and Rob will be there, that is for certain.

Now the world knows that ODA 316's motto is more than just words. Shawn, another friend of Chris' and an old warrior on 316 decided upon it, and it fit our mentality and history perfectly. "With It or On It." This was the saying the mothers and wives of the Spartans going off to do battle told their sons. What it meant was that they had better come home with their shields on their arm, or dead being carried upon it. Today we begin taking Chris down from that shield, so we can bury him and his shield together, just the way he would have wanted it.

In closing, thank you all so much for coming and honoring Chris, for those of you that knew him nothing more needs to be said. For those of you who didn't I hope this brings you closer to him.

To his parents and his brother Tim , who I cannot even begin to imagine the depths of your pain, know this: You raised a great man who was full of life, bravery, courageous, courteous, funny and loyal. You did a wonderful job raising him.

I will honor him with my memories of the times that we shared, I will always keep them close to my heart.

And lastly to our brothers who still even today find themselves on the field battle, they will honor him through their relentless pursuit and destruction of our enemies. This I know for certain. It is all they know.

Chris was a warrior and he was my friend.

WITH IT OR ON IT

Thank you, my brother—for your words, your love, your heart, your dedication, your professionalism, your vision, and most of all, for ALL that you were to Chris and are to me now!!! As I have told you more times than I can recall—You ARE the BEST man I know!

When we were waiting for ODA 316 to return from Deh Afghan, MAJ Jim and I decided to go up to Arlington before the boys got home. It was the first time either of us had been back to Arlington since Chris was interred on 22 August 2005. Chris' stone was now in place, and we both needed to go up to be with Chris, even if it was only for a few hours. So, in late January, 2006, we headed north. I was given a family parking permit by the administrator before the burial. It is a permit that allows family members to drive right out to the section where their hero is buried, rather than parking in the visitor parking lot and having to walk to the gravesite. When we got to the main entrance, there were two security guards, and Jimbo showed them the permit and they waved us past. We then turned into the actual cemetery, and there was a third security guard. He stopped us, and asked us what we were doing. I told him we were here to see my son who was buried in Section 60. The security guard asked Jimbo for the parking permit. He looked at it and then asked if we had a parking permit. I told him that what he had in his hands was the permit I was given in August when Chris was buried. And he said again, "Do you have a parking permit?" I looked at MAJ Jim, he looked at me, and then he told the security guard that he was holding the permit that I was given in August. The security guard then says, "You don't have a permit—I have your permit!" At this point, I have my hand on the door handle, when MAJ Jim looks at this moron and says, "Well, I think we can get out of this vehicle and get our permit back from you!" The guard then says, "I was just 'joshin' with ya! Have a good day!," and then he hands MAJ Jim the permit and steps out of the way of Jimbo's truck. We drove over to Section 60, and spent our time with Chris and all our other brothers who are there as well. MAJ Jim took the picture of me the first time I saw Chris' stone and I could NEVER have made it through that without MAJ Jim.

It wasn't until we got back in the truck that we started thinking about that idiot security guard! What a clown! As Chris would say from one of his favorite movie lines, "he had NO idea who he was dealing with!!!" MAJ Jim and I could have, and probably should have removed that oxygen thief from the face of the planet. We decided to go discuss his inappropriate behavior with us, but he was gone. We probably should have reported him to his supervisors, but we were both too mad to think that clearly. What an idiot!?!?

MAJ Jim is probably one of, if not, the most decorated field grade officers in all of Special Forces. He was with 5th SFG(A) during Operation Desert Storm. He has had four combat rotations to Afghanistan, and one to Iraq. I can tell you stories of MAJ Jim that—unless YOU were there—no one would believe!!! And while I wasn't there, I know and love the men, the brothers, the WARRIORS that were with MAJ Jim on those amazing battles and times that LEGENDS are made of!!! MAJ Jim was awarded the Silver Star for his valor, his courage and his bravery in Iraq on 11 December 2006. In addition to being awarded the Silver Star, MAJ Jim was also awarded the Iraqi Medal of Honor for his valor, bravery, courage, and love of his men and the Iraqi people.

Jimbo—I love you as no other. You loved my son as you love me. You share your family, your laugh, your tears and most of all, your heart with me. And you helped make OUR warrior like no other. Chris loved you more than you can possibly imagine—just as I love you now. Thank you for making Special Forces SO "special" for Chris! Thank you for helping heal my heart. Thank you, most of all, and for ALL of us, for you being YOU!!!

This is part of an email to MAJ Jim about a year ago. It summarizes my thoughts about MAJ Jim as well as anything else I could say:

> …On a separate note, I just wanted to say, even though I have said it before, and I KNOW you KNOW this, but YOU are what is so Special about Special Forces. What you have done, what you have accomplished, what you have taught so many, MANY warriors, what you have given to so many, many, MANY people, and your sharing of you, MAJ Jim, with me and the rest of ALL our family—well, that is more than anyone I know has ever done for the people they love as much as you love your men, your family and your country. I know how frustrated you are with the command and the fact they are not what they need to be, particularly now. The fact that they just don't get "it" is beyond belief. But, unfortunately it has happened, and all you can do is KNOW that YOU did ALL that you could, and you gave all you had to YOUR men and they are the warriors they are, in large part, because of and for YOU!!!

I would have given everything I have to have had the honor and privilege of serving under you, MAJ Jim. You are the officer that defines what it is to give all you can and all of YOU to your men, and while I never had that good fortune, it is so much more important to me that Chris, Tony, Scott, Dan, Shawn, JT, Markus, Chuck, Big Al and Big Ron all had YOU to show them and to give them ODA 316—for they truly know what Special Forces is because of YOU!

You are the best man I know, and your strength, your honor and you are mine now!

I love you with all my heart, my brother!

This chapter about MAJ Jim would not be complete without talking about Mack. Mack was MAJ Jim's interpreter while he was in Iraq from 2006–2007. But as with all of us that know MAJ Jim, have been lead by MAJ Jim, and love MAJ Jim—Mack became so much more than MAJ Jim's interpreter. Mack became his friend. They shared everything, and I mean EVERYTHING throughout their time in Baghdad! Mack became his brother. He loved Jim just as ALL of the men, the warriors that MAJ Jim has lead in battle. But Mack also became MAJ Jim's hero as he saved MAJ Jim's life on several occasions during their year together. Mack was there when Jim's GMV was blown up on the road to Balad. Mack was there when MAJ Jim went back and called out al-Qaida. Mack was there on 11 Dec 2006, and in fact, Mack was awarded the Iraqi Medal of Honor as well as a special award—The Office of the Secretary of Defense Award for Valor for his bravery and valor that day.

And while Chris never knew Mack on earth, he knows him now. Mack and Chris would be the same age. They would have shared their love and passion for life together. They both loved MAJ Jim as not only their team leader, but as their brother. They both learned what it takes to be a warrior from MAJ Jim, and they both became the warrior and the men they are, in large part, because of MAJ Jim.

MAJ Jim helped bring Mack and his lovely wife Alma to America after MAJ Jim came home. MAJ Jim and MAJ Giselle shared their home with Mack and Alma until Mack could get "on his feet" and acclimated to life in the United States. Mack became part of the ODA 316 family, and for who you are, and ALL that you are to Jimbo, I love you Mack as do all of MAJ Jim's brothers. You watched over MAJ Jim, kept him safe, and brought him back to us. But because you love MAJ Jim as we do, you will ALWAYS be loved by us!

One last email to share: MAJ Jim sent this to HIS men. MAJ Jim loves his men as no other man I know. He would, and HAS, done anything and everything he can for his men. This slight modification of a poem says it all …

As you know I have often used the words of my favorite author Steve Pressfield to help me verbalize my feelings. I just read the *Afghan Campaign* again for the second time. I came across these words at the end of the book. It hits exactly how I feel right now. I just changed the word "soldier" to "warrior." Soldiers are a dime a dozen. Warriors, are well, much harder to find.

IN THE COMPANY OF WARRIORS

In the company of warriors
I have no need to explain myself
In the company of warriors,
everybody understands.

In the company of warriors,
I don't have to pretend to be a person I'm not
Or strike that pose, however well-intended,
that is expected by those
who have not known me under arms.

In the company of warriors,
All my crimes are forgiven
I am safe
I am known
I am home
In the company of warriors.

13

1 LT Dan

Our heroes are those...who...act above and beyond the call of duty and in so doing, give definition to patriotism and elevate all of us...America is the land of the free BECAUSE we are the home of the brave.

—David Mahoney

1LT Dan "used to be" SSG Dan, one of the most amazing medics in all of Special Forces, and the senior medic on ODA 316 in Deh Afghan. Dan was one of the original members of ODA 316 when CPT Jim stood it up, and he was there in Mari Ghar. Two of the greatest conversations I have ever had in my entire life—and those of you that know me, KNOW I have had many, many conversations all over the world—have been with 1LT Dan!!!

The first was on 2 February 2006—the night I met ODA 316. Jimbo introduced us, and I gave Dan a hug and told him that I loved him. I had known him for about 16 seconds when he told me he had something for me, and took his KIA bracelet off his wrist and gave it to me. I was speechless! SFC Cliff had bracelets made for all of ODA 316, and they wanted to wait to meet me before they gave me one. Dan wanted me to have his, and then he would wear the one that was supposed to go to me. That simple act of love did more to fill the hole in my heart than almost anything else.

On the silver bracelet, it says:

SSG CHRIS FALKEL JR. U.S. SPECIAL FORCES
ODA 316 WARRIOR KIA 8 AUG 2005 AFGANISTAN

...and there is a SF crest on each end of the bracelet. It means so much to me that SFC Cliff would have these made up for ODA 316, but it means even more to me that 1LT Dan gave his to me. I wear it on my right wrist, and I will have it on my wrist until I cross over to be with my son and all the other warriors on the other side.

That night at Jimbo's party, after almost everyone left, Dan sat down with me on the couch and told me about Mari Ghar. He was really the first person that told me the many details that had been left out of the reports I had been given up to that time. MAJ Jim had offered to get me the AAR—After Action Report—but I told him that I wanted to hear it from Chris' brothers, and so I would wait until they got home.

Dan was the first one who actually told me how Chris died. When LTC (P) let me see Chris in his casket, I had a pretty good idea what the cause of death was. And then, when I received the official report from the Department of Defense, it gave me some more answers. But it was not until Dan told me that I actually knew what happened. I can't even imagine how hard it was for Dan to tell me—I have done many things in my life that other people would not or could not even attempt, but I have NO idea how I would have told "me" what happened to my son. I could see the pain and the hurt in Dan's eyes as he told me. I felt the love and the sorrow he had that even though he was, and still is, one of the finest medics in SF, there was nothing he could have done for Chris. And that was the hardest thing for him to deal with. Everyone on ODA 316 loved my son as I do, and when they went into battle, they were not thinking about the freedoms we enjoy in America because of the bravery and valor of our soldiers. No, they were there fighting for their brothers, the warriors on their right and their left. That was what was so hard for Dan—he had all the knowledge, skills and abilities of an SF medic, and there was nothing he could do for his little brother.

We hugged and cried in each others arms for a long time that night, and if I could take away Dan's pain, I would gladly give anything I have to do that for him. For all he has given me, for all he has given his brothers, for all he has given SF and the Army, I wish I could give that to him, but it is something we will share together for all of time.

I will remember that night for the rest of my life.

The other "conversation" I had with Dan was in August 2008 when we drove up to Arlington together. Dan had been to Arlington one other time with me, when we went up after the Memorialization in 2006 with Tony and Cliff. This time, just the two of us went, and it was something we both needed to do with and for each other. It is approximately a 5 and ½ hour drive from Fayetteville to Arlington National Cemetery, and because of Dan's work schedule we went up and back in the same day. We spent a couple of hours in Section 60 with Chris and all our other brothers who are there with him. All told, we spent about 14 hours together that day, and I would say that there was probably no more than 45 seconds when we were not talking to each other…and we were not talking about the weather!

1LT Dan is a man, a hero, a warrior and a Spartan like no other I have ever known. He has lived all over the world. He speaks multiple languages. He has a Master's degree. He enlisted in the Army to be part of the infantry, but became a Special Forces warrior and medic. Believe it or not, on 8 August 2005, both Dan and Chris were the same rank—but rank in SF is not the same as it is in "Mother Army," and Dan and Chris both were respected by their team and their command for what they knew, who they were, and what they could do. And Chris, Dan and all of ODA 316 were capable of things that "mere mortals" can NEVER imagine—for them, it was simply their SOP or Standard Operating Procedures.

My life, Chris' life and the lives of everyone that 1LT Dan loves are so much more full and complete for having him as our brother.

SSG Dan was awarded the Bronze Star with V device for the Battles of Mari Ghar. Here is the narrative:

Narrative Recommendation For Award Of The Bronze Star With "V" Device To SSG Dan, Alpha Company, 1st Battalion, 3d Special Forces Group (Airborne), Fort Bragg, North Carolina, 28310

Staff Sergeant Dan distinguished himself by exemplifying spirited bravery as the Medical Sergeant for Operational Detachment Alpha (ODA) 316, Combined Joint Special Operations Task Force-Afghanistan in support of Operation ENDURING FREEDOM from 7 August 2005 to 9 August 2005. SSG Dan distinguished himself in seven fierce enemy engagements with a well trained, tactically emplaced, and aggressive enemy during a time span of fifty-six hours while operating as the driver of the second vehicle of our element, while conducting operations in the Zabol Province of Afghanistan while deployed to A-Camp Lane. SSG Dan's calmness under fire and tactical competence were imperative to the detachment's survival. During our unit's multiple engagements that took place in Buka Ghar Valley, Cakyan Ghar Valley, and Marah Valley, SSG Dan was instrumental in positioning his vehicle so his gunner could help fix and engage the well equipped and fortified enemy positions that had the entire element pinned down by extraordinary volumes of machine gun, RPG and AK-47 fire multiple times. Each time he placed his vehicle in a position so his gunner could effectively engage, he quickly dismounted his vehicle grabbing his M249 machine gun. He quickly took up positions to actively engage enemy forces that either had members of his element pinned down or were attempting to engage the main gunner of his vehicle. He continuously did these actions without thought for his own well being or safety, thinking only of members of his element. On our fifth contact, where we had a 50 cal. machine gunner (SSG Falkel) go down, SSG Dan quickly positioned his vehicle to allow his gunner and himself to provide cover, so that individuals trying to recover SSG Falkel's body could do so without losing more members of his unit. This act drew an enormous amount of fire upon him. SSG Dan continued to engage, only thinking of the personnel trying to conduct the recovery operations and never that of his own safety. If it wasn't for the M249 fire with which he was suppressing the enemy, the recovery element would have suffered substantial losses. On the last morning and during the fiercest battle of them all, SSG Dan played a key roll in the positioning of his gun vehicle, so it could lay effective fire on the heavily armed enemy. His vehicle sustained heavy fire and munitions that knocked his gunner off his gun. If it wasn't for SSG Dan's quick thinking, instant and constant machine gun coverage with his M249, drawing fire upon himself, his gunner may not have been able to regain control of his gun. RPG fire then crippled a vehicle ahead of SSG Dan's. Instinctively with an aggressive attitude he used his severely bullet damaged vehicle to clear the kill zone so remaining vehicles could clear the intense fire. SSG Dan in between moving his gun vehicle and assisting in ammo re-distribution, still found time to actively engage the enemy with pinpoint accuracy using his M249 machine gun to greatly reduce the overwhelming numbers of enemy. SSG Dan willfully and voluntarily chose to serve in Operation ENDURING FREEDOM supporting his fellow soldiers, the legitimate Government of Afghanistan, and the United States of America in the global war on terror. The distinctive accomplishments of Staff Sergeant Dan reflect great credit upon himself, the Combined Joint Special Operations Task Force-Afghanistan and the United States Army.

Since Deh Afghan, 1LT Dan received his commission, and has been serving as an Officer in the Medical Service Corps of the U.S. Army. He has been with a unit of the 82nd Airborne Division for 15 months in Iraq, and he is now training with a transition team that deployed to Afghanistan in late 2008 to provide support and training to the Afghan National Army so they can defend their country and maintain the freedoms that Chris and so many other warriors have died for.

I love you, my brother—with every fiber of my being. You have given me what no one else could, and you will always be in my prayers and in my heart.

14

Chief

You are my hammer, my weapon for war: with you
I shatter nations. With you, I destroy kingdoms.

—Jeremiah 51: 20

On one of the worst days of my life, I met one of the best men I have known. After the Memorial Service at Ft. Bragg was over, there was a reception in the back of the JFK Chapel. I was amazed to see one of my dearest friends, Dr. Tony Abbott—who was in 5th SFG (A) during Vietnam, and retired from SF after 20 years of dedicated service—walking through the reception line. I did not know he was coming to the service, and so it was wonderful to see him there, and have him meet the warriors that called Chris "brother." There were several other special things that happened in that reception area that are discussed elsewhere in OUR book.

But for some reason during the reception, I was drawn back into the chapel. To this day, I don't know what force pulled me back into the chapel area, but it was something that I just HAD to do. As I entered the chapel, I saw a man sitting on the step to the altar area. He was someone I didn't recognize, and he had a full beard—something that is very common downrange, but unheard of at Ft. Bragg—but he looked at me, and I looked at him, and I knew that meeting him was why I was drawn back to the chapel. So I sat down and started talking to this wonderful man. He was so kind to me, and he had such tremendous things to say about my son, about ODA 316, and it was obvious that he loved Chris and the rest of the boys with all his heart. We sat there and talked, laughed, cried and hugged each other for over 20 minutes. The rest of the family had no idea where I went, and they were all waiting on me in the reception area.

As we got up, I asked him what his name was, and all he said was, "Chief." Later that day, on our way out to Markus' for the bonfire, I asked Jimbo who "Chief" was, and I told him about our amazing talk in the chapel. Jimbo got a tear in his eye and told me who Chief was, and ALL that he meant to ODA 316. When Jim first stood up ODA 316, he didn't have a team sergeant, and combat experience was lacking on the team. Chief was the one who acted as the mentor to Jim and ODA 316 as they went down the path to becoming the amazing warriors they became. He was there when ever ODA 316 needed him. He was the professional that helped them become professionals. He was the light in the storm of war, and he loved his men. That is who Chief is!

Chief also appeared to Markus when he needed him as well. It was late fall, 2005, and I was in Dallas for a meeting, when my cell phone rang. It was Markus, and I could tell something was wrong. He had tears in his voice and pain in his heart as he told me that he was up at Arlington at Chris' stone. Markus was not able to be with us when Chris was interred, and he was up in the DC area that day for a briefing prior to his next trip. So, he stopped by Section 60 on his way back to Bragg. And, Markus was the first of our family to see Chris' stone. But, Markus was not alone in his pain seeing Chris' name in the marble. All of a sudden, someone started walking toward Markus, and of all people, it was Chief. Chief was up in DC for a different meeting, and something told him to stop by Section 60, and being there for Markus turned out to be his mission. There are many of our brothers in Section 60, and so Markus and Chief left a "Chris Light"—the name ODA 316 gave for Coors Light—with Chris, and shared a beer with the rest of the brothers, and then went back to Bragg together.

I got an email from Chief several months ago after another one of his trips to Arlington. Whenever he goes, he always brings a beer for each brother, and in his email he told me that despite the solemn and sacred place that is Arlington National Cemetery, he had to laugh because there are so many brothers there now, as he put it, "it is getting expensive to buy all that beer!" It is not funny, by any means—the number of warriors that we know who are there with Chris, and Chief would never disrespect any brother who has given his life for his brothers and his country. But when I read it, I knew EXACTLY what Chief meant, and it put a smile on my face despite my tears.

The original design of the cover of OUR book was created by LTC Joe, and he sent it to me on 23 December 2007. It literally took my breathe away when I opened the email, and so the first thing I did was send it along to my family for their feedback. I have not been able to send Christmas cards since Chris left us, but this was very special, and so I sent an email literally all over the world to share "my Christmas present" from LTC Joe!

Here is the response from Chief to me and the rest of the family—it says so much about how he loved Chris and ODA 316:

> Brothers,
>
> I know I do not write often, but I think of all of you everyday.
>
> Just one quick look at the back cover of the book, seeing each of you made me so proud to have had the opportunity to work with ODA 316. Some times I am sickened by our culture, as we spend our lives seeking out and destroying those that wish to enslave, behead, and destroy our great nation and liberty around the world, while most people in their twenties know more about Brittney Spears than about the grave danger the enemy presents.
>
> Then I see a photo of you guys and I am reminded of the quote, from George Orwell, "People sleep peaceably in their beds at night only because rough men stand ready to do violence on their behalf." I cherish my pillow more because I have laid my head on enough rocks over the years. I cherish my freedom more because I fought for it. I sleep better at night because I know the rough men giving me the peace in which to enjoy it.
>
> Thank you.

Then I see a photo of Chris, and I am simply humbled to the point that my eyes well up and it is a long minute before I can gain control of my emotions.

I miss you all.

I hope and pray each of you had a Merry Christmas and will enjoy a wonderful New Year.

Chief
Jeremiah 51:20

We love you Chief, more than you will ever know!

Chief has come to my side again over the past few months. He is helping me with my Junior's Bullet Pen Company, as well as our new More Than A Name Foundation. He is currently working with LTC (P), and he is making the world and our country a safer place to live. We all owe you more than you can ever know, and for all you are to ALL of us, we love you with all our hearts.

15

CW2 Shawn— Chris' Lakota Brother

With It, Or On It…

"Shawn is a mountain of a man, Dad!" That was the first thing Chris ever told me about his brother, Shawn. Shawn was one of the medics on ODA 316 when Chris first arrived in Gereshk. Chris had only been with ODA 316 for a couple of days when he first called me to let me know he had arrived and to "introduce me" to HIS team! I don't remember exactly what he said about everyone else, but I will NEVER forget what he first said about Shawn … and Chris was so right!

I first met Shawn on 15 August 2005 at the Denver International Airport. Shawn was not with ODA 316 in Mari Ghar because he was scheduled to go to Special Forces Warrant Officer School before ODA 316 was due home. So, he was at Ft. Bragg when Chris was killed. After we got all the boys' gear, we headed over to the car rental area of the airport. Tim and I were going to escort the warriors who came with their shields to support us and protect me from the most pain I had ever had, and the first car out of the lot is a Cadillac with Shawn at the wheel! "Why not?!?" as Shawn so apply put it! That explained a great deal about all that Chris had told me about Shawn!

After we checked into the hotel, we had the boys come to our house for dinner. Several of Dianne's friends and colleagues at work had prepared food for everyone, so we headed to the house. We had only been to the house a few minutes when I noticed Shawn out on the deck in the back yard. I went out to sit down with him, and I was able to look directly into his huge heart. He told me and showed me how much he loved my son. He apologized for not being there in Mari Ghar on 8 August. We sat there together for quite a while and laughed, cried, hugged and recalled our favorite stories about Chris.

Chris was so right—Shawn IS a mountain of a man!

Later that evening, I had all the boys come down to my weight room in the basement of our house. I have several replica pieces of Lakota artwork. I wanted to leave one in the ODA 316 team room back at 1st Battalion, 3rd SFG (A) at Bragg, and the other piece would go with Chris in his casket. Without any hesitation, it was Shawn, who also has Lakota blood streaming through his veins, that said my Crazy Horse shield HAD to be in the team room, and my ceremonial pipe needed to travel with Chris. No one could argue that decision. The shield hangs over the door to ODA 316—now officially called ODA 3116 because there is now a fourth battalion in each Special Forces Group. Every time I go to visit the team room, it fills my heart to see my shield, because it is right and fitting that it is hanging there, protecting every warrior on ODA 3116.

The next day was the Memorial in Littleton, and I had asked all the boys if any of them wanted to talk at the service. Jim, Markus and Tony all wanted to say something, and so when we got to the church, they sat next to me up front. But Shawn was the one who sat behind me. When I started to lose it, he was there with his hands on my shoulder, and I felt his strength, his power, and mostly his love transfer into me to get me through the service. While Markus, then Tony, and finally Jim were up at the lectern, it was Shawn that helped me keep it together. Then, when it was my turn to get up and give my eulogy to my hero, my warrior, my son, I kept looking at Shawn and only made it through what I had to say because of his strength, and his love for Chris and for me.

Back at Bragg, the night after the Memorial there, we were supposed to have a bonfire at Markus' house, which was an ODA 316 tradition. But the pouring rain made a bonfire an impossibility. So, we moved the "party" into Markus' garage. There were two times that evening that I couldn't find Tim—the first was when he was talking to Markus, and the second was when he was talking to Shawn. When Tim and I were driving across the country in Chris' truck, he told me how much he loved talking to Shawn! Tim too, felt Shawn's strength by his mere presence and his powerful words and love for Chris, for me, and for Tim.

When we got up to Arlington for the funeral, there was a funeral home gathering on Sunday night, 21 August 2005. The U.S. Army gave us a beautiful walnut flag case to hold the flag that was on Chris coffin, and on the inside of the lid, there was a display area for Chris awards. As soon as you walked into the room at the funeral home, all I could see was Chris' coffin with our American flag draped over it. I felt like I had been hit by a truck when I walked into that room and saw the coffin. There was something so final about it, and I almost collapsed—but Shawn was there, right behind me—holding me up with his strength. We had not been in the room for more than a few minutes, when all of a sudden, Shawn looked like a bull in a china shop! It was very obvious that something was dramatically wrong, and Shawn was looking to fix what ever that was. I didn't notice it, but the medal set on the inside cover of the walnut flag case was incorrect, and Shawn was NOT going to let that happen! But, it was Sunday night—where was he going to get the right ribbons—Shawn pulled it off! After all, he is Lakota too…

That simple action showed me how very much Shawn loved my son. It was simply unacceptable that Chris' awards and medals were not correct. I can never thank Shawn enough for what he did that night, but I will spend the rest of my life trying.

On Monday, 22 August 2005, Shawn again was there to hold me up with his strength. After the grave site ceremony was over, and I walked Tim and Dianne back out to York Street, I needed to go back to the grave and talk to Chris. Within seconds, Shawn was there, standing to my left, again, with his shield protecting me and giving me strength. Tony was on my right, and Jim—being the team leader he is—was back with the rest of the family making sure they were all OK It seemed like Shawn, Tony and I stood there for hours, but I know now it was only minutes. But again, Shawn's love was my strength.

Once the funeral was over, Tony and JT were set to go wheels up and head back to Deh Afghan. But Hurricane Katrina had hit New Orleans and the Gulf coast, and so many of our Air Force transports were being diverted for bringing supplies to the survivors. So, Tony and JT were waiting for a bird to head back. Shawn felt he needed to be with ODA 316, particularly now. They were not just down a gun, they were hurting because Chris wasn't there being Chris! So, one day, Shawn went into LTC (P)'s office and asked to be sent over to be with the men. LTC (P) told Shawn that it was a very noble and courageous request, but that he needed to stay here. That was unacceptable to Shawn, and he asked again to be sent over to Afghanistan. LTC (P) said, "NO!" and told Shawn he was dismissed. Shawn told LTC (P) he would be back tomorrow to ask again, and sure enough, the next day, Shawn went to see LTC (P) again to request being sent to be with the boys. LTC (P) again commended Shawn for his commitment to the team, but he needed to stay here. Shawn told LTC (P) he was going to keep coming back EVERY DAY until LTC (P) let him go…and again, Shawn's strength won the day as he headed over to Deh Afghan in early September, 2005.

His presence on ODA 316, along with JT and Tony getting back, was just what they all needed. While all of us were grieving back here in CONUS (Continental United States), the boys were still in combat, taking it to the Taliban every day. However, they were mourning as well, and probably missed Chris even more than we did because Chris was a warrior, he was a Spartan, and he was in integral part of what made ODA 316 the team that they had become. Shawn give ODA 316 his strength, as well as his gun, and he helped them get through the remainder of that fateful tour. The boys needed Shawn as much as I needed him during all the Memorials, and I will always be eternally grateful for Shawn's dedication to his men, his professionalism and bravery, his unselfish sacrifice and most of all, his love of Chris and me.

Shawn is now a Chief Warrant Officer 2 and is the only one still on ODA 3116. He has had 2 more trips to Afghanistan since Mari Ghar, as well as, another trip with Markus to parts unknown. He has taken all that ODA 316 was, and given that warrior spirit to the new members of ODA 3116. In January, 2009, CW2 Shawn returned with ODA 3116 to Afghanistan to fight the fight again!

Shawn once said that "ODA 316 was so good, it just wasn't fair for the enemy!" He was so right!!! Shawn was also the brother to add the phrase, "With It of On It" to the ODA 316 logo, taken from Steve Pressfield's Gates of Fire, where the Spartans would either come back from battle with their shield, or being carried back on their shield because they gave their life for their brothers on each side.

CW2 Shawn is a warrior, he is a hero, he is a Spartan and he is my brother. I love you, Shawn, with all my heart—just as Chris did.

Palamo yelo, kola!

16

WO1 Markus

THE COST OF FREEDOM

No man wants peace more than the one that risks his life...
He gives You your Freedoms, your Life and your Rights So
don't ever complain about Our Red, White and Blue!!!
Because I KNOW the MEN that Have Paid ALL Your Dues

And when one man goes down and he cries out in pain
Who will stand by him, when only death remains?
I know who will be there because they stand with me now...
They hold the line strong to protect their brothers' crown

So when you see Our Flag wave Eternally Free
Remember Her Colors and what they truly mean
Red is the Blood that was shed for a brother
White were the dressings on the wounds that were covered
Blue are the Tears shed for a life that ceases to be

So Remember My Brothers
And the Price THEY Paid So that YOU could be FREE

—Mark A. Read

There were two "Guess what, Dad?" conversations with Chris that I will always remember. The first was when he graduated from AIT and told me he was going to SFAS—Special Forces Assessment and Selection. But the second was after he returned from Gereshk, and he told me, "Guess what, Dad? I am going to start building motorcycles! One of my teammates is going to build the custom motorcycles, and I am going to paint them!!! We are going to call our company, Sacred Choppers!" He was so excited—but I don't know if he was more excited about working on the bikes, or more excited about being able to work with Markus!!!

The only other person I know who wears his heart and his emotions on his sleeve more than Jimbo and me, is Markus. His mere presence changes everyone he meets. He has more "ink" that has personal meaning, than anyone I know. He can go from being one of the most fierce and lethal warriors on earth, to being a loving, caring father and brother faster than anyone I have ever seen. And, he has loved me and my sons more than we ever deserved.

Markus wrote this about his brother:

> How do I tell the story of one of the greatest heroes of all time??? How can I do his memory justice? Who am I to be so privileged? I am not worthy to write any of the words I am about to write. But, I do so out of love for my brother and so his memory Will Never Fade. Someone once said, "All men live, but few men live well." This is the story of a man that lived his life to its fullest. This is the story of a man that loved with all his soul and will cause those around him to achieve great feats within their own lives. This story is unending. This story will live on through our children and our children's children. It has changed the lives of all that knew and loved him. It is a story that causes a man to stop and think, "What have I done with my life today and what have I given to those that I will one day leave behind?" This is the story of a great warrior's life which answers the question, "What is the opposite of fear?"

> I knew Chris and I had the privilege to fight beside Chris. No, I was not in that great battle where Chris gave his life for his brothers, but I was with him in other battles. I love him and will continue to do so until I am with him in that sacred place of rest. That place where only warriors roam. It is a sacred place where they are greeted by brothers that have gone before. That place across the River Styx where only the brothers that have paid the ultimate sacrifice are allowed to go.

Our first conversation was over the "sat." phone. I told him to get some weights that the team needed and I asked him if he had read the book Gates of Fire by Steven Pressfield. He told me that he had not read the book and I told him that he had better get a copy and read it before getting to the team. I told him that we would talk about it when I saw him in Afghanistan. I told him that he needed to read the book because it defined who WE were on our team.

The first time I saw Chris, wait; Jr. which was our term of endearment for Chris. I'm not even sure were he got it from. I think it was, Big Ron, our team sergeant. There was not a single person from any other team that called Chris, Jr., not more than once. He was and will always be OUR Jr. Any one else, not on our team, that referred to Chris as Jr. learned quickly not to make that mistake again. We were all quick to enforce the fact that no one else, except us, his brothers were granted the privilege of referring to Chris as Jr. It did not matter what rank the offender might have been, he is Jr. only to us.

The first time I saw Jr. I cursed the "gods of war." What had they sent us? Chris was not a large man. I think he weighed about 165lbs. And he had the face of a boy. I was hoping for another big intimidating beast of a guy, like Scott and Tony, to work out with. I wondered to myself how this little man would be able to fit into such a team. Our team was WELL known around our unit as being the "go to" team for our Battalion Commander. We would go after ANYONE, ANYWHERE, ANYTIME. We had been through many gunfights together. Our team lived for death and destruction and that is what we delivered to our enemy at every engagement. We were a well working, finely tuned, killing machine. How was this "new guy" going to fit into such a team? We were a team of hunters, a team of wolves.

I introduced myself to Chris. I wanted to insure that he was mentally prepared to go into combat, to kill or to die if necessary. I searched deep into his eyes to look for any fault or timidity… I did not see any, and to my astonishment I saw the eyes of a wolf looking back at me. Chris and I had about a 1 hour conversation which consisted mainly of me telling Chris that he had to be an animal to be successful not only on this team but in combat. I told Chris that saying mean words don't win battles. Shoving your gun in the enemy's face and ending his life does. I told Chris "be in charge of what you find yourself in charge of." If you are a driver then drive. If you are a gunner then gun. If you are in charge then be in charge. I told Chris whatever you are doing, be the best at it! At each of these directives I again searched his eyes for weakness; I found none. And again, I found the eyes of a wolf staring back at me, fearless and unmoved.

I had just finished my "talk" with Chris when Jim, our Team Leader, hurriedly walked into our tent and called for us to "get in here"!!! Jim, solemnly, with a dead serious expression on his face stood in the middle of the tent. He waited for complete attention and silence from all team members. Jim said, "We're going to get HIM, we're going to kill UBL." Everyone immediately looked at Chris. After all, he was our "weakest link" at that time, being the newest member of the team. Chris had never been in a gun fight. Hell, his gun wasn't even zeroed. His team equipment was laid out on his cot, ready to be signed over to him. Jim, then looked straight at Chris and said, "and you're going," and then Jim looked at the team and said "get him ready." We feverishly prepared for the mission we all had dreamed of. None of us cared if we lived or died on this one, just as long as we killed HIM. All of us chipped in gearing Chris up. We were all a bit jealous, fucking new guy, 1st mission and he'll probably be the one that kills Bin Laden we all were joking. Chris's job was going to be outside security, at the breech point going into the compound, where UBL was reported to be. He was also going to carry my large aid bag for medical support if needed. We were all excited about the mission but there was a calmness in the air. This was work and the kind that we were all used to and damn good at. I had just explained this to Chris during our talk. I had explained that combat is work. We were all searching Chris for any sign of weakness. We kept looking at each other in reassurance, giving each other nods of conformation that Chris would do good. He had a confidence about him. We watched him put his gear on to make sure everything was in the right place, he put his rifle in the pocket of his shoulder to insure that his body armor and equipment harness worked together and did not impede him bringing his weapon up to fire. I noticed that he had a certain attention to detail. He was a professional. It was at that moment I knew that Chris was going to be a fine member of the team.

We got back to our camp and I showed Chris where is bunk was. As he unpacked his gear and started to settle in I threw my copy of *Gates of Fire* to him. I had this copy for 2 tours and the pages were tattered and worn. I had highlighted many passages and written notes to my individual brothers in the event that I was killed. Chris had not been able to read the book before getting to Afghanistan. The bookstore was sold out. I told him that I wanted it back when we got home. He knew what the hidden words of encouragement meant. That night I had guard duty in our watch tower. The sun was coming up and the camp was starting to wake. I saw Chris walk out of our hooch and climb on one of our 4-wheelers and start it up. He drove over to our ammo point and began loading mortar rounds on the trailer hooked to the 4-wheeler. He drove to the mortar pit and began cleaning out debris and trash that had been left behind from a previous fire mission and from what the winds had blow into the pit. He was doing his job without being told. "Fuckin' A," I said to myself, a professional. The next few days were spent in training, teaching Chris our SOP's (standard operating procedures) and during those days Chris and I talked about many things. We spoke of his father, mother, brother. How he was raised and why he joined Special Forces. Jobs he had before joining up. I learned quickly that Chris was a man. Intensely competitive, fully dedicated to his new team and he had a warriors heart. He was a breath of fresh air to the team. He brought with him a certain youth and vitality to our battle hardened team. This was our teams 2nd tour together and for a couple of us it was our 3rd tour in Afghanistan.

Chris had an innate sense of war and I soon found out that he had a great sense of humor, too. I asked him on his first mission what sector he was securing and where he was scanning with his eyes. Chris answered "well, seeing as this is a 240.... I guess I'll get the far set of buildings and that hill over there," (indicating the maximum effective range of his weapon), "I hope you got the "close in" targets with that little gun of yours," Chris joked. Chris understood war. He knew it was a team effort.

I watched Chris grow into a great warrior. He was fearless, confident and hungry. He impressed me in everything he did. I often wondered why he or how he was the way he was; a warrior. The reasons became fully apparent after I met Chris' father, mother and brother. Chris' dad raised his boys to be men. He was and is constantly involved in their training and teaching them to be the best that they can be and in everything that they do. He instilled courage in his sons and provided them with different opportunities to learn and grow. Chris' mom is the epitome of a true mother. She loves her sons with every fiber of her body but even though she knew well the possibilities of what could happen to them, she doesn't hold them back or smother them. Chris' brother is the best of brothers. Chris talked about his brother Tim a lot. He was very proud of his brother and was always telling stories of childhood their experiences. There was no doubt that Tim was one of Chris' best friends.

I remember the day that I first noticed that Jr. had "got his shield." Having "your shield" is what we refer to as having the Greek letter "L" tattooed on your body. The Greek letter "L," or Lambda, is what the great Spartan warriors had effaced on their shields. Having the Lambda tattooed on our bodies is the greatest honor on our team. This honor transcends all military awards or accolades. This is an honor because it meant that you had earned the right to "wear your shield." This is the greatest honor among the brothers of our team because it meant that you had proven yourself in battle and that you were a warrior. Our team conceived this idea from our 1st team leader Jim. Jim had "his shield" and began telling us stories of the great Spartan warriors and the story of the great Battle of Thermopylae. These stories were used to inspire and encourage us; "his" warriors. We all earned our shield on our 1st tour together in Afghanistan. We talked about going home and getting our shield "inked" on our body. A permanent reminder of where we had been together and what we had done together. The first time I saw Jr. s' shield a couple of us were having lunch and a couple beers together. I looked across the table at Jr. and I noticed that something was different. I looked directly at his ink and it didn't even occur to me that it was new. It looked as though it had always been there. It was like Chris had always had a Lambda tattooed on his left forearm. It was as if he had been with us on our 1st tour. Chris had earned his shield. He had proven to all of us that he was a wolf. He had proven that he was a hunter. He was extremely competent and dependable in battle and we all knew it.

This is the Jr. that I know and love. He could be your best friend or your worst enemy. He walked proudly and carried himself like a man and a warrior. He laughed out loud and made those around him laugh even during the hardest times. With his life he gave all. With his life he proved that the opposite of fear is love. He loved his brothers and held the line strong in battle.

I was not in that great battle, but I was with him in other battles. I love Chris and will continue to do so until I am with him in that sacred place of rest. That place where only warriors roam. It is a sacred place where they are greeted by brothers that have gone before. That place across the River Styx where only the brothers that have paid the ultimate sacrifice are allowed to go.

This is where Chris is now. I can see him standing proudly, with that wry smile on his face. He stands with his armor on. It glistens brightly in the sun, polished to perfection. His shield is on is left forearm, his sword at the ready. He has a robe of scarlet draped across his shoulders. Can you see him now? Like a flash of lightning, can you see the warrior that I love? Chris is a warrior that laid his life down for his brothers. I will never forgive…I will never forget. MOLON LABE!!!

I first met Markus at the airport in Denver, and the thing I remember the most was not his good looks, not his intimidating size, not his ink, and not even his tears—but the way he hugged me that first time. His hug told me all I needed to know: how much he loved my son, how much he missed OUR warrior, how sorry he was for me, and how he would be there for me WHENEVER I needed him. And I have felt that same hug every single time I have seen Markus since:

- At Chris' monument behind 1st BN HQ the first time I saw it with Markus. Markus was assigned the difficult task of getting the stones for SGT Jason Palmerton, Chris and CPT Chandler, who were all killed in Afghanistan within a 3 week period in 2005.

- When he came back from Yemen, and he saw what I had done to finish the office extension he started on his house waiting for his youngest son to be born.
- At the Memorial Day Ceremony at USASOC when the bugler started playing "Taps" and my total knee replacements would not hold me up.
- And when I first saw him after I found out about his "latest enemy" and the battle he is going through right now ...

Markus loves like no other man I know. His love is unconditional. His love is all encompassing. His love is genuine. His love is bigger than he is. And he loved my son, just as he loves me now. You KNOW if Markus loves you, just as you KNOW if he is ready to tear your head off!

Markus is one of the most caring people I know. He has sent me more emails to encourage me, motivate me, support me, and to let me know how much he loves me than I can possibly remember. But there was one that touched my heart as much, if not more, than any other. One of the things we talk about at great lengths is being a father. Markus has a daughter and two sons, and he is a tremendous father, but, being the true professional that he is, as well as the Spartan and warrior he has become, he wants to be even "better!" He knows how much I love my sons, and he also knew how hard my first Father's Day without Chris would be. Chris left for Deh Afghan on Father's Day, 2005, and as soon as he got downrange, he emailed me to apologize for not wishing me "Happy Father's Day" until they got to their firebase. I told him not to worry, because EVERY DAY was a "Happy Father's Day" because of my two sons!

But, as my first Father's Day without Chris approached, it affected me more than I thought it would. When I awoke on that Sunday morning, I found this in my INBOX before I headed out to the golf course to mow greens:

JUNE 2006

Dear Jeff,

I can't help but think of you. A year has passed since last Father's Day. I had just said goodbye to Chris and Tony at the airfield on Pope. I know that this is an extremely hard time for you and I can not imagine your pain...

I wanted and needed to write you not only as a father myself but as what I feel and would be honored to be,.... One of your sons, and a brother.

Jeff, I am honored to know you. I am honored to have learned of your examples as a father. I pray that I can be the type of man and father you are.

I talk of Chris often. I have shown his picture to many, many people. I want people to know of his courage and sacrifice.

Chris was the man he was and was able to do the things he did because of you. Your example, your guidance, your encouragement is an example for all fathers.

Chris will and does live on. When I think of the men that my sons will one day be I pray that they will carry themselves as Chris did, with a quiet professionalism, dedication, seriousness and with a joy of life and love of his brothers.

Jeff, I want you to know and I say this with all that I am. I LOVE YOU. I thank you for the love that you have given me. I thank you for the love that you have given MY sons.

Please know that on this Father's Day, Chris is with you. As he is with all of us that KNOW him and love him.

I know that you will be looking for him. And I know he will say he loves you still.

So, as one of your sons, I say to you as well. I love you. I thank you for the example and encourager that you are to me.

HAPPY FATHER'S DAY DAD!!!
HAPPY FATHER'S DAY BROTHER.

I needed this email on that day, and every day since—just as I need you, Markus, in my life and in my heart.

Markus was one of the medics on ODA 316 in Gereshk, but he was also one of the most lethal and violent warriors on that team. He could go from caring and compassion for the wounded, to a wolf heading straight to the throat of the enemy more quickly than anyone could imagine. Since Gereshk, Markus has had several other trips overseas, and became a Special Forces Warrant Officer in 2005.

Anyone who knows Markus would never question him as a warrior or as a Spartan. But, it has been his most recent battle that has shown ALL of us what courage, strength and love is really all about. WO1 Markus, Special Forces Medic, Warrant Officer and Warrior is fighting the battle of his life against the cancer enemy of multiple myeloma. He was diagnosed in January, 2008 and after eight months of chemotherapy, he underwent a stem cell transplant at the University of North Carolina Cancer Center in September, 2008. Markus has met this enemy head on, and has gone straight for the throat throughout his long, painful and grueling battle. He has shown us, the warriors that love him, what it means to fight, what it means to suffer, what it means to beat your enemy into submission. And he has done this with a class and a grace that I have never seen in any other cancer patient I have ever known—and I have know many—including myself! Cancer patients are trying to "beat" cancer—Markus has CRUSHED it! He refused to let it get him down. He would not let it win. He was determined to not only get rid of his multiple myeloma, but to return to his team and lead them into battle once more...because after you have destroyed this type of cancer, the Taliban or al-Qaida will be a "walk in the park"...

I love you, Markus, as I love no other. I am so grateful for all you did for Chris, and all you have done and will continue to do for me. My life is better, and I am a better man because of you. I am so proud of you as a warrior, a Spartan, a brother, a father, and a man. You are my inspiration, and KNOW that I could not have finished OUR book were it not for you and your courage. You are the definition of courage to me, and I will be your shield until I cross over to be with our brothers on the other side!

Here is one last email that Markus sent to me on Chris' birthday. Thank you for loving my son as much as you love me!

"Further On (Up The Road)"

Where the road is dark and the seed is sowed
Where the gun is cocked and the bullet's cold
Where the miles are marked in the blood and the gold
I'll meet you further on up the road

Got on my dead man's suit and my smilin' skull ring
My lucky graveyard boots and a song to sing
I got a song to sing, it keeps me out of the cold
And I'll meet you further on up the road

Further on up the road
Further on up the road
Where the way dark and the night is cold
One sunny mornin' we'll rise I know
And I'll meet you further on up the road

Now I been out in the desert, just doin' my time
Searchin' through the dust, lookin' for a sign
If there's a light up ahead well brother I don't know
But I got this fever burnin' in my soul

Further on up the road
Further on up the road
One sunny mornin' we'll rise I know
And I'll meet you further on up the road

—By Johnny Cash

I love you brother. I miss you. Please know that I will never forget you. I see your face every day. I hear your laughter. I will honor you throughout my life and my children will know your story. I know that you are watching. Please forgive me for not being there for you. When we meet again please meet me with open arms as your brother. I love you brother. It is an honor to know you and share this life with you.

Happy Birthday JR.

MARKUS
MOLON LABE

17

CSM "Buzzsaw"

BE in control of what you are in control of!

—Robert M. DeGroff

The last phase of the Q course that Chris went through before heading to his team, his ODA 316, was SERE school—Survival, Evasion, Resistance and Escape—which prepares the Special Forces warrior for the mental, physical, psychological and emotional "war" of being a prisoner of war. Chris graduated from SERE on a Friday, he had the weekend off, and first thing Monday morning, he reported to Alpha Company of 1st Battalion in 3rd Special Forces Group.

Not even SERE school could have prepared Chris for his "face-to-face" with the Company Sergeant Major! That morning, he had his first meeting with Buzzsaw!!! There are few "nicknames" that are MORE appropriate for everything about a person than "Buzzsaw" is for my brother!!! He is one of a kind, and I thank the wrathful god of war that Buzz was Chris' SGM!!! I don't remember every detail of Chris' call to me that night, but I clearly recall him saying, "Dad, wait until you meet SGM Buzzsaw. That's right, they call him Buzzsaw and now I know why!!! He is awesome, and he is even a "Chef Fan" (Buzz is a Kansas City Chief's fan—arch rivals of Chris' beloved Broncos!), so I am REALLY going to get along well with him!?!?! Chris loved verbal sparing almost as much as pulling the trigger, and he knew after his first meeting with Buzz that they were going to have a very, VERY special relationship.

This is what Buzz had to say about his first 18Xray:

> I was sitting at my desk one morning in early February 2004. In comes a new Soldier who had just signed in to the unit; his name was SGT Christopher Mathew Falkel.

Young kid of about 21 years of age, not a big fella and straight off the block.

My first 18X; the 18X program is the reinstatement of an older program which allows recruits to come straight off the block straight into Special Forces. I, too, came into SF 20 years prior through the same program. The program has received mixed reviews from throughout the force. You get a kid with no military experience except for what he has learned in basic training, advanced individual training in combat arms, and then the Special Forces Qualification Course (SFQC), also known as the Q-Course. Not a lot of experience for a guy that will be dealing with heads of state, planning and conducting combat operations, and the plethora of duties required of a Special Forces NCO. However, the good side is you get a kid without bad habits, a kid who is still hungry, one willing to learn, willing to give a 100%. That's the part I like, and with proper mentorship he will work out just fine.

What kind of Soldier would Chris turn out to be? The jury was still out on that one, only time would tell and I was about to assign him to a Team that didn't work and play well with others, ODA 316. Chris was not set up for success.

I brought Chris into my office and had him shut the door and sit down. I proceeded to give him his initial in-brief, which was a pretty thorough in-brief. We talked about why he joined the Army and how and why he chose SF and a lot of other things that would let me know more about this young Soldier. I found out that his dad had worked with SF in some capacity before and had nothing but good to say about it so Chris had decided that this was what he wanted to do. A young man who wanted to serve his Nation during a time of war and wanted to be among the best while doing it. He got what he wanted, but again, he was headed for 316.

Before I go on I'll have to clarify what it is exactly about 316 that gives me caution. First off, ODA 316 is a great Detachment and they have great leadership in Team Leader CPT Jim and the Team Sergeant MSG Big Ron. ODA 316 was at my first firebase located in Asadabad, Afghanistan when I took over as Company Sergeant Major. This was (is) a great Detachment and they were modern day warriors. They were focused on the mission; find kill/capture the enemy! They went out on numerous missions and were always mission focused. They played to win as opposed to playing not to lose. They were aggressive in every aspect of the game. They trained hard and never, ever, took things for granted. They had a training plan that they routinely used after every refit and recovery to get them back on tract without exception. They made sure that prior to every mission that they were as prepared as possible, that's just good leadership. However, they were their own entity. They were fiercely loyal to one another. A bond between brothers that are few and far between.

Would this new, young kid be able to make it with team? I don't know because the jury was still out. I would just have to do my part and ensure that he at least gets a fair shot. After he finished in-processing I turned him over to 311 Team Sergeant, JC with the guidance to get him ready for combat because he leaves in less than 30 days to go to 316.

ODA 311, another great detachment, had many ranges and a great training plan laid on in preparation for their Team's deployment in the spring. I knew that JC would get him where he needed to be in the short time that we had and most importantly, he would tell me if he was not ready. I got good reports from JC from the very beginning; SGT Falkel was performing well and was eager to learn. In addition he proved to be good with both his rifle and his pistol.

The day before he was scheduled to depart for Afghanistan I told him that he could take the day off to do whatever it was that he may have needed or wanted to do and that he didn't have to come in and do physical training (PT) with us in case he wanted to have a few beers before deploying since he would not be able to partake once in theatre. I remember him saying that he would see me Monday morning for PT. Again, I told him that he didn't have to but it was his choice. Guess who didn't show up for PT that Monday? He showed up around noon with that "I had too much to drink" look on his face but was rearing to go down range.

Soon after, Chris got on the plane and was headed to Afghanistan and to join his new detachment, ODA 316. The next time that I would see him would be when I and the rest of the B-Team came to Firebase Gereshk.

Upon Chris' arrival in the company and my determining where I would put him, I had called to Afghanistan and talked to the Team Sergeant, MSG Big Ron. I told him that I would be sending a new kid, an 18X to join his team. I also told him that I had supported the removal of the last guy that I put on that team but would really scrutinize any issues this time around. Bottom line is I told him I liked this kid and if the Team had any issues with him to fix it. Mold him into the kind of Soldier that you want but you are not sending him back; his success or failure would be up to him. In addition, I told him to ensure that the rest of the guys on the Team gave him a fair shot. He, as always, stated "Roger Boss" and that was that.

I periodically checked on Chris' performance and received good reports from his Team Sergeant. I would be making my own assessment soon enough because I was headed to the same firebase.

Early in March 2004, I arrived with the rest of the B-Team onto Firebase Gereshk. It was like an old homecoming, man-hugs and pats on the back. Yes 316 was one of my favorite teams and we were going to be sharing a Firebase together again. As all the embracing was taking place I'm looking around for Chris, as he wasn't there to welcome the Team to the Firebase. Then I see him moving out with a purpose with a weapon part, or a target, or something in his hands.

For the next few weeks, everyday I saw SGT Chris Falkel doing something with a weapon system, setting up a range or fixing and repairing a vehicle but I never saw him in the gym or out doing Physical Training (PT). On one occasion I asked how things were going and he said great. Then I asked him when the last time he did PT and he said that he didn't have time for PT. I looked down at his gut, not that there was much of a gut there, and said looks like you have time to eat. I told him that if he has time to eat he has time to do PT. Now that I think about it I still don't remember if I ever saw him do PT on that trip.

The Battalion Commander came out to Firebase Gereshk for a command visit and while he was there we had a little situation at one of the check points. The Commander, LTC(P) wanted to roll out there to see what was going on so we loaded up one of the vehicles and headed out to the check point. After we had gotten out there it wasn't anything more than a green on green skirmish so we returned to base. Once we arrived back at the firebase, the M-2 heavy machine gunner could not extract the round out of the chamber so he called to me. I too tried to extract the round out of the weapon but it was lodged into where I could not get it extracted. There were no immediate action drills left to try so I called over to Big Ron to get his assistance and he looked at it and called out to "Junior"; that was the nickname that they gave SGT Chris Falkel. It took Junior about two seconds to clear the weapon and with that cocky look on his face he said "what else you got Sergeant Major?" I scolded him for being so damned cocky and sent him off with a thank you. He walked on with his business with a confident smile on his face knowing that he had just fixed something that the SGM couldn't fix and he used to be a Weapons Sergeant.

One of the last memories that I have of SGT Chris Falkel is on the day when he became Staff Sergeant Chris Falkel. His new Team Sergeant, Big Al, recommended him for the Promotion Board after they came back from his first deployment and I had to ask the Command Sergeant Major to board him in his absence because of some reason or another and he accepted. I was working pretty close with the promotions clerk to ascertain when Jr. would be promoted. I knew that we had boarded him too early as far as "time in grade and time in service" and did not expect it to happen but assumed a little risk to see what would happen. To my surprise we had promotion orders in hand promoting young Falkel in 32 months time in service. Most importantly, we were promoting a deserving Soldier/Warrior. This was not a gift, not from 316 and certainly not from me. He had proven himself tenfold that he was worthy and capable of performing the duties of a Staff Sergeant. He had CPT Jim pin his rank and I know that it is a memory that will carry with Jim to his grave.

The following account is by far the part in which I would prefer not to revisit. It is very painful because of my emotional attachment to the men in which I have served with. For the record I have never reached out to any of the five Soldier's Families that were in my Company that gave their lives in defense of our great Nation. The reason for this is simple; I am weak. I cannot imagine the pain that they must feel and the amount of suffering that they will endure. I do not want to share that with them, I want to avoid it at all cost.

316 left on one of the earlier flights out of the U.S. enroute to Afghanistan so I was at the airfield to see them off as it was likely that they would already be at the firebase when I and the rest of the B-Team arrived in country. Routine stuff, don't get caught with baseball caps on your head and take care and be safe. Jim was also there and he told me to please get in touch with him immediately if anything happened to one of his boys. I then promised, which I rarely do, that if anything happened that I would contact him immediately.

I believe it was a Sunday morning not more than a couple of days after I had returned back to the states to do a Permanent Change of Station (PCS) move as my time as a Company Sergeant Major was over. There was a call from Command Sergeant Major, the 1st Battalion CSM, to my home phone. My wife Crystal answered the phone and told me it was him. I knew immediately that Dave was keeping his promise to me and was calling to let me know that something had happened to one of my boys. As he provided with me the bad news I again went through that the same sick feeling that I experienced too many times before. It is really a numbing feeling of true deep regret and sorrow for the family and the men that he served with. I thanked Dave and called immediately to Jim to tell him the news. I now wished I hadn't made him that promise. Jim was pretty much in shock and was not thinking very straight so he said he would call back soon as he was boarding a flight.

The next day I was back in the shop and we were making all of the arrangements for Chris' memorial service and sharing memories of Chris waiting for the notification to be completed. Soon the phone rang with a man identifying himself as Jeff Falkel, Chris' dad, on the other end of the phone. He called to thank me for everything that I had done for Chris and was telling me how much I meant to Chris. This is why I cannot reach out to families, to Dads and to Moms; I don't know what to say. I told him how sorry I was and we shared some tears but I did not know what to say. I soon met Chris' Dad when I delayed my PCS move and went out to Colorado to meet him in person and be at the memorial at his home.

In closing I just want to say that Chris Falkel did not die in vain. He died for a cause, he died for his Country. This great Nation that we live in was formed by men like Chris; men who made huge sacrifices so that others will have a better way of life. Most importantly and especially in the line of work that we are in, Chris was a Warrior! A Warrior who took the fight to the enemy and the type of Warrior, who would at all cost, not let his Teammates down, even if it meant giving his own life. I was told that before he was shot that he had a big smile on his face because he was doing exactly what he wanted to do in life and he was killing bad guys with well aimed shots. This is the Staff Sergeant Christopher Falkel that will live in my thoughts forever.

I am sorry, Buzz, but just like Chris, I love you more than mere words can describe, and you are stuck with me for the rest of your life!

There was one other story about Buzz and Chris that the CSM "forgot" to mention. The day before Chris was scheduled to go wheels up for his first trip to Afghanistan, Chris stopped by Buzzsaw's office to say good bye. But, his primary mission in that visit was to tell Buzz that he did not have a weapon, and that he was concerned that he would get off the plane and "not be ready!" Buzz told Chris that he could have HIS weapon on one condition: But before Buzz could tell Chris what the condition was, my wise-guy son said, "I know—make sure I give it back to you clean!"

Buzz said, "NO, make sure you use it for what it is intended to do!"

"Roger that, CSM" with that smile that Buzz and I know ALL too well!

Buzz knows his men, and he knew EXACTLY how to get Chris' "attention"—Whenever Chris was getting too rambunctious or "needed to be brought back to 'reality,'" Buzz knew just what to say to Chris. All he had to do was threaten to send Chris to Scuba School, and he had Chris' undivided attention!!! Chris was not a big fan of the water—the 50 yard swim test in full BDU and boots was the ONLY evaluation that Chris failed throughout SFAS and the Q course, and it ALMOST kept him out of SF—so the last school on earth that Chris wanted to attend was scuba school. Then once, Chris figured that tactic out, Buzz needed some 'bigger' ammunition to keep his attitude in line with Buzz's. Again, Buzz came up with the answer—threaten to send Chris to Ranger School at the "Benning School for Boys!"

I am not sure whom Chris disliked more: Marines, Officers, or Rangers! So, the threat of Ranger School worked REALLY well!

One of my fondest memories of CSM Buzzsaw was my visit "home" just prior to Christmas, 2006. I enjoy woodworking and building furniture as my only real "hobby," and I wanted to make something for everyone. I made doll cradles for all the little girls, I made wooden GMV's and Bradley tanks for all the little boys—LTC (P) liked the GMV I made one for him last month, and it proudly sits on his desk—and I made coffee tables for all the boys. There were two marble squares on each end of the top, and in the center was a glass display area for all the awards and medals they had earned. While I did not have an exact list of everyone's awards, I had a pretty good idea of what to include.

So when I got to Buzzsaw's coffee table, in addition to all his medals—including his Bronze Star with V device for his heroic efforts in Desert Storm—I included a Ranger Tab on his "tower of power." Tim and I brought the table over to Buzz's house and he was very surprised, because I had not told anyone what I had made for them. Buzz thanked me from the bottom of his heart, and told me it was going in his office at Battalion as soon as Christmas leave was over. Well, on my next visit "home," I stopped by Buzzsaw's office to say hello, and I was so pleased to see his coffee table in his office. One of his support personnel came in to give him a message, and Buzz proudly told this E-4 that I was the one who had made the coffee table. This young soldier came over to get a better look, and said to Buzz, "CSM, I didn't know you were a Ranger?"

Buzz told him, "I'm not, but if Jeff put a Ranger Tab in my coffee table, I'm keeping that Tab right where it is!" That is the Buzz we all love!

I asked Buzz for the Narrative for his Bronze Star with V he earned for a fierce contact during Desert Storm, but he was unable to find it, and in digging around, no one else could. Suffice it to say, were it not for Buzzsaw's courage, valor, and calmness under intense enemy fire, his entire 5th SFG (A) team would have been destroyed by the Iraqi Republican Guard. Buzz's efforts enabled all of his team to live to fight another day!

In August, 2008, CSM Buzzsaw became Command Sergeant Major for one of the Civil Affairs Battalions at Ft. Bragg, and it was a great honor for me to attend his "Change of Responsibility" ceremony. Buzz is a man of few, but powerful words, and so when he thanked me and Chris for what we mean to him, it was something that was not only unexpected, but it filled my heart to know that I mean as much to Buzz as he does to Chris and to me. I love you, my brother, with all I am, and I am so very grateful that Chris had YOU as his SGM!!!

18

SGM Big Ron—
Chris' First Team Sergeant

*Death is a constant companion for those who serve
in a time of war. Although able to sever the physical tie,
it is incapable of breaking the bonds of the spirit.*

—COL Nick Rowe

I will NEVER forget the first time I met Big Ron!!! Like the rest of the members of ODA 316, Chris had talked about Big Ron constantly, and I felt like I knew him well before we ever actually met. Big Ron was not in Mari Ghar on 8 August 2005. He had left ODA 316 with Jim to go over to another team in 3rd SFG (A), and he was not available to come to Littleton for the first Memorial we had for Chris. So, I met him for the first time on 18 August 2005 in the reception area of the JFK Chapel at Ft. Bragg.

The Memorial had just concluded, and we were all in the reception area, meeting the warriors and heroes at Ft. Bragg that loved my son. As the people moved through the reception area, they came up to me to hug me, share a tear with me, and tell me what a warrior and man my son was. But then, all of a sudden, up walks someone with a smile as big as the Grand Canyon! EVERYONE else is either crying, or has tears welled up in their eyes, and this guy is smiling from ear to ear—it was Big Ron!

And it was EXACTLY what I needed to see at that moment and given the whirlwind that the previous 10 days had been! You have given me many, many gifts, my brother, but the gift of your smile that day is one of the BEST things I have or will ever receive!!! It was a smile that said, "I was so very lucky to have known Chris!" It said, "I will always remember laughing my ass off with Chris!" And it said, "Chris wants you, Dad, to remember his smile and his laugh RIGHT NOW—and that's an order!!!"

I went up to Big Ron, and gave him a hug like I have never hugged anyone before—and every time I see him, he gets that same, unique hug because I love him so very much!!! We moved away from the rest of the crowd, and talked, laughed and cried together about the antics, humor, and courage of my son. But, he also told me something that I had never heard before, and I will let Big Ron tell you:

Chris Falkel showed up to a Detachment that was closed to most outsiders (anybody), he was welcomed and subsequently he became a member of ODA-316 very quickly. I remember thinking about this new Soldier (18X) showing up to this team in a combat environment; what was his work ethic, how will he react in a fire fight, and how much will he have to be trained before we take him out on his first mission. Answers came very quickly to these questions once Chris got settled in. I remember being extremely impressed with his ability to perform as an 18B so quickly after his arrival. The weapons were always ready on the vehicles, as well as, around the perimeter of the fire base, he took a basic fire base defensive plan and ensured everybody that was assigned to the base camp was briefed of what their responsibility was in case we got attacked. He showed early on that he was extremely capable of teaching techniques and procedures to enable each detachment member to operate all weapon systems. And lastly I looked at Chris and saw my son in so many ways. His gestures and mannerisms constantly reminded me of my son Jacen. Chris and the team had many great times together, here is just a few that I want to recall.

We were notified of an in-coming new guy named Chris Falkel. Jim and I told the other members of the team about the "New 18B" coming to the team. Immediately the guys began to laugh and make fun of the last name of Chris, they would all say over and over "FOKER" from the movie. Anyway I remember the guidance from me and Jim was to ensure we train this guy correctly and welcome him to the Team. The guys assured us with their typical devious laughter that they would take good care of "Foker." We decided the fastest way to get Chris was to pick him up at KAF; we were already scheduled to go there to get more money. We all met Chris—damn what a young looking dude. We were there for overnight, and a mission came down to get the number one dude in the country. We were all very excited, and the boys were telling Chris how lucky he was to have this as the first mission with the team. Things happened and the mission did not go, even after a very eventful evening with Jim and the planning of this thing. We finished our business and we departed back to our Firebase. Chris was brought to the team hooch to find his place next to the wall where he will rest his head. I remembered looking at Chris and thinking damn this kid looks younger then my son. I asked him his age, and when he responded, I started calling him Junior from that day on; the rest of the guys caught on and started calling him Junior, as well. The guys decorated the wall above his bed with graffiti and ribbing immediately. Chris had a very short time to throw his bag on the floor and the boys took him on a tour of the Firebase.

I got a message from Task Force 31 referencing the New Guy had previously received a DUI and never had a mental evaluation (as required by the US Army). I was instructed to ensure he gets on the next Re-Supply and get him back to Bagram to get his mental examination. Chris was on duty in the guard tower that day when I ask him if he had been arrested previously. I remember Chris looking at me and saying "No." Then I asked him more pointedly if he has ever been arrested for DUI, then he told me his story. I ask him why he did not tell me the deal from the beginning. He responded with he did not want us to look at him like he was a screw-up. I responded to Chris that what was done was done, and starting immediately was all I cared about.

One of the funniest times I personally had with Chris was when we were all watching the movie "DEEDs." We laughed about everything that Adam Sadler said, especially when he states "I'll bring the beers," "I'll bring the beers," with his hand over his heart. Chris and I had greeted each other daily both cracking up after we said it to each other , it seems like we did this for months after seeing that movie. Chris had so many lines of that movie memorized, all were hilarious when he would say them.

Another movie we use to discuss was "Dumb and Dumber," the part we constantly laughed about was when Lloyd and Harry got pulled over, and the cop asks what was in the open bottles on their floor of the "Shagging Wagon." Harry tried to tell the cop it was not what he thought and the cop insisted on taking a drink to test what he thought was alcohol. After the cop took a sip he immediately started to twitch and get sick, I remember Chris reenacting that scene over and over. We laughed uncontrollably each time, just as my son and I use to laugh about the same exact scene in previous years.

One day, while ODA 316 was in Gereshk, I got a call from Chris, and he told me he was up in Kandahar for a "psych eval"—my initial concern was combat stress had gotten to him, but he assured me that he was fine, and that they had "lost" his evaluation from the Q course, and it was just a routine evaluation. That made more sense, and so we continued our great conversation about other things.

Well, when Ron told me about the DUI during language school, I was as mad at Chris as I had ever been! And when I see you, my son, we WILL discuss that—you can be sure of that!

I never had any fear about Chris being killed in combat. I prayed each and every day that he and all of ODA 316 were safe during their contacts, but if he died in combat, that was how a warrior was supposed to die. No, my worse fear was that Chris would be killed in a car accident.

Chris loved to party, and he loved being the "life of the party" but, at the same time, it was my worse nightmare. So, in addition to getting a second DUI, he did it while in the Q course when he was SO close to finishing the course—it could have easily gotten him thrown out of the Q course and SF—and he KNEW that—but even more so, he didn't tell me the truth about it.

Oh yes, Chris—we will talk about this!

I found this letter that Chris wrote to the cadre of the Special Forces Qualification Course (SFQC) after his DUI when I was going through his things. It does not change the fact Chris took a risk that could have cost him everything he worked so hard for, but it takes a man to admit your mistakes, and to ask for a second chance:

To Whom It May Concern,

Sirs, I am writing this letter with much regret for the actions that I have committed and the way that I have conducted myself over the past several weeks. As you already know, I was arrested on the night of 2 November 2003 for operating a motor vehicle under the influence of alcohol. I have no justifications for my actions of that night other than the fact that I executed very poor judgment and should never have been driving in the condition that I was in. I write this letter to you to plead for my continuation in the Special Forces Qualification Course.

I began this course in April of 2002 at SOPC, and had did not know where I would end up. I found that over the duration of this course, I made better friends with my fellow students/soldiers than I ever had my whole life. Over the different phases of training, some people failed to make the grade and did not move on. I did lose several friends to these mishaps, but at the culmination of each phase, I felt more and more a part of a new family. This brotherhood that I have since joined is a place where I would consider myself at home. Given the extensive training and enduring the rigorous challenges that I have met and overcome, I truly see the US ARMY Special Forces as a place where I want to belong and I feel that I do belong. I have elapsed this course with above average scores in every phase that I have gone through, and I shall continue to take my future with SF just as seriously as I have during the Q-Course. Ever since I was a child, all I ever wanted to do with my life was join the ARMY. As I have started to fulfill this lifelong goal, I see that I sincerely want to defend America's freedom while fighting on an SFODA. I am currently studying the Arabic language and I will take my DLPT on Tuesday, 18 November 2003. Sir, I beg that you let me finish the course and graduate with my peers. Staying in the SFQC, and graduating, is more important to me now than anything else in my life. I am willing to do anything to remain a student in this course whatever actions may follow.

Again Sir, my future, career, and my rest of my life are in your hands, and I pray that you give me the chance to become a member of a SFODA and continue my career as an 18B weapons sergeant. I had planned on making/spending my career in the Special Forces and I truly hope that this mistake does not eliminate the possibility of me doing so. Once more I give you my deepest apologies on the way that I have conducted myself and vouch that I shall never act in this manner for the rest of my career to come in the United States Army.

Falkel, Christopher M.
SPC, USA

But, again, Big Ron knew exactly what to say when it needed to be said, and we concluded our first of many, MANY amazing talks laughing at Chris and his unique ability to have exactly the right movie line at exactly the right moment! Chris was the master of movie lines. In fact, the day I was typing this it just so happened that "Mr. Deeds" was on TV, and while I had seen that movie several times before, it was that much more special this time because I felt Big Ron and Chris with me watching and laughing/crying hysterically at the movie.

I was also honored to attend Big Ron's graduation from the Sergeant Major Academy in May, 2007 at Ft. Bliss, Texas. I had a meeting in Las Cruces, NM, and El Paso is only about an hour away. So I drove over to see Ron and his family and then go to his graduation ceremony. I drove over to the graduation ceremony with Big Ron. We had no sooner gotten out of the car, and one of his classmates yells out at the top of his lungs to Big Ron, "Hey Rambo!" I almost got hit by a car pulling into the parking lot because I was laughing so hard I didn't see it coming right at me!!! It was an amazing graduation, and the part I will always laugh at was the Command Sergeant Major of the Sergeant Major Academy, "commanding" over 400 Sergeant Majors like they were a bunch of E-1 privates!!! It was so ironic, it was comical! However, every American should witness that graduation ceremony! The men and women in that auditorium will go out and be the leaders of the greatest Army on earth! It was an incredibly powerful experience for me.

And in keeping with Big Ron's innate ability to say exactly the right thing at the right time, he made me even more proud of Chris than I ever thought possible. Every one of the new SGMs (Sergeant Majors) that Big Ron introduced me to, he told them of Chris. I could see in Ron's eyes and hear in his voice how proud he was of Chris, and then the look on the face of these great NCOs when they heard about Chris made my heart soar. Big Ron would always mention that Chris was only 22 when he crossed over, and that fact alone would cause almost shock on the faces of the SGMs.

Big Ron loved my son, and I love him!

There is one more story that I want to share about Big Ron—one that touches my heart.

One of the hardest things for me to see is the homecoming celebrations whenever a unit returns from Afghanistan or Iraq. When Chris came home from Gereshk, I had told him I would be there when he got off the plane. However, being the professional he was, Chris told me that as soon as he got home, he would have so much to do to in-process all the team's weapons. So he asked me to stay in Colorado, and he would call as soon as he got back, and then he would fly home once he was done. I had to respect his request, and I was so very proud of his maturity. But, I never got to see Chris get off that plane and that is one thing I don't think I will ever be able to get over. And because of all the emotions that we all had when ODA 316 got back in February 2006, we decided it would be better for me to wait a day or so to meet the boys for the first time, and I am so glad we made that decision.

Then, when anyone else in my family returned from combat, it seemed that I was always out of town, and many times, out of the country. However, in May 2008, I was "home" when Big Ron came back from Afghanistan. His wonderful wife called me, and invited me to be there at Green Ramp over at Pope Air Force Base. Ron had told her that he knew I was at Bragg for the Memorialization, but he was afraid that I probably had gone back to Colorado, and he was so disappointed that he would have missed me by just a few days. So, Brenda and I decided we would surprise Big Ron! It was not the same as seeing Chris get off the plane, but it was a very special day for me because Big Ron means that much to me!

And last, but certainly not least—Big Ron's house warming party! After he returned from El Paso, he and his family moved into a new house on the outskirts of Fayetteville. But he was only home for a short period of time when he was sent to Afghanistan as Charlie Company SGM for 2nd Battalion/3rd SFG (A). So, he never got to "properly" christen the house! So, on 9 August 2008, Big Ron started a new tradition in the family, and had a party I will never, EVER forget! I was "home" to be with everyone on the third anniversary of Chris' crossing, and to help Markus with his kitchen renovation. Big Ron took the opportunity to have a party while I was there, and it was just what I needed on that day! I have never laughed so hard, or so much in my life!!! I got to meet my brother, "Felix" that I had heard so much about, and have shared so many "little" emails with. Big Ron gave me the chance to look Felix in the eye, to thank him for all he is to my brothers, and to tell him that I love him!

It was a night I will never forget, and will always cherish—just as I cherish Big Ron's love for me, for Chris, and for all his men in 3rd SFG (A)!

…"And, I'll bring the beers!" my brother!

Big Ron—you are a warrior, you are a hero, you are my brother, and I love you with all my heart. Your influence has gone beyond your wildest dreams! Your example is being followed by team sergeants on the best ODA's in SF right now, and for that and ALL you have done for YOUR men, you have my unending gratitude, and all my love.

19

MSG Big Al—The Consummate Special Forces Team Sergeant

There is a choice you have to make, in everything you do. And you must always keep in mind the choice you make, makes you.

—Anonymous

When Chris first arrived on ODA 316 in January, 2004, Big Al was the 18 Fox, or intel sergeant on the team. While they were in Gereshk, Big Al was promoted to Master Sergeant, and I remember Chris emailing me after the promotion ceremony, and him telling me what a great NCO—non-commissioned officer—Big Al was, and how he had learned so much from Big Al while he was in Gereshk. Soon after ODA 316 returned from that trip, Big Ron who had been the team sergeant was scheduled to go to the Sergeant Major Academy at Fort Hood, so Big Al became the team sergeant for ODA 316. Big Al was responsible for coordinating all training schools for ODA 316 as one of his duties, and Chris "loved" Big Al because he was able to get Chris a slot in both SFARTAETC—Special Forces Advanced Reconnaissance, Target Analysis and Exploitation Techniques Course and his favorite school, SOTIC—Special Operations Target Interdiction Course (SF sniper school). It takes most SF weapons sergeants several years to get into either of these advanced schools, but Big Al got Chris in both within one year! Big Al saw in Chris what I always knew was there—Chris wanted to be the BEST Special Forces weapons sergeant in the U.S. Army, and Big Al was going to give Chris every opportunity to make that goal come true.

Big Al has a quiet strength. He is the textbook of the "quiet professional" that Special Forces NCO's should strive for. But Big Al is also a warrior and a Spartan. He has the vision and experience to lead his men under any circumstance, and the 54 hour battle in Mari Ghar became Big Al's shining moment and worse nightmare.

Big Al was in vehicle #3 with Chris. When Chris was shot, it was Big Al's job to tell not only the rest of ODA 316 that Chris was gone, but also up the chain of command. For all the battles, for all the years, and for all the experiences of ODA 316, Chris was the first member of the team to die in combat, and while every warrior knows he is potentially seconds away from death, when it first happens, it affects you like you cannot imagine. This was particularly strong in the case of Chris and his brothers on ODA 316. Chris was the youngest, he was their "little brother," and he was "invincible"—so Chris couldn't be dead—but he was. Big Al had to muster all his strength, all his professionalism, and all his love for HIS men to remain calm in the face of unthinkable tragedy, and he shined like the brightest star in the heavens. He kept his head, kept his emotions in check, he was the professional he had to be, and because of Big Al, and the consummate team sergeant he was on that fateful day, Chris was the ONLY casualty during the 54 hour Battles of Mari Ghar.

For that, I owe Big Al everything, because if someone else had died during that battle, I don't think I could have handled it. Big Al kept his men, Chris' brothers, alive so they could fight another day. And fight they did because the most fierce battle of the seven would be the morning after Chris died.

But, Big Al loved Chris, and for a long time, it was so very hard for him because he did not bring all his men home. As Jimbo and I have told him and the rest of ODA 316, 99 percent of the 54 hour Battles of Mari Ghar was what legends are made of, and as Jim said in his eulogy, "will live in the annuals of Special Force history." The only bad part was losing Chris. Were it not for Big Al, the probability of the entire team being wiped out was almost a certainty. He did what needed to be done to save the lives of everyone else.

For that, I owe you more, Big Al, than anyone on the face of the earth. You brought back our brothers. You did what only you could do. And I love you as no other. I can never thank you for giving me OUR family, and while I miss Chris more with every passing day, my life is so much more complete and full of love because of everyone that you DID bring home. I can NEVER adequately thank you for that, my brother.

After Deh Afghan, Big Al went to the "school house" and he became the First Sergeant of the Special Forces Qualification Course Language School. He brought his skills, talent and professionalism to young men striving to become Special Forces, and they are all better soldiers today because of Big Al giving of himself to HIS students.

MSG Big Al and MSG Chuck both did something after they returned home from Deh Afghan that will forever hold a special place in my heart. They both withdrew their nominations for the Silver Star that they most certainly deserved for everything that they did during the Battles of Mari Ghar. Again, Big Al was more concerned for his men, and their careers, and that is why he withdrew his nomination. Is there a better definition of love than that?

Here is the narrative for the Silver Star that should have been the minimal award that MSG Big Al desired for the Battles of Mari Ghar:

Narrative Recommendation For Award Of The Silver Star To Master Sergeant Big Al, Alpha Company, 1st Battalion, 3d Special Forces Group (Airborne), Fort Bragg, North Carolina, 28310

Master Sergeant Big Al distinguished himself by exemplifying spirited bravery as the Team Sergeant for Operational Detachment Alpha (ODA) 316, Combined Joint Special Operations Task Force-Afghanistan in support of Operation ENDURING FREEDOM from 7 August 2005 to 9 August 2005. MSG Big Al distinguished himself in seven fierce enemy engagements with a well trained, tactically emplaced, and aggressive enemy during a time span of fifty-six hours while operating as the tactical commander of the third vehicle of our element, while conducting operations in the Zabol Province of Afghanistan while deployed to A-Camp Lane. MSG Big Al's calmness under fire and tactical competence were imperative to the detachment's survival. During our second contact in Buka Ghar Valley, MSG Big Al maneuvered his vehicle so his gunner could put down heavy volumes of fire on well emplaced machine gun positions. MSG Big Al took charge of the element while receiving enormous amounts of fire, while his team leader and another member of the ODA moved to pinned down Afghanistan National Army (ANA) elements that were part of our patrol and help consolidate, assess, and get control of their situation. Our unit continued to receive heavy volumes of machine gun fire and RPGs from numerous positions. MSG Big Al continued to lead the element until the dismounted element had gained control of the ANA soldiers. Once the ANA fires could be directed, MSG Big Al then took charge of the 60mm mortars and directed a heavy barrage of fires against a well emplaced enemy positions. The intensity and accuracy of the 60mm fires forced the enemy to break contact, therefore ensuring that the ANA soldiers and the ODA could consolidate and continue pursuit of the enemy. Our elements continued to pursue the enemy during their retreat when they sent ahead for reinforcements to set up what was to be the third ambush. When the third Anti Coalition Member (ACM) ambush commenced, MSG Big Al immediately located and put his vehicle in a position so his gunner could fire upon the well emplaced and trained enemy. MSG Big Al once again took charge of the element when the team leader and another member of the element dismounted in an attempt to flank the ACM positions that were slowing the maneuver of our ANA elements. His bravery and direction of fires allowed our ANA element to maneuver on the larger ACM element. The remaining ACM elements broke contact again, only to reform and gather more experienced and trained fighters further down our route. We intercepted ACM communications that again said they were reorganizing at a location that they had success with in the past. MSG Big Al demanded that we continue on and finish the enemy. As we entered Cakyan Ghar Valley, the ACM element opened up on our lead element as before with extraordinary volumes of machine gun, RPG and AK-47 fire. MSG Big Al immediately maneuvered his gun vehicle to a position to engage this highly trained, numerically superior, and well equipped ACM force that we had been dealing with and pursuing for the past thirty hours. MSG Big Al got out of his vehicle and engaged the enemy without care for his own life. His only concerns were for the care of his fellow team mates and trying to eliminate, or draw some of the fire from those machine gun positions that had our ANA element pinned down. MSG Big Al continued engaging the well emplaced enemy positions, when the rest of the ACM ambush opened up with an enormous amount of fire on the entire element. The third vehicle sustained a KIA (SSG Falkel) and MSG Big Al continued to return fire so that the gun turret could be re-occupied. MSG Big Al, with no regard for his own life, recovered SSG Falkel while being engaged by enormous amounts of highly accurate machine gun and sniper fire. At that point, the vehicles could start to maneuver to cover. MSG Big Al took charge of his vehicle, while returning fire, to maneuver the vehicle out of the kill zone. Throughout the following evening MSG Big Al directed and supervised the defense of the NDP (Night Defensive Position). The following morning our element began its final pursuit of the ACM forces in the Marah Valley and link up with our ground quick reaction force (QRF) element. MSG Big Al manned a 50 cal. machine gun while continuing to lead the third vehicle of the element. Shortly after we made link up and movement, we began our seventh contact, with what would turn out to be our largest most violent ACM force of all the contacts we had faced in the prior fifty six hours. MSG Big Al maneuvered his gun vehicle so he the gunner could begin to lay down heavy volumes of fire on the ACM element that opened up on our lead element and his vehicle with extraordinary volumes of machine gun, RPG and AK-47 fire. MSG Big Al's vehicle was struck numerous times and yet again he continued to fiercely lay down fire so the rest of his element could clear the choke point on which the enemy had directed tremendous amounts of fire at the moment. His continuous engagement without concern for his own well being allowed our heavily suppressed elements to get to positions of better cover and his relentless punishment to the enemy while fully exposed later caused them to retreat. MSG Big Al willfully and voluntarily chose to serve in Operation ENDURING FREEDOM supporting his fellow soldiers, the legitimate Government of Afghanistan, and the United States of America in the global war on terror. The distinctive accomplishments of Master Sergeant Big Al reflect great credit upon himself, the Combined Joint Special Operations Task Force-Afghanistan and the United States Army.

Chris' life, my life and the lives of our ENTIRE 316 family are that much more enriched because of you, our brother, Big Al! I love you with every fiber of my being and will for the rest of time.

20

MSG Chuck

A warrior didn't try to stand out from the band of warriors. He strove to act bravely and honorably, to help the group in whatever way he could to accomplish its mission.

—Lakota Warrior

There are few words to accurately describe Chuck! He is as unique a man, a warrior, a Spartan as anyone I have ever known!!! He was one of the 18 Echoes or Communications Sergeants, on ODA 316 and eventually became the 18 Fox for ODA 316. He is a computer genius, and as fierce a warrior as you have ever seen. He could play computer goes for days at a time, and be ready to roll out the wire in seconds. One of my favorite stories about Chuck occurred while Chris and I were skiing together in Utah. The rest of ODA 316 was heading out for a training exercise, and they stopped at the Commissary on post for some last minute supplies. They were all ready to go, but couldn't find Chuck. After some extensive recon, they saw him with several cases of SoBe energy drink. When Dan asked him, "Chuck, what are you doing, and where are we going to put all that SoBe?" Chuck simply responded that he got a free T-shirt if he bought that many cases!!!

When Tim and I went to Bragg for the Memorialization in May, 2006, we stayed at Chuck's house, and there was STILL SoBe there from that bargain shopping spree!!!

But, Chuck did something for me that I will NEVER be able to repay. Chuck was the commander of vehicle 2 on 8 August 2005 in Mari Ghar. After Chris was shot, there were bullets flying all over vehicle 3, but Chuck was not about to let Chris lay there. He told Dan he was going to get Chris down, and despite fierce fire from all directions, Chuck ran back to vehicle 3 to get Chris down. Dan told me that story the night I got to finally meet ODA 316 at Jimbo's house in February 2006, and as Paul Harvey says, "the rest of the story" is that just before Chuck ran back to get Chris down, all Dan could think to tell him was, "Well, be careful!" Dan told me while we were sitting on Jimbo's couch that of all the things he could have said to Chuck, or SHOULD have said to Chuck at that moment, he couldn't believe that he told him to "be careful!!!"

That is Chuck! But that act of bravery and of his ultimate love for my son is just about the most amazing gift that anyone has ever given me. The courage, the professionalism, the total disregard for his own life to keep my son from suffering any further, and to get up in Chris' turret and continue to lay down fire to keep the rest of ODA 316 alive is something that mere words can not adequately describe. To me, that act is the definition of love for your brother, and that is the love I feel for Chuck because what he did for Chris and for me.

You are my hero, Chuck, and I love you as no other!

But, there is another story that the world needs to know about Chuck and Big Al. Both Chuck and Al knew that they were going to retire soon after they returned from Deh Afghan in 2006. And, they both wanted the rest of ODA 316 to be recognized for their valor and bravery during the battles in Mari Ghar. So, rather than having their nominations for their medals of valor going forward for consideration, BOTH Chuck and Al pulled their nominations. It was something that they didn't have to do, and should not have done, but they did because of their love for their team.

How do you describe that kind of love? It goes beyond words, it goes beyond what almost anyone else would have ever thought about doing. But Chuck and Big Al are more than most—they are true American and Special Forces heroes.

Here is the narrative of the Bronze Star with Valor that Chuck should have been awarded:

Narrative Recommendation For Award Of The Bronze Star With "V" Device To SFC Chuck, Alpha Company, 1st Battalion, 3d Special Forces Group (Airborne), Fort Bragg, North Carolina, 28310

Sergeant First Class Chuck distinguished himself by exemplifying spirited bravery as the Intelligence Sergeant for Operational Detachment Alpha (ODA) 316, Combined Joint Special Operations Task Force-Afghanistan in support of Operation ENDURING FREEDOM from 7 August 2005 to 9 August 2005. SFC Chuck distinguished himself in seven fierce enemy engagements with a well trained, tactically emplaced, and aggressive enemy during a time span of fifty-six hours while operating as the Tactical Commander of the second vehicle of our element, while conducting operations in the Zabol Province of Afghanistan while deployed to A-Camp Lane. SFC Chuck's calmness under fire and tactical competence were imperative to the detachment's survival. During our unit's multiple engagements that took place in Buka Ghar Valley, Cakyan Ghar Valley, and Marah Valley, SFC Chuck was instrumental in positioning his vehicle so his gunner could help fix and engage the well equipped and fortified enemy positions that had the entire element pinned down by extraordinary volumes of machine gun, RPG and AK-47 fire multiple times. The most notable act of bravery out of all the engagements was about thirty hours into our operation. We had already had four major fire fights with Anti Coalition Forces (ACM), which were highly trained, numerically superior, and looking to eliminate our entire element. It was in our fifth contact with this fierce enemy that we lost the machine gunner on our last vehicle (SSG Falkel). SFC Chuck upon seeing the down gunner and the vehicle being suppressed with heavy volumes of fire, maneuvered on foot over to the pinned down vehicle exposing his whole body numerous times to the fierce incoming fire. SFC Chuck then assisted the remaining vehicle crew in moving SSG Falkel's body down from the turret so SFC Chuck could later occupy the turret and gun. His ability to quickly re-acquire and engage the enemy that had been laying down extraordinary amounts of effective fire on our element was essential to the survival of our element. SFC Chuck continued to engage enemy forces while exposing himself without care or safety for himself, thinking only of that of his fellow teammates was a key factor in the entire element being able to move to a position of cover. On the following morning and during the fiercest battle of them all, SFC Chuck played a key roll in the positioning of his gun vehicle, so it could lay effective fire on the heavily armed enemy. He participated in redistributing ammo to machine guns that were either out or critically low on ammo. SFC Chuck moved *ammo from one truck to another while receiving heavy volumes of fire during the entire time of ammo re-distribution. SFC Chuck and his interpreter also played a key role in our pursuit of the enemy, as well as giving our element vital information on enemy ambushes that were emplaced ahead of our element. Our unit would have suffered much greater losses without this vital information. SFC Chuck willfully and voluntarily chose to serve in his fourth rotation of Operation ENDURING FREEDOM supporting his fellow soldiers, the legitimate Government of Afghanistan, and the United States of America in the global war on terror. The distinctive accomplishments of Sergeant First Class Chuck reflect great credit upon himself, the Combined Joint Special Operations Task Force-Afghanistan and the United States Army.*

As I said, you are my hero, Chuck!

Chuck has retired to Phoenix, Arizona but he will always be in my heart. I can NEVER thank Chuck enough for all he was to Chris, and all he did for Chris. I would gladly give my life for you, my brother. I love you with all my heart, Chuck!

21

MSG Tony—"T"

The path to my fixed purpose is laid on iron rails in which my soul is grooved to ride

—Herman Melville in *Moby Dick*

It has been said to me that writing OUR book has been a labor of love. Love—absolutely! The two words used most frequently in OUR book are Chris and Love!!! But, labor—I am not sure about that word. It is paradoxical in that it is one of the hardest things I have ever done, but yet, it is probably the best thing I have ever written. It has been anything but easy—in fact, it was exhausting at times! But, my thoughts flowed as easily as my tears—until I got to this chapter. It is the only time in my life of writing that I wrote something, and tore it up. And I did it TWICE for OUR chapter about Tony!!! I have never had that happen before, and I wasn't sure why at first. But then it hit me—this is the chapter about MSG Tony—Chris' Tony. He is the one that loved my son as no other, and my son loved him with all his heart. Tony and Chris had a very special love that goes beyond what warriors or brothers have for each other, and Tony is the only one that can truly tell THEIR story!

…but I will try…

Here is the first email I received from Tony as soon as they got back to their firebase after the Battles of Mari Ghar—it is one that I will have with me for the rest of my life:

Dear Sir,

There are no words to express how sorry I am for your loss. Introductions are in order; however I'd rather do that in person when I return. Right now I just want to extend my sympathy to you and convey that even though I do not know the grief a father feels in a moment like this, your grief is shared by all of us. I don't know how much Junior spoke about us to you; he and I were very close. He spoke about you frequently and I'll share those stories with you when we are seated across from each other.

We fought for fifty four hours. I can not disclose any details at this time, but we were in the biggest contact this theater has had to date. Junior fought brilliantly. He did everything perfectly with a warrior's heart. I can still remember exchanging smiles with him after the fourth firefight of that day. I promise you that I and all his other brothers fought as hard and as well as we know how. I personally packed all Junior's belongings and have a separate container of his possessions that I thought he would want you to have. We are trying to persuade our command to allow us to escort Junior home. The outcome is still undetermined. I apologize for being brief. I'm having a difficult time with our loss as well. If this letter is in anyway inappropriate, again I apologize.

I am my brother's keeper,
SFC Tony
USSF

In my first email to MSG Tony, I told him that Chris didn't speak of him often, he spoke of him CONSTANTLY! When people in Fayetteville or at Ft. Bragg saw Tony, there was Chris by his side. If MSG Tony had a "date," she had better like Chris or the date was off! And while I had never actually talked to MSG Tony until he was on his way back to CONUS with Chris, of all the members of ODA 316, I knew the most about MSG Tony.

MSG Tony was the senior 18 Charlie or engineer on ODA 316. Chris used to get the biggest kick out of me asking, "Now, is Tony an "Echo"—NO Dad, he is the Charlie; Scott and Chuck are the Echoes!"

After a while, I must admit, I would "mess with Chris" when I actually DID remember who was the Charlie and who was the Echo! A Special Forces engineer is not only responsible for "blowing shit up," but for building and designing new facilities. One of my favorite emails from Gereshk was one where Chris told me that he and Tony were building some storage areas in their firebase, and he was asking my advice about how to best undertake the construction. It made my heart soar that Chris was using some of the skills I taught him about woodworking and construction.

Well, the most difficult construction job that MSG Tony has ever had to undertake, was rebuilding our family after we lost Chris. All of ODA 316 wanted to escort Chris home, but command needed them to stay and continue to take it to the enemy. They were told that only one of them would escort Chris back, and they unanimously choose MSG Tony for that job. I can't even begin to imagine how difficult it was for Tony to fly back with Chris. Tony handled that task like the true professional that he is! Each stage of the trip home, he either emailed me or called me to let me know their status. Again, I can't comprehend how he was able to accomplish this painful journey, but know this, Tony did it with the class, the excellence and the professionalism of a warrior, of a Spartan. I am so grateful that Tony had the courage and the strength to bring my son back to me because I was unable to. It was just another testament to the love that he had for his brother.

MSG Tony took Chris under his wing as soon as Chris got to Gereshk. Tony once told me that as soon as he met Chris, he knew that Chris was a warrior, and that Chris would teach him as much as he would teach Chris. They pushed each other—in EVERYTHING! Chris used to love going up to Washington D.C. with Tony for some of Grandma's cooking, but also because he loved doing anything and everything with Tony! Apparently after a night at the Royal Lee Bar, Tony got up for a run, and even though Chris would have rather slept, he laced them up and off they went. The run ends with a long staircase, and despite being sick as a dog from too many at the Royal Lee, Chris was not going to concede and neither was Tony!!! They both pushed themselves and each other in that run, and everything they did. Tony showed Chris what it was to be a professional, and Chris keep Tony sharp and on his toes at all times!

Tony loved my son. And my son LOVED "T"!!! I can remember so many phone conversations with Chris where practically every other sentence had the word, "Tony" included in it! Well, now that I know MSG Tony as well as I do, the word "Chris" is practically in every other sentence that Tony says. They had a very special relationship, as they were cut from the same mold. They are both perfectionists, and refuse to accept mediocrity. They love to have fun, but they love to fight equally as much. They are both WARRIORS, and they made each other BETTER warriors!!! And because they were who they were, they made ODA 316 better.

I have said it before, but I can never say it enough—I am so grateful that Chris got to experience what is so SPECIAL about Special Forces BECAUSE of the men that were ODA 316! Chris wanted to be SF almost his entire life, and the fact that his SF experience was with you, Tony and all your brothers on ODA 316, fills my heart with joy. Chris LOVED being on HIS team, YOUR team, and if he had been on any other team, he would have never experienced what SF should be all about. You were a tremendous part of Chris' SF life, and for that, and everything you were to Chris and are to me, I love you as no other.

Tony spoke about his brother at the Memorials in Littleton and at the JFK Chapel. Here are the amazing words, that my amazing brother had to say about my amazing son—they touch my heart like no others:

Anyone who knew Chris can stand here and talk all day long about what a wonderful son, brother or friend he was. He touched each of our lives in a unique and very special way. I am going to tell you a little about Chris, the warrior. He wanted to be a "Green Beret" since he was 8 years old, when he tacked his first "Long Tab and Arrowhead" his father gave him above his bed. Coincidently, Chris' passion was creating weapons and strategically placing them around the house in case of an "attack."

Chris was contagiously enthusiastic every day, and strived to be the best at everything we did, which was pretty bold considering the men he worked with. However, we realized how talented and competitive he was, and being who we are, welcomed his tenacity and respected his abilities. He made us better. It wasn't long before Chris established his name amongst his peers in Special Forces, and more importantly, amongst his brothers whom he would fight beside. Chris was loved first because he was a warrior. All his other qualities we came to know and love, were eventually revealed to us in time.

Chris was our little brother. He was ALWAYS close by and constantly made his presence known with his humor and antics. However, when it was time to work, and the team rolled out the wire, Chris was a lion amongst men. I used to brag about him like proud older brothers do, and always had an eye on him, protecting him when we spent time together at home.

In battle, he wasn't my little brother whom I had to guide and protect. He stood beside us and held the line under any adversity. I felt a sense of pride and comfort in knowing that Chris was beside me, because at our worst hour, I knew he would be at his best.

I caught glimpses of him in his final battles. He fought brilliantly and executed perfectly. He stood behind his gun and faced a determined, relentless enemy with valor and tenacity. He never let up, he didn't flinch. Chris was a lion among men.

Chris' favorite saying to me was, "I want to go out in a blaze of glory." What I remember most about that day is his smiling face and a focused, determined look in his eyes after each engagement.

Those battles are over. Chris made his mark on history and will be remembered by those of us who fought beside him that day, and those of you that hear the tale, as the warrior he was, at his best.

Now, I am his big brother again. Swelling with pride, and bragging about him. His spirit will be with us in battles to come. And when the time comes for us to hold the line once again, I will find comfort in that.

T, your words touched not only me, but everyone that heard them. What I heard in your words was your pride in OUR Chris. What I felt in your words was the pain in your heart—not that Chris died—but that he would not be there with you the next time you "have some scheme up your sleeve!" What I know from your words is how much you love OUR Chris.

There is another story about Tony that I want to share because it further defines the man, the warrior, the Spartan that MSG Tony is: When we went to the Memorialization in 2006, Tim and I went out a few days early, and Jim wanted to have a party—what a surprise—and the best day to have that party was on Saturday, 20 May 2006. Well, MAJ Jim didn't know it when he was planning that party, but 20 May 2006 just happened to be Tim's 21st birthday. I am sure it is a birthday that Tim will NEVER forget, but what I will always remember about that party was when we were giving out our gifts to everyone. When it was MSG Tony's turn, he asked Tim to come up. He hugged Tim, and told him that while he can never replace Chris, Tony was going to be Tim's big brother now and forever. He then reached into his back pocket, and Tony gave Tim his ODA 316 war hat. One of the "perks" of being SF—despite CSM Buzzsaw's 'protests'—was being able to wear baseball style hats around post and the firebase when downrange. Picking out your 'war hat' was a special thing, and that hat went through things that most people would never believe.

Tony wanted Tim to have the hat that he wore throughout ODA 316's entire rotation in Deh Afghan. It was a gift that touched Tim like no other gift he has ever received. I saw a look on Tim's face that I had never seen before—well maybe one time in England when we found your Manchester United long sleeve kit jersey, right Tim?!?!—and T's war hat is one of Tim's most prized possessions.

Also, it almost got Tim busted going through security at DIA on our way back to Honolulu for Tim's fall semester at University of Hawai'i!!! I have so much metal in me that I always set off the metal detectors, but Tim was the one that they stopped and searched his carry-on bag. Something set the detector off, so the TSA agents went through his entire backpack. The backpack Tim had was one that I got for Chris when he graduated from Basic Training, and other than his laptop and a couple of DVD's, the rest of the contents were primarily Tim's collection of baseball hats. The TSA agents looked and looked through his stuff, but didn't find anything, so Tim re-packed his bag, and we were on our way to Paradise. Tim wondered what the search was all about, and the ONLY thing I can think of was the gunpowder residue that was on Tony's war hat!!! It made for an interesting trip to say the least!

MSG Tony is now a team sergeant for an ODA in 3rd SFG (A), and he has all his experiences while on ODA 316 to guide him and his new team. He told MAJ Jim and me when he got back from Afghanistan after his 6th deployment in the last 7 years, that his new team was using the SOP's that ODA 316 had developed so many years ago. When MSG Tony started laughing while his new team was reviewing their procedures, one of his men asked what was so funny. "I wrote those SOP's with MAJ Jim years ago—they worked then, and they will work now!!!" His new team is so very fortunate to have MSG Tony as their 18 Zulu, and what he brings from ODA 316 to his new team. They had a very successful rotation, and the Taliban would be the first to confirm that assessment!!! MSG Tony and his team left for Afghanistan again in January, 2009.

MSG Tony is one of the most decorated warriors in Special Forces. MSG Tony has been nominated for the Distinguished Service Cross (DSC) for his valor, bravery, courage, professionalism and love of his brothers during the Battles of Mari Ghar. The DSC is the second highest military award for valor and bravery in combat, with only the Medal of Honor being the highest award. Even though it has been over three years, there is still a chance that MSG Tony will receive the award he deserves. As OUR book is being written, several warriors who know what T did are actively trying to get him recognized for his amazing actions. If MSG Tony does not receive the DSC, he will be awarded the Silver Star, but I hope with all my heart that the "powers above" will do the right thing, and award my brother what he so valiantly deserves.

This will be the narrative that will accompany what ever award MSG Tony receives (Tony was Sergeant First Class—SFC—during the rotation to Deh Afghan):

Narrative Recommendation For Award Of The Distinguished Service Cross Or Silver Star To SFC Tony, Alpha Company, 1st Battalion, 3d Special Forces Group (Airborne), Fort Bragg, North Carolina, 28310

Sergeant First Class Tony distinguished himself by exemplifying spirited bravery as the Engineer Sergeant for Operational Detachment Alpha (ODA) 316, Combined Joint Special Operations Task Force-

Afghanistan in support of Operation ENDURING FREEDOM from 7 August 2005 to 9 August 2005. SFC Tony distinguished himself in seven fierce enemy engagements with a well trained, tactically emplaced, and aggressive enemy during a time span of fifty-six hours while operating as the driver of the first vehicle of our element, while conducting operations in the Zabol Province of Afghanistan while deployed to A-Camp Lane. SFC Tony's calmness under fire and tactical competence were imperative to the detachment's survival. During our second contact in Buka Ghar Valley, SFC Tony maneuvered his vehicle so his gunner could put down heavy volumes of fire on well emplaced machine gun positions. SFC Tony and another member dismounted their gun vehicle and moved up while receiving enormous amounts of fire, to pinned down Afghanistan National Army (ANA) elements that were part of our patrol and help consolidate, assess, and get control of their situation. Our unit continued to receive heavy volumes of machine gun fire and RPGs from numerous positions. He played a crucial role in reorganizing and focusing the fires of the ANA and our gun vehicles on the heavily fortified positions that had the ANA element pinned down. SFC Tony's movement to a position to gain positive control of our ANA element and focusing their fires was essential. Our element wouldn't have been able to positively engage with pinpoint accuracy the element that had the ANA pinned down. The numerically superior forces would have taken advantage of the lack of organization of the ANA element and would have destroyed their unit. Our elements continued to pursue the enemy during their retreat when they sent ahead for reinforcements to set up what was to be the third ambush. Upon the third Anti Coalition Member (ACM) ambush, SFC Tony immediately located and put his vehicle in a position so his gunner could fire upon the well emplaced and trained enemy. SFC Tony once again dismounted with another member of his vehicle to attempt to flank the ACM positions that were slowing the maneuver of our ANA elements. His bravery allowed our ANA element to maneuver on the larger ACM element, later causing the enemy to maneuver to a location they thought would give them a tactical advantage. This only led them to a better vantage point for our gun vehicles to eliminate them during their maneuver to what would have been a position devastating to our ANA element. The remaining ACM elements broke contact again, only to reform and gather more experienced and trained fighters further *down our route. We intercepted ACM communications that again said they were reorganizing at a location that they had success with in the past. SFC Tony demanded that we continue on and finish the enemy. As we entered Cakyan Ghar Valley, the ACM element opened up on our lead element as before with extraordinary volumes of machine gun, RPG and AK-47 fire. SFC Tony immediately maneuvered his gun vehicle to a position to engage this highly trained, numerically superior, and well equipped ACM force that we had been dealing with and pursuing for the past thirty hours. SFC Tony got out of his vehicle and engaged without care for his own life. His only concerns were for the care of his fellow team mates and trying to eliminate, or draw some of the fire from those machine gun positions that had our ANA element pinned down. SFC Tony continued engaging the well emplaced enemy positions, when the rest of the ACM ambush opened up with an enormous amount of fire on the entire element. Within minutes he saw SFC Cliff's turret burst into flames caused by the incoming rounds. SFC Cliff continued to engage without care for his own welfare or safety, he continued engaging the fierce enemy with pinpoint accuracy until SFC Tony pulled him down from his gun position because of the intense fire that had raged around SFC Cliff. Once he pulled SFC Cliff down to safety, SFC Tony started to maneuver back to our rear vehicle of the element, that had a downed turret gunner which was in it and being suppressed by an enormous amount of fire. Upon arriving at the downed vehicle, SFC Tony was essential to the movement of SSG Falkel into the rear of the vehicle so the gun turret could be re-occupied. At that point, the vehicles could start to maneuver to reach adequate cover. SFC Tony took it upon himself to stay behind, knowing the danger that he faced but only thinking of the ANA soldiers that were trapped by the fierce fires. He maneuvered, ensuring that he gathered up all the ANA soldiers that were scattered throughout the enemy kill zone. If it wasn't for the bravery of SFC Tony moving under enormous amounts of fire ensuring no ANA were left behind, the ANA element would have sustained tremendous losses. The following morning our element began its final pursuit of the ACM forces in the Marah Valley to link up with our ground quick reaction force (QRF) element. Shortly after we made link up, our seventh contact began, with what would turn out to be our largest most violent ACM force of all the contacts that we had faced in the prior fifty six hours. SFC Tony maneuvered his gun vehicle so the gunner could begin to lay down heavy volumes of fire on the ACM element that opened up on our lead element and his vehicle with extraordinary volumes of machine gun, RPG and AK-47 fire. SFC Tony's vehicle was struck numerous times and yet again he continued to fiercely lay down fire so the rest of his element could clear the choke point which the enemy was engaging with tremendous amounts of fire at the moment. His continuous engagement without concern for his own well being allowed our heavily suppressed elements to get to positions of better cover and his relentless punishment to the enemy while fully exposed later caused them to retreat. SFC Tony willfully and voluntarily chose to serve in Operation ENDURING FREEDOM supporting his fellow soldiers, the legitimate Government of Afghanistan, and the United States of America in the global war on terror. The distinctive accomplishments of Sergeant First Class Tony reflect great credit upon himself, the Combined Joint Special Operations Task Force-Afghanistan and the United States Army.*

Tony, you gave my son your heart. You gave my son your spirit. You gave my son your love. And you love him as no one has ever loved anyone—except for my love for you. Thank you for loving Chris and Tim as you do. Thank you for giving my heart my grandchildren. Thank you for keeping the rest of Chris' team alive when they should have all crossed over with Chris. Thank you for being MSG "T" and all that you now give to your new team, and for making them the great ODA they have become.

Thank you for being my brother and my son. I love you with all my heart, and you have given me that which I thought was lost forever.

22

Scott

That Which Does Not Kill Us, Makes Us Stronger

—Nietzsche and "Conan the Barbarian"

During my first phone call from Chris once he arrived at Firebase Gereshk in 2004, I asked him if he had access to email. After giving me shit like, "I had no idea you knew how to use email, Dad!?!" he gave me his email address in an email a day or two later. In that email, he told me something that made me smile, and has changed my life forever...

Chris wrote, "Well, Dad, you are no longer the strongest man I know!," and he was absolutely right!!! That was my introduction to Scott. But what I didn't realize when Chris first wrote that about Scott, was that his strength goes so far beyond his physical stature—which, by the way, is indeed HUGE!!!

I knew a great deal about Scott before we ever met. Scott was the BIG brother Chris never had. He probably spent as much, if not more time at Scott's house than he did at his own apartment. And one of the things that I was so proud of Chris for having was his relationship with Scott and his family. Chris was one of the family, and Scott's family became Chris' family. Chris would help fix things around their house that needed repair—in fact, I remember Chris calling me late one night to ask how to re-hang a door because he was working on something at Scott's house. Those were the phone calls and questions that made me so very proud of my son—he had become a man in every sense of the word, and that is something that makes all fathers swell with pride.

I know how much Scott misses Chris, because I miss him just as much. But Scott's amazing strength has given me the strength to do things I never thought I could. The best example I can share was the first SSG Christopher M. Falkel Memorial Scholarship presentation at the National Strength and Conditioning Association meeting in Washington, DC, in July 2006. I had been a member of the NSCA for many years, and I knew how important strength and conditioning is for SF, so our family decided to offer a scholarship to a member of the military so they could continue their education in the field of strength and conditioning. The first winner of the award was CPT Theodore Croy of the 75th Ranger Battalion—I know, Chris: a Ranger AND an officer, but he truly deserved your award—and seeing that the award was going to be presented in Washington DC, I invited all of ODA 316 to attend as my guests.

Scott was the only one who could make it, and I would not have been able to make my presentation to CPT Croy were it not for Scott being there. When they called my name to come up on stage and present the award, I had Scott come up on the stage with me. This annual meeting was the first time I had seen many of my dearest professional friends and colleagues since Chris was killed, and it was also the first time since the Memorial that I had spoken to a group about Chris. I was oblivious to the size of the crowd at the Awards Banquet that night until Scott and I got up on stage and we saw almost 2,000 people standing on their feet, giving Scott and Chris a standing ovation for almost five minutes! It was truly a moving experience for both Scott and for me. Before I started to talk about Chris, and introduced CPT Croy, I had Scott come forward to be recognized. I have thrown a lot of weights around for most of my life, but I have never felt strength like I did on that stage standing next to Scott. His strength, his power, his love filled me and let me get through my speech. There is NO WAY I could have done it were it not for Scott!

We headed over to Arlington before we left for "home" the next day. It was the first time Scott had been to Arlington since Chris was interred, and it was a day that will live in my heart forever. Scott told me things he had not told me before, and hearing those stories further explained how much Scott loved Chris, and the special relationship that they had, and that I now have with Scott.

Our relationship is very strong and very personal, and for that, we decided to keep it to ourselves, just as I have done with my dreams about Chris. Scotty, you are my strength. You are my heart. You will always be with me, and I love you with all my heart, for you love me as you loved OUR Chris.

23

SSG JT—The "Quiet" Quiet Professional!

The legend of the Cherokee Indian youth's rite of passage

His father takes him into the forest blindfolds him and leaves him alone. He is required to sit on a stump the whole night and not remove the blindfold until the rays of the morning sun shine through it. He cannot cry out for help to anyone. Once he survives the night, he is a MAN.

He cannot tell the other boys of this experience, because each lad must come into manhood on his own. The boy is naturally terrified. He can hear all kinds of noises. Wild beasts must surely be all around him. Maybe even some human might do him harm. The wind blew the grass and earth, and shook his stump, but he sat stoically, never removing the blindfold. It would be the only way he could become a man!

Finally, after a horrific night the sun appeared and he removed his blindfold. It was then that he discovered his father sitting on the stump next to him. He had been at watch the entire night, protecting his son from harm.

—Unknown Author

SSG JT is one in a zillion! He is a member of 19th Special Forces Group (Airborne), which is an Army National Guard unit, but he was destined to become a member of ODA 316. SSG JT is a medic, but he is also a warrior. JT was with ODA 316 in 2004 when they were in Gereshk, and that is where Chris met JT. Chris would talk about JT as "the quiet one" but he loved to 'be Chris' with JT, scheming ways to get the rest of ODA 316 with some prank.

My most vivid memory of JT was during all the Memorials and at Arlington. I was torn apart, and felt I needed to be everywhere for everyone. But the one person I really felt I needed to be there for was Tim. I knew Tim was hurting like we all were, but he kept his emotions and his pain to himself. I was really worried about Tim, particularly because I had so many things to do, I couldn't be there for Tim. And that is where JT came in—JT was Tim's shield! He was by Tim's side from the moment he came off the escalator with Jim, Tony, Markus, Buzz, and Shawn. When ever I looked to see if Tim was OK, SSG JT was there right by his side. In fact, I can not remember a moment when JT was not right by Tim's side.

SSG JT was Tim's big brother for the most difficult week of Tim's life. I will NEVER be able to thank JT for ALL that he did for Tim, and for me that week, but I will spend the rest of my life trying. Even today, Tim is probably closer to JT than anyone else on Chris' team, and Tim knows how much JT loved Chris, because Tim loves JT just as much!

After all the Memorials and the burial at Arlington, SSG JT asked to go over to Deh Afghan to be with ODA 316. He and Tony had to wait longer than normal for a bird to be available due to the relief efforts after Hurricane Katrina. I remember talking to JT while he was waiting, and it was driving both SSG JT and MSG Tony "crazy" to have to sit and wait, knowing that ODA 316 needed them, just as much as they both needed to get over to Afghanistan so they could actually DO something about Chris' death. The rest of us who had to stay here could do nothing about it, and it was so very difficult for us to deal with. But I remember SSG JT telling me, "don't worry, I will take care of things for you," just like Chris used to say to me all the time! And, JT did just that! His getting to the team with Tony was the physical and psychological boost that the team needed. In one of my first talks with 1LT Dan when ODA 316 returned in February 2006—on JT and Chrissa's birthday to be exact—Dan told me how much it meant to the boys when JT, Tony and then Shawn got to Deh Afghan. I will always remember the look on Dan's face as he told me that—it was a look of confidence, relief, pride and love—all the things that JT brought to ODA 316.

For the past two years, SSG JT had been working for a contractor in Iraq, in and around his National Guard duties. After OUR book is done, and out for the world to see, I will head up to the Pacific Northwest to help JT renovate his house, and I can't wait!!! Just to be able to spend time with JT fills my heart. I owe JT more than I can ever possibly repay. JT is a hero, a warrior and a Spartan. While he was in Gereshk in 2004, JT was nominated for a Bronze Star. SSG JT is now enrolled in firefighter and paramedic school, and to those lucky people in the Pacific Northwest, you truly will be able to sleep safe in your beds at night with SSG JT standing watch over you!

Thank you, JT, for loving BOTH of my sons as only you can! Thank you for being there for Tim, for me, and then for the rest of the boys when we ALL needed you more than you can ever imagine!!!

I love you, JT, with all I am!

24

James, Jon, Cliff and Brandon

There were four other members of ODA 316 in Deh Afghan:

James—During the Battles of Mari Ghar, James was up in Kandahar, doing his AST—Administrative Support Tech—assignment. When I first met James at Jimbo's house on 2 Feb 2006, James pulled me aside and with tears in his eyes, told me that he was not there, and that he would have given anything and everything to have been there in Chris' place. It takes a great man to tell me that, and so, thank you, James, for loving my son that much!

Jon—Jon was the driver of vehicle 3, and he was the first person on ODA 316 to tell me what actually happened. I had decided that even though I could have seen the official reports of the Battles of Mari Ghar, I wanted to hear it from his teammates first. And Jon was the first one to tell me what I knew as soon as I opened Chris' casket, reached in and touched my son's head for the last time. Jon told me that Chris was killed with a single sniper shot, and that is what I knew when I put my hand behind Chris' head. I asked if he had his Kevlar—helmet—on, or was he wearing his "Coor's Light" hat, and Jon told me that he did indeed have his Kevlar on. Jon also told me that the sound the sniper's .50 cal amour piercing round made when it hit Chris' helmet is a sound that will haunt Jon for the rest of his life. I reached over and hugged him and thanked him for being there with Chris at the end. I am so sorry that he has to carry that with him for the rest of his life, but I hope with all my heart that he knows that I know that he did everything he could and his actions helped keep the rest of ODA 316 alive.

For his valor, John was awarded the Bronze Star with "V" device, and here is the narrative for his award:

Narrative Recommendation For Award Of The Bronze Star With "V" Device To SGT Jon, Alpha Company, 1st Battalion, 3d Special Forces Group (Airborne), Fort Bragg, North Carolina, 28310

Sergeant Jon distinguished himself by exemplifying spirited bravery as the Engineer Sergeant for Operational Detachment Alpha (ODA) 316, Combined Joint Special Operations Task Force-Afghanistan in support of Operation ENDURING FREEDOM from 7 August 2005 to 9 August 2005. SGT Jon distinguished himself in seven fierce enemy engagements with a well trained, tactically emplaced, and aggressive enemy during a time span of fifty-six hours while operating as the driver of the last vehicle of our element, while conducting operations in the Zabol Province of Afghanistan while deployed to A-Camp Lane. SGT Jon's calmness under fire and tactical competence were imperative to the detachment's survival. During our unit's multiple engagements which took place in Buka Ghar Valley, Cakyan Ghar Valley, and Marah Valley. SGT Jon was instrumental in positioning his vehicle so his gunner could help fix and engage the well equipped and fortified enemy positions that had our entire element pinned down by extraordinary volumes of machine gun, RPG and AK-47 fire multiple times. The most notable act of bravery out of all the engagements was about twenty-four hours into our operation. We had already had one fire fight with Anti Coalition Forces (ACM), which were highly trained, numerically superior, and looking to eliminate our entire element. It was in our second contact with this fierce enemy that we had elements pinned down by heavy volumes of enemy fire coming from numerous well emplaced, fortified Anti Coalition Members (ACM) positions. SGT Jon quickly helped emplace and take part in mortar operations to help eliminate those ACM positions that had elements of his unit pinned down. He conducted these operations out in the open, exposing his body constantly to enemy fire. He continued to assist without thought of his own safety, thinking only of that of members of his unit that had been pinned down. Without his help in the mortar operations, the unit would have suffered great losses. Upon losing our gunner (SSG Falkel), he played a key role in providing cover fire with his M203, so other members of the element could recover SSG Falkel's body and put it in the rear of the vehicle. If it wasn't for the 40mm rounds used to suppress the enemy, the recovery element would have suffered substantial losses. On the last morning, when the fiercest battle of them all erupted, SGT Jon played a key roll in the positioning of his gun vehicle, so it could lay effective fire on the heavily armed enemy. He participated in redistributing ammo to machine guns that were either out or critically low on ammo. SGT Jon moved ammo from one truck to another while receiving heavy *volumes of fire during the entire time of ammo re-distribution. SGT Jon in between moving his gun vehicle, assisting in ammo re-distribution, still found time to actively engage the enemy with pinpoint accuracy using his M203 to reduce the overwhelming numbers of enemy forces. SGT Jon willfully and voluntarily chose to serve in Operation ENDURING FREEDOM supporting his fellow soldiers, the legitimate Government of Afghanistan, and the United States of America in the global war on terror. The distinctive accomplishments of Sergeant Jon reflect great credit upon himself, the Combined Joint Special Operations Task Force-Afghanistan and the United States Army.*

Cliff—Cliff was the other 18 Bravo—weapons sergeant—on ODA 316 during the Deh Afghan rotation, and he was one of the gunners in vehicle 1. During the Battles of Mari Ghar, Cliff performed brilliantly, and for his actions and valor, Cliff was awarded the Silver Star. Here is the narrative of Cliff's award:

Narrative Recommendation For Award Of The Silver Star To SFC Cliff, Alpha Company, 1st Battalion, 3d Special Forces Group (Airborne), Fort Bragg, North Carolina, 28310

Sergeant First Class Cliff distinguished himself by exemplifying spirited bravery as the Weapons Sergeant for Operational Detachment Alpha (ODA) 316, Combined Joint Special Operations Task Force-Afghanistan in support of Operation ENDURING FREEDOM from 7 August 2005 to 9 August 2005. SFC Cliff distinguished himself in seven fierce enemy engagements with a well trained, tactically emplaced, and aggressive enemy during a time span of fifty-six hours while operating as the M240B machine gunner on the first vehicle of our element, while conducting operations in the Zabol Province of Afghanistan while deployed to A-Camp Lane. SFC Cliff's calmness under fire and tactical competence were imperative to the detachment's survival. During our unit's first engagement in the Buka Ghar Valley, SFC Cliff was instrumental in helping fix and engage enemy positions that had the entire element pinned down. His continuous engagement without concern for his own well being allowed our heavily suppressed elements to get to positions of better cover and his relentless punishment to the enemy while fully exposed later caused them to retreat. During our second contact in Buka Ghar Valley, SFC Cliff once again was instrumental in accurately putting down heavy volumes of fire on well emplaced machine gun positions so other members of his gun vehicle could move up to pinned down Afghanistan National Army (ANA) elements that were part of our patrol and help consolidate, assess, and get control of their situation. Our unit continued to receive heavy volumes of machine gun fire and RPGs from numerous positions. He played a crucial role in the final elimination and forced withdrawal of the enemy by providing cover for the ODA's mortar team while they engaged the extremely fortified machine gun positions. If it wasn't for the cover fire and marking of these positions by SFC Cliff, our element would have been seriously devastated by the well emplaced, heavily armed and numerically superior forces. Our element continued to pursue the enemy during their retreat when they sent ahead for reinforcements to set up what was to be the third ambush. Upon the third Anti Coalition Member (ACM) ambush, SFC Cliff immediately located and fired upon the well emplaced and trained enemy force without care for his own life while being engaged himself by multiple positions. His bravery allowed our ANA element to maneuver on the larger ACM element, later causing the enemy to maneuver to a location they thought would give them a tactical advantage. This only led them to a better vantage point for SFC Cliff, who was able to eliminate them during their maneuver to what would have been a position devastating to our ANA element. The remaining ACM elements broke contact again, only to reform and gather more experienced and trained fighters further down our route. The fourth ACM contact opened up on our lead element with concentrated fire, but SFC Cliff's close proximity allowed him to quickly and effectively respond as he had done in the previous contacts, knowing that he would draw fire upon himself. Immediately to the rear flank of his vehicle the major portion of the ambush opened up with an extraordinary amount of heavy machine gun fire. SFC Cliff, while fully exposed, quickly and effectively spun his turret and machine gun in the direction of the greater fire and began to engage. The whole time rounds were impacting all around his vehicle and himself. He continued to engage without care for his own welfare or safety, his only care being that of his fellow team members. He continued to suppress the well concealed enemy until aircraft came on station. SFC Cliff was able to spot and lay down effective fire so the aircraft knew where to fire to completely eliminate the enemy threat. We intercepted ACM communications that again said they were reorganizing at a location that they had success with in the past. SFC Cliff demanded that we continue on and finish the enemy. As we entered Cakyan Ghar Valley, the ACM element opened up on our lead element as before with extraordinary volumes of machine gun, RPG and AK-47 fire. SFC Cliff immediately pinpointed and engaged this highly trained, numerically superior, and well equipped ACM force that we had been dealing with and pursuing for the past thirty hours. SFC Cliff continued to engage without care for his own life. His only concerns were for the care of his fellow team mates and trying to eliminate, or draw some of the fire from those machine gun positions that had our ANA element pinned down. No sooner had SFC Cliff begun to engage the well emplaced enemy positions, when the rest of the ACM ambush opened up with an enormous amount of fire on the entire element. Within minutes, SFC Cliff's turret burst into flames caused by the incoming rounds. SFC Cliff continued to engage without care for his own welfare or safety, engaging the fierce enemy with pinpoint accuracy until his driver pulled him down from his gun position because of the intense fire that raged around SFC Cliff. The following morning our element began its final pursuit of the ACM forces in the Marah Valley. Our element didn't get thirty minutes down our route when we made our sixth contact with the highly trained enemy force, once again. SFC Cliff quickly fixed the enemy positions and engaged them with pinpoint accuracy, allowing the second and third vehicle to pick up and engage in the same fashion. This was instrumental in our element being able to clear the switchback pass and make link up with our ground quick reaction force (QRF). Within minutes of link up and movement with our QRF element, we made our seventh contact with what would turn out to be our largest, most violent ACM force of all the contacts that we had faced in the prior fifty six hours. SFC Cliff quickly fixed and began to lay down heavy volumes of fire on the ACM element that opened up on our lead element and his vehicle with extraordinary volumes of machine gun, RPG and AK-47 fire. SFC Cliff's vehicle was struck numerous times and yet again he continued to fiercely lay down fire so the rest of his element could clear the choke point which the enemy was engaging with tremendous amounts of fire at the moment. His continuous engagement without concern for his own well being allowed our heavily suppressed elements to get to positions of better cover *and his relentless punishment to the enemy while fully exposed later caused them to retreat. SFC Cliff willfully and voluntarily chose to serve in Operation ENDURING FREEDOM supporting his fellow soldiers, the legitimate Government of Afghanistan, and the United States of America in the global war on terror. The distinctive accomplishments of Sergeant First Class Cliff reflect great credit upon himself, the Combined Joint Special Operations Task Force-Afghanistan and the United States Army.*

Brandon—Brandon was the team leader of ODA 316 in Deh Afghan. Brandon was awarded the Silver Star, and here is the narrative for his award:

Narrative Recommendation For Award Of The Silver Star To CPT Brandon, Alpha Company, 1st Battalion, 3d Special Forces Group (Airborne), Fort Bragg, North Carolina, 28310

CPT Brandon distinguished himself by exemplifying spirited bravery as the Team Leader for Operational Detachment Alpha (ODA) 316, Combined Joint Special Operations Task Force-Afghanistan in support of Operation ENDURING FREEDOM from 7 August 2005 to 9 August 2005. CPT Brandon distinguished himself in seven fierce enemy engagements with a well trained, tactically emplaced, and aggressive enemy during a time span of fifty-six hours while acting as the overall on ground commander and the tactical commander of vehicle one of our element, while conducting operations in the Zabol Province of Afghanistan while deployed to A-Camp Lane. CPT Brandon's calmness under fire and tactical competence were imperative to the detachment's survival. During our unit's first engagement in the Buka Ghar Valley, CPT Brandon was instrumental in helping fix and focus gun vehicle fires on enemy positions that had the entire element pinned down. His continuous assessment and movement within the battle space without concern for his own well being allowed our heavily suppressed elements to get to positions of better cover, and his relentless punishment to the enemy while fully exposed later caused them to retreat. During our second contact in Buka Ghar Valley, CPT Brandon immediately placed his gun vehicle so it could accurately put down heavy volumes of fire on well emplaced machine gun positions, so he and his driver could move up fully exposed under heavy fire to pinned down Afghanistan National

Army (ANA) elements that were part of our patrol and help consolidate, assess, and get control of their situation. While moving CPT Brandon's helmet was struck. We continued to receive heavy volumes of machine gun fire and RPGs from numerous positions. CPT Brandon quickly assessed the situation, marked the heavily fortified enemy position with the AT-4 that he carried, and refocused our element's fires. If it wasn't for the refocusing of fires by CPT Brandon, our element would have been seriously devastated by the well emplaced, heavily armed and numerically superior forces. Our element continued to pursue the enemy during their retreat when they sent ahead for reinforcements to set up what was to be the third ambush. Upon the third Anti Coalition Member (ACM) ambush, CPT Brandon immediately placed his gun vehicle in a position to fire upon the well emplaced and trained enemy force. Without care for his own life but only that of the element he was leading, CPT Brandon and his driver dismounted their vehicle and maneuvered on foot to cut off ACM elements that were attempting to flank our pursuing ANA element. This act of bravery allowed our ANA element to maneuver on the larger ACM element, later causing the enemy to maneuver to a location they thought would give them a tactical advantage. This only led them to a better vantage point for our gun vehicles, which were able to eliminate them during their maneuver to what would have been a position devastating to our ANA element. The remaining ACM elements broke contact again, only to reform and gather more experienced and trained fighters further down our route. The fourth ACM contact opened up on our lead element with concentrated fire, but CPT Brandon quickly and effectively responded as he had done in the previous contacts, knowing that he would draw fire upon himself. Immediately to the rear flank of his vehicle, the major portion of the ambush opened up with an extraordinary amount of heavy machine gun fire. CPT Brandon, while fully exposed, quickly and effectively maneuvered fire in the direction of the larger enemy element. The whole time rounds were impacting all around his vehicle and him. He continued to engage without care for his own welfare or safety, his only care being that of his fellow team members. He continued to suppress the well concealed enemy until aircraft came on station and aided in completely eliminating the enemy threat. We intercepted ACM communications that again said they were reorganizing at a location that they had success with in the past. CPT Brandon motivated the element to continue on and finish the enemy by his own actions. As we entered Cakyan Ghar Valley, the ACM element opened up on our lead element as before with extraordinary volumes of machine gun, RPG and AK-47 fire. CPT Brandon immediately pinpointed and engaged this highly trained, numerically superior, and well equipped ACM force that we had been dealing with and pursuing for the past thirty hours. CPT Brandon continued to engage without care for his own life. His only concerns were for the care of his fellow team mates and trying to eliminate, or draw some of the fire from those machine gun positions that had our lead element pinned down. No sooner had CPT Brandon begun to engage the well emplaced enemy positions, when the rest of the ACM ambush opened up with an enormous amount of fire on the entire element. Within minutes our element was down to one machine gun still in operation and engaging the fierce enemy with pinpoint accuracy. CPT Brandon quickly assessed the situation and began to maneuver vehicles to the safety of cover in between aircraft gun runs. Throughout the night CPT Brandon continued to asses the enemy situation and communicate with the ground Quick Reaction Force (QRF) as they made their approach into the area advising them of the upcoming possible ambushes they may encounter. The following morning our element began its final pursuit of the ACM forces in the Marah Valley. Our element didn't get thirty minutes down our route when we made our sixth contact with the highly trained enemy force. Once again, CPT Brandon assessed the situation and focused our gun vehicle fires. This was instrumental in our element being able to clear the pass and make link up with our QRF. Within minutes of link up and movement with our QRF element, our seventh contact began with what would turn out to be our largest, most violent ACM force of all the contacts that we had faced in the prior fifty six hours. CPT Brandon quickly fixed and began to lay down heavy volumes of fire on the ACM element that opened up on our lead element with extraordinary volumes of machine gun, RPG and AK-47 fire. Within minutes a vehicle in front of his was hit by an RPG, during an attempt to lock us in their very violent well emplaced ambush. CPT Brandon immediately dismounted his vehicle to help assist injured members of the QRF, fully exposing himself to the rage of incoming fire. CPT Brandon helped his element clear the choke point at which the enemy had directed tremendous amounts of fire at the moment, in the hopes that the RPG disabled vehicle would trap CPT Brandon, the two ODAs, and ANA element in their violent kill zone allowing them to finish off our element. Upon clearing the enemy's well planned and numerically superior kill zone. CPT Brandon maneuvered our elements to high ground where he assisted cross loading ammunition that we were critically low on, so our element could finish off the enemy element. CPT Brandon willfully and voluntarily chose to serve in Operation ENDURING FREEDOM supporting his fellow soldiers, the legitimate Government of Afghanistan, and the United States of America in the global war on terror. The distinctive accomplishments of CPT Brandon reflect great credit upon himself, the Combined Joint Special Operations Task Force-Afghanistan and the United States Army.

25

3 – 1 – 6 in OUR Family!

Numbers are the universal language offered by the deity to humans as confirmation of the truth.

—St. Augustine of Hippo

As I have said before in OUR book and I will say again, the ODA 316 family is truly special in all of Special Forces. There are indeed "special forces" that connect all of us together. I firmly believe that it was more than co-incidence that this group of men and their families were MEANT to be together! I am incredibly grateful that Chris was a member of this amazing family, and I am even more grateful and lucky to part of OUR family now!

I firmly believe there is a bond, a connection that links us all together. And the fact that we are part of the ODA 3 – 1 – 6 family is no coincidence either! It is almost spooky how many times the numbers 3, 1 and 6 are part of OUR family—here are just a few examples:

- Chris' birthday is 24 September at 1831 EDT or 6:31 PM
- My birthday is the 16th of the month
- Dianne's birthday is the 13th of the month
- My dad's birthday is the 8th of the month—8 +16 = 24
- Markus' birthday is the 6th of the month
- Markus' son Gabriel's birthday is the 31st of the month
- Scott and Chrissa's daughter Ruby's birthday is the 13th of the month
- Tony's twins—Christopher and Malia—were born on the 26th of the month
- CSM Buzzsaw's birthday is the 13th of the month in 1960
- Markus' son Zeth weighed 6 pounds, 13 ounces when he was born.
- The last four digits of my cell phone number are 3166

- There were 300 Spartans…
- Chris' number in soccer was 13, and he played defensive midfield—the 6th position.
- The elevation at Chris' room at our house in Littleton, CO is 6,013 feet
- The registration number on Chris' challenge coin from SOTIC is # 0166
- The registration number on Chris' Yarborough knife that he was given when he graduated from Special Forces Qualification Course is #1636
- The registration on Chris' M4 was BFI 427 163
- The registration number on the case of "Chris Light" (Coors Light) that Markus left in the ODA 316 team room when they returned from Deh Afghan was Serial # 000316
- MAJ Jim studied the great warriors of history, and one of his favorites was Alexander. Alexander made famous his "Phalanx Formation," which consisted of 16 men across and 16 rows of men deep.
- When I first started mowing out at Fox Hollow Golf course, I used to mow green #3, then green #1, and then green #6—in that order
- My favorite mowers at Fox Hollow are #61 and #63
- Chris, Tim and my favorite golf hole at Fox Hollow Golf Course is #16, which is a par 3
- The odometer reading on Chris' truck when Tim and I stopped at Section 60 of Arlington National Cemetery in December 2006 was 58316
- The odometer reading on Chris' truck after Tim and I went to see the "Bourne Ultimatum" (Chris loved the first two Jason Bourne movies!) on 8 August 2007 was 66316.
- On Father's Day in 2006, Dianne, Tim and I went to the Texas Road House Restaurant in Littleton. Chris used to go to the Fayetteville Texas Road House all the time during SFQC. On that first Father's Day after Chris crossed over, we were seated in Section 31, at table #6
- Markus got cancer when he was 36, and he has "Lambda Light chains" in his blood
- Special Forces has 13 letters in it

- Two of OUR favorite Bible verses are: John 3:16, "For God so loved the world that He gave his only son, that whoever believes in Him will not perish but will have eternal life." And 1 John 3:16, "The way we came to understand love was that he laid down his life for us; we too must lay down our lives for our brothers."
- Over the past several weeks, every day I have been getting up at 0316 to finish writing OUR book!
- SSG Chris Falkel Drive was dedicated in Littleton, Colorado on 3/16/2009.
- …And the list goes on and on!!!

26

OUR Spartan Women

In the end, it was the women who galvanized the Spartans into action.

"Death stands close upon us now," the king spoke. "Can you feel him, brothers? I do. I am human and I fear him." Leonidas continued softly. "Shall I tell you where I find the strength, friends? In the eyes of our sons in scarlet before us, yes. But more than that, my heart finds courage from these, our women, who watch in tearless silence as we go."

—Steven Pressfield in *Gates of Fire*

We have OUR Spartan women as part of the ODA 316 family. They are truly amazing, beautiful, committed, loyal, and strong women. They HAVE to be to put up with us!!!

I would NEVER think of arguing with "Leonidas," as I know I will see him on the other side—and Chris will be kicking my ass enough for what I have done—but I have a slightly different opinion on the strength of OUR Spartan women. I have spent the vast majority of my life involved with exercise, and strength training has been a huge part of my career. I started strength training "back in the day" when, if a coach caught you lifting weights, you would actually be punished, because "weights made you muscle bound." As the old school coaches were not familiar with strength training, they were afraid of what they did not understand. As an athlete, coach, teacher, physical therapist, and exercise physiologist—I have a fairly good understanding about strength. We are all born with a certain amount, and unless we test that strength, we will not adapt and develop even greater strength. But, strength must be gradually developed as well. Too much "overload," or too little, and our strength will not improve.

And I think they same applies to OUR Spartan women. Yes, they are tremendously strong ladies. They have had to endure undue amounts of stress over all these years, and if they did not have a certain level of personal strength initially, they would not have been able to put up with us in the first place. But, hopefully, we have helped them develop their strength through our strength. I think this is how the Spartan women of old became the rock and foundation of the Spartan society, and I am sure this is how OUR Spartan women have become as strong as they are! Here are OUR Spartan women—the women that Chris loved, and that we love and could not do what we do without:

Giselle

MAJ Giselle is MAJ Jim's beautiful wife. As I have told Jim and Giselle over and over again since she has become such a tremendous part of my life, "There are few constants in life, and Giselle being Giselle is one of them!!!"

MAJ Giselle is an officer in the U.S. Army, and she has had an amazing career. She is currently working for the U.S. Army Special Operations Command, and if there was ever a Spartan woman that understood what it takes to be Special Forces, it is Giselle. Giselle has been there when Jim has left for combat. She has had to work and raise their tremendous children, Tristen and Scout, alone for much of the kid's lives because Jim has been downrange so much due to the Global War on Terrorism. She has been the "hostess with the mostess," sharing her home with Jim's men for all these years, and she has done all this and ALL she does with a smile, and with love.

I have had the honor and privilege of getting to know Giselle, and she has made my life so much more full and complete. We have talked for hours on my visits "home." Giselle has a love of learning, and it has been so much fun to share my knowledge of woodworking and construction with Giselle to help her prepare for a possible career after she retires from the Army in 2009. We have talked about life and death—we have laughed and we have cried together. She has shown me how much she loves Jim, me and ODA 316, and for that and all you have done for me, I will love you for all of time.

She loved my son. She welcomed Chris into her home, into her heart, and into her life. She shared her children with Chris, and taught him what it was like and what was needed to be a parent. She also shared her husband with Chris and all of ODA 316. These things take a very Special woman, and Giselle is just such a Spartan woman.

Giselle is such an integral part of the 316 family—we would not be what we are were it not for Giselle. I love you Giselle with all my heart, and just as you have been there for me, I will ALWAYS be here for you!

Chrissa

Chrissa is Scott's beautiful wife, and Ruby's amazing mommy! But Chrissa is so much more than that. When ever ODA 316 was deployed, Chrissa was there holding the line for everyone back home. Chrissa showed Chris what it took to be a mother and a wife. She shared her heart with my son, just as she shares it with me now.

I don't remember the first time I met Chrissa in person exactly. I know it was at the JFK Chapel, but I don't remember much about that meeting. What I do remember, though, was our first long talk together. I had gone out to Jim's house to wait for 316 to come home, and they were waiting on the tarmac at Kandahar Air Field for what seemed forever. Chrissa and Ruby came over to Jim's house, and while Ruby was playing with Scout and Jim was bar-b-queing our dinner, Chrissa and I sat in Jim and Giselle's kitchen and talked. And talked and talked and talked! But after a while, she became very quiet, and I was not exactly sure why. That night, she sent me an email and told me why. She said that she heard Chris talking through me. She saw Chris' smile and felt his laugh in me, and while it made her sad because she missed Chris so very much, she could see where Chris got "it" from. It was an email that will forever be part of my heart. I have shared much of my heart in OUR book, but THAT email is just for me.

But, I will give everyone a look into the heart of this Spartan woman. Chrissa is currently finishing her college degree and she had to write a paper about heroes, and she has graciously allowed me to share this with you:

I'm with this guy!

One winter morning early in 2005 I found myself staring blankly at my computer screen at work. I was bored and distracted. I had been working a job in real estate I had absolutely no passion for, it regretfully left me in a desk for way too many hours, and frankly was a waste of time. To add to my list of complaints my husband was away again, in Georgia this time, suffering, surviving, and succeeding at becoming a ranger for the US Army. I was so proud and am still to this day, but as all who love each other, and bear the burden of separation, I was lonely. My toddler while she was a handful, and a piece of grace all wrapped into one, was not doing much of anything to relieve the stress of life. There I sat watching the clock tick.....waiting to break free into the cold morning air just outside the office door, when to my pleasant surprise that very door opened and my day got better, right there at my desk, paperwork and all!

A dear friend of mine, whom we all called Jr. Had just decided to drop in that morning, I had forgotten in my pity party that he had his sniper school field test that morning. How I forgot I'll never know, because the two of us had talked for the last two days about it. You see it was Chris' (Jr.) Dream to be a Green Beret sniper. Chris was what we in the SF community refer to as an SF baby. When he joined the army he signed up to be a Green Beret right out of basic training. He went straight through SF selection and became a green beret. This made him significantly younger than most of his coworkers. Most SF men had a minimum, four to five years of military experience before even going through SF training, thus the nickname, Jr.

That moment I saw him this morning, looking as though the sun itself lit his eyes up, I knew he had succeeded and was officially a Green Beret sniper. As he walked across the office to my desk and its mountains of paperwork I was simply awe struck. Here he was so young and glorious with the smell of fresh dreams oozing from his being. I was so proud and so honored he came to tell me in person I could hardly keep my butt in my seat. Chris sat down with that sheepish grin of his BDU's ruffled and crazy hat head hair. He put his hand on my desk as he sat down on the other side as if to emphasize he had an announcement. I was grinning from ear to ear, waiting on him to say anything. The suspense was killing me even though I knew he did well. We played a game of cat and mouse, I asked how his morning was and he mine. I could bare it no more. "How does it feel I asked?" "What?" he asked, acting confused for a moment then catching on. "To accomplish a dream before 10 AM ?" I asked. We began to laugh, and he of course began detail by detail and moment by moment replaying his field test.

Let me intrude my female, SF, wife, opinion here. There is something magical about these men as they tell the tales of being a Green Beret, after hearing a few I somehow have become like others in my midst and tune out some of the tale, and tune into the new parts, the parts I've never heard, the rest I have learned to lay to the way side. As I get to know the men my husband surrounds himself with, I learn from each what part of his story to tune into. What was special about this particular story of Chris' momentous journey, if you will, was the way he was telling it. I knew that it was still fresh in his memory, and I saw how he became excited and began to move around while telling me. He mentioned the weather and I thought yes, yes, I was outside then I remember a few hours ago the rain, and so I was able to connect, which was unusual considering I usually get the stories months later, after they are back in the states. Not today! Today, I got a front row, first time listener special event replay from Chris himself. I was the proudest big sis on the planet in those moments.... I wanted a t-shirt; I'm With This Guy and He is an SF Sniper...What Did You Do Today? I wanted to make an announcement, or call the news station, something, and anything to let the world know. Instead, I did what my dear friend always did for me, I listened...I listened for me and for my husband who could not hear, as the two were nearly inseparable while they were both home.

After recalling this glorious tale, and awakening me from my pity, Chris decided to get on with his day, and leave me to the somehow less depressing office that held me prisoner, but not before we made plans for a celebration diner, and beer, later that day. As I sit here now, I can not even recall what must have been another day filled with endless customer complaints, being late for appointments, and having the boss breathing down my neck. I don't remember racing to pickup my daughter or getting the mail, what I remember was my diner with Chris.

We met up at a local burger joint, the three of us, as usual. Chris and my daughter played their silly little games while I got a much needed moment to breathe. We talked about how bad my husband must want a burger or a nap, and how we anticipated seeing him graduate. It was not a diner unlike many we had had before. In fact, with the exception of Uncle Chris saving my daughter when she got trapped under the table, I would almost say it was uneventful! Why bring it up you ask? Because of all the moments I spent with Chris, and all the times we shared, there was one that night that is written on the memory of my soul.

After the somewhat ordinary dinner that we enjoyed to commemorate Chris' achievement, we stepped into chilly night air. Chris and I immediately became the audience to my little girl's excited shrieks, clapping , and pointing. The local carnival and all its penny pinching glory was lit up across the street. Twenty feet tall rides with lights top to bottom. Eye candy for a two year old. Chris and I laughed, and he took her hand to walk us to the car as he was always a gentleman. I walked in front of the two of them and listened as he entertained her gibberish by acting as excited about the lights as she was. While I busied myself with the keys and diaper bags I remember thinking how thankful I was for his willingness to be a part of her life while her daddy was away. I readied the car seat, and prepared to collect my daughter. As I turned around laughter from both Chris and my daughter filled the air. Chris had whisked her off the ground, and above his head. I stood there for a moment and watched as the colorful lights lit the night behind the two of them and they laughed. My eyes teared with thankfulness. How kind he is I thought, as a friend. And how wonderful it was to know men who love my husband like a brother and are willing to look after those he loves while he is away. Here he is, this friend of mine, this brother to the man I love, this uncle to my daughter, this dream catcher, this wonderful spirit, here he is in our lives.

As many of you reading this know Chris died in combat a few short months later. My heart still spills tears for my family and his, at our loss. This memory of Chris though shines through so many of those tears, it is a memory recorded in the roots of my spirit and soul. It is one that my grandchildren will know about and one that they will tell their own children. It is proof that there are heroes among us, people like Chris. People who inspire you and humble you as you watch them spread their wings into life and soar on the winds of ambition and courage. People who change you forever.

Chrissa Marie—December 13, 2006

We are all, in large part, who we are because of who is part of our lives. Chris was in LARGE part who he was because of Chrissa and he learned about love from you, Scott and Ruby. For that, and for loving me as you do, I will never be able to thank you enough, but I will spend the rest of my life trying. I love you with all my heart!

Jamie

Jamie is Shawn's amazing wife and Callie, Addie and Wyatt's terrific mom. She is as no-nonsense as Shawn is—maybe even more so if that is humanly possible. She will tell you what she thinks, and she will do all she can to convince you she is right! Ha! Ha! When it comes to juggling, Jamie is a wizard! She teaches, takes care of the kids, puts up with Shawn, welcomes us into her home, and she does this all with a smile on her face and love in her heart! My life, and Chris' life are that much more complete because of Jamie—a Spartan wife and mother. Thank you from the bottom of my heart for taking us into your life, and for loving Shawn, Chris and me as you do. I hope you know how much we love you!!!

Brenda

Brenda is Big Ron's wonderful wife, and I have never NOT seen a smile on her face—of course, living with Big Ron that is not only easy, but is a requirement!!!

My most vivid memory of Brenda was sitting with her, waiting for Big Ron to get back from Afghanistan in May, 2008. He had been downrange for many months, and it had been an exceptionally stressful rotation, and that stress had crossed the globe to Brenda as well. She wanted me to be there to welcome Big Ron home, because I meant so much to Ron, not knowing how important it was to me to be there, as I would never be there to welcome Chris home again. We waited and waited, and just as his plane was about to land, it was diverted to another airfield in North Carolina because of the weather at Pope Air Force Base. Everyone else, all the wives, kids, parents and friends were extremely dejected, having waited so long for their heroes and loved ones to get home, but not Brenda. She still smiled and while she was disappointed, she didn't show it, and she was the strength for everyone else waiting for their loved ones. The plan was for Big Ron and his men to "commandeer" some vehicles and drive "home"—arriving back at Bragg at 2300 rather than the scheduled 1600 local time. Brenda called me and told me I BETTER be there, so of course I was. Even though it was dark, I will always remember the look on Brenda's face when Big Ron got off that shuttle bus. If there was ever a look that defined love, it was the look on Brenda's face. She KNEW Big Ron would be the last one off the bus, so that his men could get to their families first—that is Big Ron—so she was not anxious, but as soon as she saw him, I saw what love is all about!

Thank you for allowing me to share that moment with you—it is one I have missed, and having been there with you and your beautiful daughters, has helped heal the hole in my heart. Thank you for "The Party"—that made my heart soar, and put a smile on my soul that had been missing for three years. And thank you for loving me and my son—we love you with all our hearts!

Rocio

I so wish Chris could have known Rocio better. She started dating Markus just before ODA 316 left for Deh Afghan. But, I know he is looking down on Rocio now, and he knows how much she loved him.

Few people in life ever find their soul mates—Markus and Rocio have found each other! They are exactly what each other needs, and they have made each other better in the process. Rocio is one of the hardest working people I have ever known, and I have known many! How she is able to do all she does boggles my mind, but the fact that she does it all so well is even more amazing!

She has been the strength that Markus needed to get through his multiple myeloma—from the diagnosis through the long months of treatments, and on into the unknown future. Markus WILL beat this, and he will because of Rocio and her strength, her will, her love.

Rocio has shown me a new definition of love. She has welcomed me into their home, and has shared her children with me. The love, the laughter, the joy of her family has given me back my smile, and brightened my world. I love you, Rocio, and you know I will always be there for you, just as I know you are ALWAYS here for me!

Tara

Tara is McKenna, Christopher and Malia's mommy. She is the newest member of our 316 family, and we are all blessed to have her with us now! She learned a few months ago what being part of the 316 is all about. Tony was still in Afghanistan, and Tara had taken McKenna to dance class about 0930 local time. When Tara and the kids got back to their condo, the front door was open and there had been a robbery at their home. Within minutes, Chrissa, 1 LT Dan and MAJ Jim were all there to do what needed to be done. Were I not on my way to China, I would have been there in 8 hours. Tara and the kids stayed with Chrissa and Ruby until the front door could be fixed. Dan and Jim took care of security issues, and even though they lost some expensive material things, everyone was safe, and Tara knew how much she and her beautiful children were loved.

Dianne and I had decided many years before she was pregnant with Chris that we were going to name our first son Christopher Matthew. Many people have names for their children picked out before they are born. This was "initially" what Tara had done as well. There was a boy's name that she liked, and if she had a son, that was what she was going to name her son. When Tony and Tara found out they were going to have twins, and one was going to be a boy, Tony asked Tara if they could name him Christopher Matthew after he asked me "if it was alright!?!?!" Even though she had never met Chris, she knew how important Chris was to Tony, and how much he was loved by Tony and all of us, so there was no hesitation in wanting her son to be named after my son.

Thank you, Tara, for loving OUR Tony! Thank you, Tara, for sharing your children with Grandpa Jeff! Those three angels have done more to heal this old warrior than I can possibly ever explain. I see their beautiful faces in my dreams, but when I get "home" I realize they are not a dream when I get to hug and kiss them—and if you haven't noticed already, I am going to spoil them like no other!!! Thank you, Tara, for giving me hope, making my soul smile, and healing the hole in my heart that I thought would never be filled again.

I love you, Tara, with all my "healing" heart!

Mom

Dianne is Chris and Tim's mom and my dear wife. As with all of OUR Spartan women, Dianne has had her share of battles putting up with me all these years. There were many times that I have been gone, and she was always there for our boys. There have been many days when she did not know what would happen to me, and she "held the line." And she has been there for OUR boys, sharing her strength with them, and helping them get through OUR losing our hero, our warrior, our son.

Dianne is a dedicated and disciplined woman. She sees something, and she does what ever needs to be done to make her dream and wishes come true. She has amazing talents, and one she is sharing now with OUR family is her quilting. She started quilting about four years ago, having perfected several other craft skills. One day, unexpectedly in May 2006, I received a tax-refund as a death benefit—those words are so hard for me to type, much less say—and I knew Chris would want Mom to have the best quilting machine available, so that is what he gave her for the first Mother's Day after he left us. She has put it to good use, having made quilts for many of OUR boys—and if you haven't gotten yours YET, it is on the way!!! She has been involved in a project with other quilters to make quilts for our wounded warriors. And she has started a quilting group where she shares her talent and skills with others.

I am so glad that Dianne was able to talk to Chris on his last phone call home. He called the morning that ODA 316 rolled out of the wire on 7 August 2005, which was Saturday evening back in Colorado. Dianne answered the phone, and even though she didn't get to talk to Chris for very long, he was able to wish her a happy birthday, as he knew he would not be able to call her on her actual birthday, 13 August. I am so thankful she got that time to talk to Chris one last time.

Thank you, my dear wife, for giving me the greatest gifts a man could possibly have—our two sons. I am sorry for all I have put you through over all these years, but I am a better man because of you. And never forget how much I love you.

There is a poem that SGM Big Ron sent me several weeks ago that I would like to include here for those of you who are reading OUR story who do not personally know a Military Wife. They are truly unique, strong, and wonderful women who needs to be recognized for the life they lead, and the men they love:

WHAT IS A MILITARY WIFE???

Each one may look different and each is wonderfully unique,

But this they have in common:

Lots of moving—
Moving
Moving
Moving far from home
Moving two cars, three kids and one dog—all riding with HER of course
Moving sofas to basements because they won't go in THIS house
Moving curtains that won't fit
Moving jobs and certifications and professional development hours
Moving away from friends
Moving toward new friends
Moving her most important luggage—her trunk full of memories

Often waiting—
Waiting
Waiting
Waiting for housing
Waiting for orders
Waiting for deployment
Waiting for phones calls
Waiting for reunion
Waiting for the new curtains to arrive
Waiting for him to come home
For dinner—AGAIN!

They call her 'Military Dependent', but she knows better:

She is fiercely IN-dependent

She can balance a checkbook
Handle the yard work
Fix a noisy toilet

Bury the family pet...

She is intimately familiar with drywall anchors and toggle bolts.

She can file the taxes
Sell a house
Buy a car
Or set up a move—

—all with ONE Power of Attorney
She welcomes neighbors that don't welcome her.

*She reinvents her career with every PCS (Permanent Change of
Station);*
Locates a house in the desert
The Arctic
Or the deep south
And learns to call them all 'home'.

She MAKES them all home.

Military Wives are somewhat hasty—
They leap into:
Decorating
Leadership
Volunteering
Career alternatives
Churches
And friendships

They don't have 15 years to get to know people.

Their roots are short but flexible.

They plant annuals for themselves and perennials for those who come after them.

Military Wives quickly learn to value each other.

They connect over coffee
Rely on the spouse-network
Accept offers of friendship and favors
Record addresses in pencil...

Military Wives have a common bond:

The Military Wife has a husband unlike other husbands; his commitment is unique.
He doesn't have a 'JOB'
He has a 'MISSION' that he can't just decide to quit
He's on-call for his country 24/7

But for her, he's the most unreliable guy in town!

His language is foreign
TDY
PCS
OPR
ACC
BDU
TAD

And so, a Military Wife is a translator for her family and his.

...and to ALL military wives, ALL over the world—you have OUR unending admiration and eternal love! We would NOT be who we are if not for you!!!

27

Chris' "Kids"

You can discover more about a person in an hour of play than in a year of conversation.

—Plato

Ever since Chris became Tim's big brother, he was around young children. He would go with me to my coaching sessions with young players, and he loved being my "assistant coach" with the little kids! Chris had a patience and understanding of young children, and they not only seem to gravitate towards him, but they sensed in Chris, someone that cared about them. I was always so proud of Chris' interest and caring about not only Tim and his friends, but any young child that he came in contact with—and there were many! Young children know more than we give them credit for, and one of the things they KNOW is when someone is genuine, when someone cares about them, and when someone will actually listen to them. Chris got that from his old man, and we always had a good time being around young kids.

One of the things I will miss the most about Chris is that he never had the chance to become a dad! He would have been an amazing father, and I feel so sorry for the world that Chris never had children of his own.

But, he did have his "kids!" The children of his teammates on ODA 316 were his as well, and he loved them, and loved playing with them. That was one of the first things that Giselle, Chrissa, and Jamie told me at the Memorial at the JFK Chapel on 18 August 2005—was how much Chris loved their children, and how comfortable and how good he was around the kids! Chris would play "army" with them at team parties, including setting up ambushes for anyone that arrived late to the party!!! He would play video games with the kids. He would read them bedtime stories. He would get on the floor and play with their toys with them—

even if it meant Chris playing with the toy one of his "kids" wanted to play with—he was always "teaching Tim how to share!!!"

I can remember many of our phone calls when he would talk for hours about one of his "kids" and the antics and tricks they played on the rest of the team. I could hear in his voice how much he truly loved his brothers' children, and now that I have had the honor and privilege of getting to know them, I know how much they loved and miss Chris as well.

I, too, have grown to love Chris' "kids," just as my son did. They are the light of my life. I love being with them, watching them grow, and seeing how much they mean to the men and women I love the most. I am so lucky to have them in my life, and they are so lucky to have known Chris, even if it was only for such a short time. I know their dads will never let them forget who Chris was, and how much he loved them, and that is something I will do for the rest of my life as well. One of Chris' teammates told me something that will stay with me for the rest of my life. He told me that when he sees me playing with his kids, it is like watching Chris when he played with the kids! That is one of the greatest compliments I have ever received! Chris had a very special relationship with "his kids," just as I do now. The kids know how much Chris loved them, and how much I love them now. And to hear them call me, "Uncle Jeff" or "Grandpa Jeff" is the BEST thing I have ever been called in my life! I realize I have very big shoes to fill because they loved their Uncle Chris, and they miss him as much as I do. But it is their love for Chris and for me that has probably done more to heal the hole in my heart than anything else. So sharing my love with the "kids" Chris never had is one of the best ways I can honor my son. Chris touched so many people, and now it is my turn to be part of the lives that were such a tremendous part of Chris' life.

Here are some of the stories of Chris' "kids" that I cherish the most:

Tristen

Tristen is Jim and Giselle's son. Chris used to love playing video games with Tristen. I vividly remember after one party at Jim's house—and there were WAY more than "one" party at Jim's house!!!—when Chris told me about playing a football video game against Tristen. Tristen must have only been 6 or 7 at the time, but Chris played against him as he would against anyone—full out and taking no prisoners—and I don't remember the final score, but he beat Tristen like a rug!!! One of the first stories Jim told me about Chris was the same story, and how much it meant to Jim that Chris didn't "go easy" on Tristen.

I first met Tristen at the JFK Chapel on 18 August 2005. He was such a little gentleman, and when Giselle introduced me to him, the first thing he did was come up to me and gave me a hug. He didn't know me from a hole in the wall, but he knew Chris, and if I was Chris' dad, than I was OK in his book! That hug has been as important to me as any I have ever received because it told me how much Tristen loved Chris, and how much he loves me now.

Later that day, out at Markus' house before it started to pour, Tristen and Scout—Jim and Giselle's daughter—wanted to play soccer with Tim and me. Tim also has Chris' gift for loving and caring for young kids, and Tristen instantly took to Tim as I am sure he took to Chris. So, after we established where the goals would be on Markus' front lawn, we started to play—Tim and me vs. Tristen and Scout! Tristen had played soccer for a couple of seasons, and he was a good little player.

I had the ball and I was going to pass the ball to Tim so he could go in and score. I could have made a simple pass to Tim along the ground, but, being a wise-ass, I decided to flick the ball over Tristen's head and have some fun with that pass. Sounded like a good idea at the time—but, I accidentally put a little too much "flick" on the pass, and hit poor Tristen right in the throat! It knocked the wind out of him, and made me feel like a fool! I rushed to comfort Tristen, but he took it like a man. But what he said after that told me more about the person Tristen is than anything else—he told me he was OK, and that he didn't want me to go easy on him, but he asked if I wouldn't go "quite that hard" as the ball that knocked the wind out of him! My little man!

The other thing that Tristen did that makes my heart soar was a conversation he had with his dad, Jim, about a month after Chris left us. Jim was driving Tristen and Scout to school, and Tristen asked, "Dad, who will replace Chris on ODA 316?" Jim told Tristen that while no one could replace Chris, JT and Shawn were going to go over to be with 316. Tristen thought about it for a few seconds and then told Jim, "Well, Dad, I will become a Green Beret so I can replace Chris on 316!" When Jim told me this story, I wrote the following letter to Tristen:

Dear Tristen,

How are you doing, buddy? I can't wait to see you in January or February when the rest of 316 gets back from Afghanistan!

Your dad told me what you said about wanting to become a Green Beret, and that you wanted to do it to replace Chris on his team. Of all the wonderful things that have been said about Chris since he was killed in action, that, my little buddy, was the most wonderful thing of all. I will always remember it, and I will always love you for saying it.

I am positive that you will become a Green Beret someday; I know that with all my heart. I will always remember the first time I met you, and kicked the soccer ball at your neck and you came back for more (…and kicked my butt playing soccer on Markus' front yard as well!). So, I want you to have something. When Chris was about your age, he too, had decided that he wanted to become a Green Beret. So I gave him a Long Tab and Arrowhead, which he put on the wall over his bed so that every night before he went to sleep, and every morning when he first woke up that is what he saw, because he wanted to become a Green Beret that much. So, I want you to take this Long Tab and Arrowhead that belonged to Chris and put it on the wall over your bed. Chris loved playing soldier with you, and I am so proud of you and what you want to do with your future.

And, I will be there when you graduate from the Q course and walk across that stage…I will have something special for you then as well.

Have fun today, and I look forward to seeing you soon!

I love you,

Jeff

I used to play a game with Chris and Tim when they were young—it was called the Money Game, and I would let them guess how much money I had, either in my pocket or my wallet, and if they guessed EXACTLY, they "won" the money. Chris came within a few cents one time of guessing, and so whenever I go "home," I still play the Money Game with Tristen and Scout—and I have no doubt that one of these days, Tristen will clean me out!!!

I love you, buddy and thank you so much for loving Chris and loving me!

Scout

Scout is Jim and Giselle' beautiful daughter. Scout is no longer a little girl as she has become a lovely young lady! Scout was about 5 when Chris died, but she still has very vivid memories of Chris. I love to talk to her about Chris, and I know she knows how much it means to me!

Scout is my helper! I made wooden baby cradles for all the little girls, and when I got to Fayetteville to meet ODA 316 when they got back from Deh Afghan, Scout helped me stain and varnish all 5 of the cradles! When Giselle and Jim moved into their new home in July 2007, Scout helped me build the shelves for storing all of Dad's stuff! And it reminds me so much of my first little helper when I was doing projects around the home—Chris!

I have not kept every email I have gotten from my 316 family, but of all the emails I have ever gotten, including those from Chris in Afghanistan, the following email from Jim is not only my favorite, but it has touched my soul and it is something I will always remember:

Jeff,

Scout told me something on the way to school this morning, completely out of the blue… "daddy, when I miss Chris, I just look up into the sky...."

"Me, too, Scout, me too..."

I love you.

Jim

So, I sent Scout the following letter with a marble falcon that Chris had given me as a present when he was about 5 years old. He had bought it at a Christmas Fair at his elementary school, and it had been one of me favorite gifts I had ever received up to that point:

Dear Scout!

Your dad sent me an email yesterday that I will never forget! You had told him that when you miss Chris, all you have to do is look up to the sky. I do that too, sweetie, many times each day and even though I miss him more everyday, I know he is looking out for you, your dad and everyone of us that loved him so very much.

There is something else you can do to see Chris. Have your dad show you what a falcon looks like. Chris' last name, in Lakota Indian language, means "little falcon," and when ever I see a falcon flying over my head, I know Chris is there with me, looking out for me, and sharing my day with me.

So, here is a little falcon for you. This was one of the very first presents Chris ever gave me that he bought for me when he was just about your age. It has sat on my desk for many, many years, but it is time for this little falcon to be with you, just as Chris is always with you and your dad. Chris used to love to tell me about the times he spent playing with you and Tristen, and how much fun you guys used to have. I can't wait to do the same!

Have fun today, and give your mom, dad and Tristen a big hug for me

I love you!

Jeff

I never had a daughter, but I have you, Scout! You fill my heart with your beauty and I love you with all my heart!

Sean

Sean is Dan's "little man!" He is one of, if not, the smartest people I have ever known, and as Chris would always say—"disregardless" of age!!! One of my favorite pictures is of Chris and Sean, and it is included in OUR book because not only the look on their faces, but the "accessories" in their hands are in my mind and in my heart for all of time!

I first met Sean at the JFK Chapel, and on one of the worst days of my life, Sean was a shining light that I will always remember. He had a black ODA 316 t-shirt on, and he was just about the cutest little man I had ever seen—and even at the age of 4, he was indeed a little man! That is what Chris always called Sean, and he was so well behaved, and looking at his handsome face, it did more to help me get through that Memorial service than anything else.

Over the past 3 years, Sean's dad has been downrange way too much, and so I don't get to see Sean as much as I would like. But Sean and Tristen are my wooden toy consultants! They let me know what wooden vehicle I should make next, and so far, they have made terrific choices: a GMV, Bradley tank, APC—Armored Personnel Carrier—and most recently, a MRAP—Mine Resistant Anti-Personnel vehicle. They are deciding between an Apache and an A-10 for the next toy. Sean is leaning towards the Apache because it is an Army "weapon" and the A-10 is just a support aircraft from the Air Force! That is our little man!

Sean, I love you with all my heart! You are your dad's reason for being, and for all you are to me and ALL you are for your Dad, I love you and always will!

Ruby

Ruby is the beautiful daughter of Scott and Chrissa. Chris probably spent more time with Ruby than any of his other kids. He loved Ruby, and I clearly remember one night Chris called me to tell me about "Ruby being Ruby!" It made my heart soar to hear him tell me about her, to hear him laugh about her antics, and I could tell from his voice how much Ruby meant to Chris. Then, he told me something I NEVER thought I would hear Chris say—"You, know Dad, I wouldn't mind having a daughter, if she could be like Ruby!"

I can NEVER thank Chrissa and Scotty for sharing your daughter with my son! Ruby was as close to Chris' daughter as anyone will ever be, and I am so grateful that Chris had that experience. The world will never be the same, because Chris will never have a daughter or a son, but at least he had Ruby, and he got to know what the love of a child means. And, I can NEVER thank Chrissa and Scott enough for sharing Ruby with me! Watching her grow, seeing her become a young lady, being part of her life is the joy of my life.

I want to share my favorite Ruby story with you. On 8 August, 2008, Chrissa took Ruby to the back of 1st BN, 3rd SFG (A) where the Memorial Stones for the warriors of 3rd SFG (A) are located. Chrissa wanted to place some flowers at Chris' stone. Ruby didn't have any flowers, so when they got to the stone, and Chrissa put the flowers by the stone, Ruby ran over to a bush near the entrance to the walkway. She gently pulled off several leaves, ran back to Mommy, and carefully placed them on Chris' stone. "There…" she softly whispered.

I can see my precious Ruby doing this, and it is something I will always remember! I love you, Roo, and we will always tell you about your Uncle Chris and how much he loved you!

Callie and Addie

Chris' other little girls were Shawn and Jamie's daughters, Callie and Addie. They were very young when Chris was still with us, and I remember him telling me how much he enjoyed watching them grow. I can remember the first time I met them. They were hanging on Shawn's legs, and we were playing "hide and seek" around the people in the JFK Chapel. They are such loving little girls, and it fills my heart to see how they are growing today into such wonderful and beautiful young ladies. I am so lucky to have you in my life, and I love you both with all my heart!

Wyatt

Wyatt is Shawn and Jamie's son. And as much as Shawn loves his two beautiful daughters, I know he really was hoping for a son when he found out he and Jamie were going to have another child. Wyatt is amazing! One of my favorite pictures of ALL time is the Christmas photos of Shawn and Jamie's wonderful family. The picture that captured my heart was one where Wyatt's little hand is holding onto his daddy's huge finger, with Shawn's SF ring in the picture as well. I can see in my mind's eye a picture like that of Chris with his child, and that is why that picture is so special to me.

Wyatt is my "toy tester"—and Daddy's toes can attest to that! I can't wait to watch you grow into the man your father is, and being part of your life, Wyatt, is so very, very special to me. I love you, Wyatt, with all my heart, and we will have many, many great days together!

The "Rest" of OUR kids!

There are six gifts that unfortunately Chris never got to know here, but I know he looks down and smiles on them each and every day—and they do, and will continue to know who Chris was because their marvelous parents loved Chris as much as I do.

Randi

Randi is Markus and Rocio's beautiful daughter. Randi has some memory of Chris, but he was training and getting ready for Deh Afghan when Markus and Rocio brought Randi into Chris' life. Randi is such a wonderful young lady. She is one of the greatest joys of my life. Whenever I stay with Markus and Rocio, Randi INSISTS that Uncle Jeff stays in her room! She is an amazing big sister to Gabe and Zeth, and it is truly an honor for me to be part of her life, because you are SUCH an important part of mine! I love you with all my heart.

Gabe

Gabe is Markus and Rocio's oldest son. He was only a couple of months old when Chris and ODA 316 was deployed to Deh Afghan, so Chris never really got to know Gabe. He is a great little guy! He has a smile that will light up a room. He has a heart that makes your heart smile. And he is one of the greatest joys of my life. I love you Gabe, and I'll have your train the next time I see you!!!

Zeth

Zeth Ronin is Markus and Rocio's youngest son. He reminds me so much of Chris when he was that age, it is almost scary! I first met Zeth at the Memorialization in 2006, and then got to know him better when I went out to help finish an addition on Markus' house. Markus had started working on it while waiting for Zeth to come into our lives, but then he had to head back "to work," so I came out in July and worked on the room for him. Zeth has a mind of his own, and he doesn't mind if you don't—and if you do, he doesn't!?!?!

Watching Zeth grow has been one of the greatest gifts of my life. We are great buddies, and I want to share with everyone a story from this past 8 August. I was helping Markus with an extension of the kitchen, and so after dinner, I sat down to type an email to our family on the third anniversary of Chris crossing over. As you might guess, I started to cry while I was typing, and I didn't see Zeth come into the room. Next thing I knew, he had come up to me and handed me a dish towel for me to wipe my eyes. That sweet, innocent gesture is something I will always remember, and whenever I think of Zeth, I will think of that wonderful gesture of love.

You are truly a very special little man, my Zeth, and Uncle Jeff loves you with all my heart!

McKenna

McKenna is Tony and Tara's oldest daughter. She is an amazing big sister, and Kenna is one of the smartest little ladies I have ever known. She fills my heart with her smile, her laugh and her love. I am so very lucky to have you, McKenna, as such a big part of my life, and I love you and always will.

Christopher Matthew and Malia Jaden

Sometime in the spring of 2007, Tony called me on my cell phone. He had emailed me earlier in the week, telling me that he had something to tell me, but wanted to wait until we could talk on the phone. With T, you NEVER knew what that might be, so I was anxiously awaiting that phone call.

So when I answered the phone, he asked me a very simple question, but one that I thought I would never hear—"Do you want to be a grandpa?!?!" Tony and Tara were going to have a baby, sometime in October. I was speechless and my heart soared as it hadn't soared in many, MANY moons! I couldn't wait to tell Uncle Tim and Grandma Dianne! Tony didn't have much time to talk, as he was leaving on a training mission, but we would have more time to talk in a few weeks.

Well, a few weeks later, I had just parked Chris' truck in the parking lot of a store when my cell phone rang, and it was Tony. He started this conversation with a request—seeing he and Tara were having TWINS, a boy and a girl, he wanted my permission to name his son Christopher Matthew, after my son and his brother. I have shed many tears in the last three years, but my tears that day in the parking lot were tears of my greatest joy and honor!!! In fact, the ONLY thing that has filled the hole in my heart more, was on 26 October, 2008 when I got to meet my grandchildren—Christopher Matthew and Malia Jaden! Chris is two minutes older than Malia, but they were both the most beautiful babies I have ever seen—including my own! Holding them fills me with such hope, joy, happiness and love—I can not adequately describe it in words. Looking into their smiling eyes, I see a world I thought had been taken away from me forever. When I hear their laugh, I hear Chris' laugh.

As I told Tony on the day they were born, I didn't think I would ever be happy again—but Christopher Matthew and Malia Jaden have changed all that!

You are Grandpa Jeff's greatest joy and I love you both as no other.

Jay Harmon Falkel

In our society today, the word, "warrior" is used way too often. A "warrior" is a special person, and MY definition of the word, "warrior" can be seen on the back cover of OUR book! These men, to me, are the definition and the embodiment of what it means to be a warrior. And to that extent, the word warrior throughout OUR book has been used only when it truly describes what it is to be a warrior.

When Chris crossed over, he was met by warriors from the beginning of time. The Spartans, the great Lakota warriors, and two other warriors from my family. When I cross over, before I am greeted by the warriors who have gone before me, I will first be greeted by three warriors: my dad, my son, and my nephew—Jay Harmon Falkel.

When Chris finished SFAS, and had 10 days leave before starting the Q course in the summer of 2002, Tim, Chris and I drove out to California to help my brother and my wonderful sister-in-law prepare their house and Grandma's house for the arrival of their first child. Unaware of the baby's sex, they had names picked out for a boy or a girl. If it was a boy, they decided to call him Jay (Lisa's maiden name is "Jay") Harmon, which was my dad's name. He was delivered via emergency C-Section on 15 July 2002. When we got out there about 5 July, Lisa had been admitted to the hospital, holding off pre-term labor. The doctors all said everything was fine, she just needed to be monitored and to hold off the birth with medication as long as possible, as the baby wasn't due for seven more weeks. Chris needed to be back "home" by 16 July, so we were driving his car back, and we were somewhere in Missouri when Jay was to be born. We actually had a really great talk about kids for several hours before Jay's birth. Well, we waited and waited and waited for the phone call from my brother, but it didn't come. Finally I got a call from one of my sisters, and she was hysterical. There was a problem—Jay was born without kidneys. The doctors had a Life-Flight helicopter flown to Monterey from Children's Hospital in San Francisco, but after all their evaluations, they determined that even if he made it up to Children's Hospital, his chance of living was very poor. So, the family made the decision to let him go, and 7 hours after he came into this world, he left to be with his grandfather.

Jay was a WARRIOR. He fought a battle that no one could have possibly survived, and he was a blessing to our family. After we heard about Jay crossing over, we stopped in a rest area, and Chris and I went for a walk. I could see how much it affected Chris. Chris loved his Uncle Mic, my brother, and he was so sad that Uncle Mic would not have the chance to do all he wanted to do with Jay, or be able to do all the things Chris and I had done. It truly touched Chris, and he told me in our talk before ODA 316 went wheels up for Deh Afghan that if something happened to him, he would introduce me to Jay when I made the journey.

Take care of Grandpa and your cousin, my son. I will be there soon, but not soon enough. I miss all three of you more than words can express, but I am so glad the three of you are all there together, watching over us, and letting us know that you are all where you need to be. I can't wait for Uncle Jeff to hug you, Jay, and I love you with all my heart!

28

Liz

*I hope that I may desire more than I can
accomplish.*

—Michelangelo

As with all of my ODA 316 family, I knew about Liz before I ever met her. When Chris came home after completing SFAS, he told me he had a "surprise" for me—which you NEVER knew what that might be with Chris! Well, his surprise was his first tattoo! It was on his left shoulder, and it depicted the Grim Reaper with a .357 Magnum! While he liked the idea, he was not happy with how the "ink" came out. Now, if you have ever been to Fayetteville, North Carolina—there are "a couple"—of 100—tattoo shops in town! But there is only one shop that is an art studio, and that is Smokin' Guns! So once Chris got to ODA 316, and he wanted to get some more ink, his brothers took him to THE tattoo shop they all used, and that was Smokin' Guns. Chris' next ink after returning from Gereshk was a dragon on his right shoulder, and as fate would have it, he got his tattoo from Liz. Liz is truly an artist, and is as talented as any artist I have ever seen! The only difference is the "canvas" Liz uses is the skin, and she makes her art come alive on her canvas!!!

Liz is able to take a design, and MAKE it what the person wants to say with their tattoo. And once Chris saw how incredibly talented Liz was, she was the only one that he used for his ink, including the lambda he got on his left forearm. She puts her heart and soul into her work, and the results are there for the world to see. And Liz becomes one with her masterpiece as she communicates what needs to be said with her tattoos.

When Chris and I had our conversation the night before he left for Gereshk, one of the things we talked about was "ink." He asked me to do two things for him if something happened: first, was to have Tim get some ink from Liz. Tim and Chris had talked about ink for several years, and while Tim had always told Chris he wanted some ink, he had not found the right idea yet. Tim wanted to wait until he found the perfect design. Chris told me that Liz could do WHAT EVER Tim wanted, and that he just needed to get it done! But the second thing he asked me to do for him, was to get a lambda on my left arm if something were to happen to him. I did not have any ink in 2005, and had no desire to have any, but I told Chris I would honor his request, but that it probably would not be needed.

The night before the Memorial at Ft. Bragg, Jim, Markus, Tony and JT took me to see Liz. Jim told her who I was, and why I was there, and I could see in her eyes the honor and yet the sadness she felt in giving me my lambda. I had never even been in a tattoo shop before, and there I was, getting my first tattoo! Throughout the process, which didn't take that long, Jim kept wincing, as he HATES the process of putting ink into his skin, but he loves what his ink means to him. Markus was there for moral support, but what I remember most was Liz, and the look on her face, and the smile in her eyes. After she finished my lambda, she gave JT his. Throughout this process, I remember looking at Tim, and seeing in his eyes that Liz was indeed going to be the one to do his tattoo—he just needed to figure out what that would be.

Her next masterpiece was for Tony. After the Memorial, we went out to Markus' house for the traditional bonfire. No one knew where Tony was, because he was supposed to be there, and Tony NEVER missed a party. Well, when he finally arrived, we found out where he had been. Liz had added to his lambda, and he had her put a dedication to Chris around his lambda. It was magnificent—it was perfect. When Tim saw Tony's new ink, he was even more envious, and wanted to get his ink for Chris that much more.

So, over the next few months, Tim worked on a design—when he should have been doing his homework!?!? He wanted something dedicated to his brother, he wanted something Greek, and he knew he wanted it on his back, just as Chris always had Tim's back while they were growing up. He sent Liz some of his ideas, but it wasn't until we got back "home" for the Memorialization in May, 2006 that Tim finally saw the design Liz had created. When she showed us her ideas about

Tim's design, we both just stood there in shock. Without knowing it, she had created EXACTLY what Tim had in mind, and the most amazing thing about her creation, was the Spartan in the middle of the design. Chris' favorite picture of Chris was taken while he was in AIT at Ft. Benning, and it is a picture of him in his BDU's with his M-16, and he is stalking his prey. The foliage in the background blended in perfectly with the design on his BDU's and you could barely see Chris! He loved that picture, as do I. Well, even though Liz had NEVER seen that picture, the way she drew the Spartan is in exactly the same posture as Chris is in his favorite picture of himself! The resemblance is uncanny! Tim looked at me, I looked at him, and we simultaneously told Liz it was perfect!!!

When I was going through Chris' things, I found a design he had been working on for the ink he would get when he got home from Deh Afghan. It was a falcon, in the colors of 3rd SFG (A) and the Lakota colors of black, red, white and yellow. As soon as I saw this drawing, I knew what needed to be done—I had Liz put Chris' design on my back.

Another thing Chris asked me to do that involved Liz was that if something happened to him, he knew that it would greatly affect Scott, and so he wanted me to get some ink for Scott. So, that is what I did. I went to see Liz with Chrissa before Scott got back in February, 2006 from Deh Afghan, and told Liz what Chris had asked me to do. Again, she was honored and humbled to be asked to do this, and she told us that of course, she would do what ever Scott wanted. Scott was deeply moved by his "little brother's" gesture, and after thinking about it for awhile, he came up with a design that Liz put on his calf, and is with Scott everyday, just as Chris is always with him.

Liz is part of our family. She is one of us because she has shared her talent, her love and her heart with all of us through her work. She has been able to tell our story through her masterpieces, and we are so very lucky that she loves us as she does to give us the amazing gift of her, and OUR ink! Whenever I see my lambda on my arm, it reminds me what Chris wanted it to do—to let me know how much he loved me. The ink may be on my arm and my back, but it goes straight to my heart.

Liz, you will ALWAYS have a very special place in my heart for all that you have done for the family I love—and for that, I will always love you!

29

Michael Reagan—
An Angel Among Us!

*There are in the end three things that last: faith,
hope and love… and the Greatest of these, is LOVE!*

—1 Corinthians 13:13

It has been said that there are angels among us. Some people believe, some don't—and that is their loss. But few people that I know ACTUALLY know an angel.

Well, for me and thousands of other Gold Star Families, we DO indeed know an angel—His name is Michael Reagan!!!

Who is Michael Reagan? Michael lives in Edmonds, Washington, and at an early age after a football injury prevented him from playing, he started drawing. His first drawing was based on a magazine picture of Katherine Hepburn, and after he finished it, he realized "how good it made me feel." When friends and family saw how talented he was, he found out quickly "how much I also enjoyed that"—making people feel the joy he felt in drawing. That was the start of a lifetime of love—the love that Michael feels for his work and the love he shares with those people that he draws.

During Vietnam, Michael was a United States Marine (…but we don't hold that against him!) and when he returned, he wondered why he was spared when so many of his brothers in arms were killed. He drew portraits of many Marines "whose pictures came home, but they didn't" as Michael has said many times. He found he had a gift of sharing his talents to help others through his drawings. It wasn't until many years later that he realized what a very, VERY special gift his drawing was.

Mike believes it is his duty to share that gift, as he does now with the families of our fallen warriors and heroes from the Global War on Terror in Afghanistan and Iraq.

Michael has drawn thousands of portraits in the last thirty years. He has donated over $10,000,000 dollars to various charities from the portraits he has put his heart and soul into. But he found his true calling after the wife of a fallen hero asked him to draw a portrait of her husband. Ms. Cherice Johnson, the wife of Navy Hospital Corpsman 3rd Class Michael Vann Johnson, Jr., 25, of Little Rock, Arkansas, who was killed in combat 25 March 2003, saw a story about Michael's artwork on the Seattle's Evening Magazine show. Michael's heart went out to Cherice and her family having been a combat war veteran, and after completing the portrait, he gave it to Cherice and refused any payment for the commission. As Michael has said, "Being a combat veteran that was fortunate to make it home has me thanking God everyday. Because I truly consider all of us that have fought or are fighting for this country to be brothers, there just isn't any way I could charge for the picture."

That first drawing of Corpsman Michael Johnson has become Michael's life work. And since that first drawing of Corpsman Johnson, everyday, Mike draws up to two portraits of our fallen warriors. All a family of a fallen hero needs to do is ask Michael to draw their loved one, and provide a picture—his magical talent does the rest! And to date, Michael has drawn over 1600 portraits for the families of our warriors!!!

I became aware of Michael Reagan on 22 September 2006. A friend of mine called me to tell me he saw on the NBC Nightly News that Friday a segment about an artist that was drawing portraits of our fallen brothers. I got on the NBC website and found the information about Michael. I immediately emailed him that night, telling him about OUR warrior, Chris, and asking if he would honor me by drawing one of his portraits of Chris. I told Michael that Chris was with me everyday in my heart, and having a portrait of him would mean the world to me.

Little did I know that night how much Michael's gift and his love would mean to me...

The next morning, 23 September 2006, I received an email from Michael. He started off by saying how sorry he was for my loss, and how PROUD he would be to draw Chris' portrait!!! All he needed was a picture of Chris and he would take care of the rest. I was blown away—NEVER in my wildest dreams would I have thought someone would do this for me, and that that someone would do it so quickly! I have many pictures of Chris, but there was one that I thought would be best for the portrait. It was a picture in his Class A uniform, and there was always something in the eyes of that picture that spoke right to my heart. I never saw the picture until I was going through Chris' things after he crossed over, so it was especially meaningful to me.

That would be the picture. But, I had a special request of Michael. Our name means "little falcon" in Lakota and falcons have always played a special part of our lives, as seen in Chapter 9 of OUR book. So, I asked Michael if he could draw a small picture of a falcon soaring over Chris. Michael emailed me back almost immediately and told me that while he had never done that before, he would try if I could send him a picture of a falcon. No problem, as I have hundreds of falcon pictures to choose from. So I emailed him two of my favorites and waited.

The next weekend, I was asked by one of my brothers to come to Florida to be the key note speaker at his graduation ceremony. Tony was a member of 5th SFG (A) in Vietnam, and was also attached to 7th and 8th SFG (A) until he retired from the Army after 20 years of service. He worked with the NASA program on fitness for our astronauts. About 25 years ago, he started Fitness Institute International, a two year program to prepare people to work in the fitness and conditioning industry. Tony asked me to give the key note speech about Chris and the fitness needed to be a member of Special Forces today, given the demands of the Global War on Terror. I called the speech, "Fit to be a Hero." I told him I would be honored, but that I had no idea how my speech would come off. It was the first time since the Memorial in Littleton that I had spoken in public about Chris, and while I knew WHAT I wanted to say, I had no idea HOW I would be able to hold it together and actually give my speech.

So, on 30 September 2006, I was in Ft. Lauderdale, Florida for the Fitness Institute's graduation ceremony. Being the man of honor and integrity that Tony is, he also had another of our brothers, Dr. Tom Baechle, come to the graduation ceremony to receive a special award. Tom started the National Strength and Conditioning Association's Certification Commission almost 20 years earlier. He was going to retire, so Tony wanted to give Tom the recognition he so greatly deserved because of ALL that Tom and his contributions to the profession have meant for all of Tony's students over all the years. Tom is one of my dearest friends and closest brothers—in fact, it was Tom that got me started in the strength and conditioning profession and it was Tom that I called first after I heard that Chris had been killed in action. It was great to see Tom, and there was only one other time in the almost 30 years that I have known Tom that it was better to see him—and that was at Arlington on 22 August 2005 when we interred Chris. I did not expect to see him there, and it gave me a strength on the second "worse" day of my life that I did not know I had. I was hoping on that Saturday night in Florida that Tom would somehow give me some of his strength again as I gave my speech.

Well, big help he was—while we were sitting next to each other, not paying attention to the speakers before me—he leans over and asks, "How in the world are you going to get through your speech? I know I couldn't do it! What are you going to do??? " Thanks, brother! But at about 1930 (7:30 PM), I got up and gave it my best shot.

I have given hundreds, if not thousands of lectures all over the world, and this one was probably the best one I have ever given. To this day, when I go back and look at my PowerPoint slides, I have NO clue how I was able to stand up and talk about Chris the way I did! I have given many speeches about Chris over the past three years—some of them are included in OUR book—but this one was special. After a standing ovation for Chris, and then meeting Tony's students at the reception afterward, I finally got up to my hotel room about 2230 (10:30 PM). It was only when I opened my email, then and ONLY then, that I knew HOW I was able to get through my speech.

At 1931 local time in Ft. Lauderdale, FL, I received an email from Michael Reagan. When I opened the email I was absolutely speechless— and for those of you that know me, that is pretty much impossible! But what left me speechless on 30 September 2006 was seeing a digital picture of the portrait that Michael had drawn of Chris. I was absolutely blown away! Several people knocked on my hotel door for me to go have a drink with them and I just sat on the chair in the hotel room in utter amazement at what Michael had done! And done so fast—it was just one week earlier that I had emailed him the pictures of Chris!!!

The first things I saw were Chris' eyes. From the day he was born, his eyes gave him away. Sure, he could be as stealth as any Special Forces operative has EVER been, but he better have sunglasses on, because his eyes always told me exactly what he was thinking, what he was feeling, and what scheme he had up his sleeve! Michael captured Chris' eyes like nothing I had ever seen before.

In fact, it was probably several minutes until I noticed where Michael had placed the falcon. He was below Chris and to his left, and again, the drawing of the falcon was unbelievable, and Michael was also able to capture this magnificent creature's eyes—the path to his soul. After marveling at this amazing gift that a complete stranger had made for me, I must admit I was somewhat confused by where Michael had placed the falcon. In my mind, I thought having the falcon soaring over Chris' head would be where Michael would have placed the falcon—keeping his eyes on Chris, just as my falcon brothers soar over me more times than I can possibly recall. Falcons are such an important part of OUR story about Chris that they have there own chapter in OUR book!

By now, it was after midnight, so I emailed Michael to thank him from the bottom of my heart for one of the most wonderful gifts I had ever received. And I did ask Michael why he put the falcon where he did. Well, when I got back to Colorado later that Sunday, I had an email from Michael waiting for me. He told me that he had drawn 14 portraits that week, but for some reason, he felt compelled to take a digital picture of Chris and email it to me as soon as he finished the portrait. Michael said that he had never done that before and that he usually doesn't even download the images from his camera that soon! But, as he said in his email to me, "All through this project (the fallen hero's portraits) things like this have happened. It amazes me, but it just reinforces how much love surrounds it all!" Amen to that, my brother!!!

Michael also told me why he placed the falcon where he did. As he was drawing Chris' portrait, he had this overwhelming sense that he should put the falcon below Chris—and then it hit him: Chris was now flying on the wings of our falcon, looking down together and watching over all of us that love him as we do. It is EXACTLY where the falcon should be!!! The falcon is also on Chris' left, where the Spartans wore their shields, which were used to protect their brother—just as OUR falcons are there to protect us!

After I got this email from Michael, Chris' portrait was electronically sent, literally, around the world! His brothers, his teammates, were deployed to various regions, and my list of family keeps growing and growing, and they all needed to see what gift of love I had just received. Of all the emails I have sent out since Chris left us, the response to this one was not only the fastest and most complete, but EVERYONE was equally as amazed as I was! Particularly because almost no one knew that Michael was doing this for ALL of us! With Michael's permission, I had the digital print copied and gave framed portraits to OUR brothers and my family. Whenever I go to one of their homes, or offices, and see Chris on their wall, it fills me with a joy that is difficult to explain. They all receive the same love from their portraits that I have with the original. And each and every person I have given a copy to has said the same thing about Chris' eyes—they not only follow them wherever they go, but there is something comforting in his eyes to let them know that Chris is fine, and that he loves each of us and watches over us, just as our falcons do..

There are some things that all I have to do is think about them, and I get very emotional—knowing that Michael has Chris on our falcon's wings is one of those things. The original portrait hangs in our family room in Colorado, right over my chair—in perfect line of sight to the T.V. for watching Bronco football games!!! No matter where I go in that room, Chris' eyes follow me; just as they did all the while he was growing up. It will obviously never take the place of my warrior, my hero, my son. But Michael's masterpiece has given me more love and more hope than I can possibly ever express. I said in my eulogy that there was a hole in my heart that I did not know if it could ever be filled. Michael Reagan—with his talent, his compassion, his caring, his dedication and most of all, his LOVE—has done more to fill the hole in my heart than I ever thought possible.

I would like to share an email I found that Michael had sent out around the holidays to the families of the heroes he has drawn up to that time. It gives a small "snap-shot" of the man, the angel, that Michael Reagan is:

Dear All:

I know this is a very hard time for all of you. But I wanted to let you all know I'm keeping my promise. I will never forget your family and your sacrifice for me, my family and our country, and I'm not allowing anyone else to either. I've now worked with 510 families and each of you is thought of constantly. This year I was asked to be the speaker at the Marine Corps Ball in Seattle. It was an experience I will always be proud of. I spent the evening with true heroes. I told them all about all of you. They all care deeply for all of you.

I also want to say thank you. It is because of all of you spreading the word of this project that's allowed me to reach so many families. Please keep that up. I will be doing these free portraits until I am no longer asked to do them, or there are no more to do. When I say this, I mean this—I love you all. If you ever need to talk or just write, please do. This project has taught me a new definition of the word love. It's a place I never thought existed, but it does. It has changed me.

Thank you for trusting me to do these portraits for you. I care!

Mike

...For ALL of us that Michael has touched, you are now part of OUR definition of what love is all about!

It has taken me over 3 years to finish OUR book. I have an office downstairs in the basement of our house, and I have written articles, books, emails and almost everything else at the desk in my office. But, when I sat down there to finish OUR book, for some reason, the thoughts would not flow. Well, one night, I was sitting in my recliner, under the portrait of Chris in our TV room, and the "flood gates" opened and the words flew onto my laptop. It was then and ONLY then that I realized why—Chris was looking down on me and helping me do what I didn't have the strength to do WITHOUT him! Mike, YOU made that possible, and OUR story might not have EVER been told were it not for your amazing gift!!!

When OUR book is finished, the first copy will be taken to Arlington National Cemetery, Section 60, Grave 8212. But the second copy will be taken to Edmonds, Washington, so I can look Michael Reagan in the eye, hug him as only a brother can, and try to thank him personally for all that he has given me and every other Gold Star family that his love and his talent have touched.

30

What I Miss ...

Fallen Soldier

A Soldier has fallen
He will not be forgotten
His spirit dwells in those
Whose lives he touched
He has lead us
He has taught us
He has shown us the way
He gave us all of himself
Because he was made that way
He gave birth to an idea
That will never go away
He did this all
To save us some day
As all heroes do

—by CW3 Roque Gonzalez

I miss you, my son, more than mere words can possibly express. One of my dear friends asked me once how I get through the day—and back then, I really didn't have an answer for him. I have so many memories, and we have tried to share those throughout OUR book. But I think it is because of all these memories, I miss you most...

I miss hearing his laugh, and seeing his smile. I can hear his laugh in my mind, and I can see his smile in my heart, and even in my moments of greatest despair, all I have to do is think about something that we laughed at, or that would have made Chris smile, and I will actually laugh out loud. But, I will miss those things until we are together again.

I miss feeling the excitement Chris used to have when ever we talked about his team—his brothers. I now have those same feelings when I talk to them and when we talk about Chris, but there was always something very special in his voice, and it used to speak directly to my heart.

I miss our phone calls. We used to talk about every thing and ANY THING! It was not unusual for us to literally talk for hours. But there were many times, we didn't talk at all, yet we could not hang up the phone—it was the way we stayed connected to each other.

I miss talking "shop" with Chris. When he went into the Army, and as he progressed through his training, we would talk about everything he was experiencing. It had been many years since I got to "talk-the-talk" and when Chris would call and we would speak a language that is only familiar to the military, it made my heart soar. I get to talk with OUR family now, and it is something I love doing more than I can possibly express, but it was always so very special for mae to talk "shop" with Chris.

I miss going skiing/snowboarding with you. The last time I saw Chris was on our trip to Utah right after he graduated from SOTIC. It was the best trip of my life. We talked, laughed, cried, and we had such a great trip! In fact, we were so engrossed in a conversation once while we were on the chair lift, we actually FORGOT to get off! We had to ride the lift around to the bottom of the hill, and then back up to the top. But the memories of that trip will last forever, and I am so grateful that we had that time together—it was THE time of my life. One of the last things we did on that trip before I dropped Chris off at the Salt Lake City Airport, was plan our next ski trips. We were going to ski at Whistler in British Columbia next. Then we were going to take Tim to Europe. We also decided that we would ski on every continent—and that is something I WILL do for you, my son—but it will not be the same without you there next to me. To this day, it tears my heart apart to land in the Salt Lake City airport, knowing that you will not be there to greet me.

I miss not seeing you get off that bird with the rest of your team. It hurts my heart to see the return ceremonies of our troops when they are re-united with their families. While my heart soars with happiness for their loved ones being able to make it home, my son will never get off that plane again. I will never forget the day I came home from a trip when Chris was eight years old. Due to increases in security even back then, people meeting a flight could not go out to the gate to meet the plane—they had to wait at the end of the terminal. Well, Dianne brought Chris and Tim to the airport to greet me, but as soon as Chris saw me in the crowd getting off the plane, he ran through security, and into my arms. He got in trouble, I got in trouble, but it didn't matter—I will have the look on his face, his smile and the love that he had for me in my heart and my mind forever. I never got to do that for him, and it hurts more than I can describe. Until I get to run into your arms on the other side … I will miss you every second of every minute for the rest of my life.

I miss not watching Chris become even more of a man than what he became in his 22 years with us. My heart would swell with pride as I saw you grow before my eyes, and I miss all you would have become, my son.

I miss not being able to share your life with me, and my life with you.

I miss loving your children as I love you and Tim, and I will miss watching you become the Dad I know you would have been.

I miss seeing you and Tim playing with our black Labrador retriever, Splash. Right after Chris died, for several weeks Splash slept in Chris' room—something she had never done before. And in 2007, when Splash was almost 14 years old, we had to put her to sleep because her hips would dislocate every time she stood up. The hardest part of that day was not putting her to sleep, but knowing that Splash was going to be with you and it was not my time to cross over and hug you again.

What Chris Wanted to Do...

Chris had some pretty lofty goals, but to those of us who knew Chris and loved him as only we can, those goals were very achievable! Here are just a few of the things Chris wanted to do:

- He wanted to learn to play the guitar
- He wanted to go to HALO school
- He wanted to become a Dad

- He wanted to ski with me on every continent
- He wanted to be one of the first people to snowboard in Afghanistan—and Chris and Tony had already started working on his snowboard when he was killed
- He wanted to rebuild a muscle car
- He wanted a ride in an F-16, or some other "fast mover!"
- He wanted to race a Porsche on the Autobahn
- He wanted to hike the entire Appalachian Trail. In fact, we were going to start our hike when 316 got back from Deh Afghan
- He wanted to hike the highlands of Scotland and Japan with Tim and me
- He wanted to hike the path of the 300 Spartans to Thermopylae
- He wanted to buy land in Colorado where he could have a firing range starting at the front porch of his cabin that we were going to build together
- He wanted to try out for either Safety or Corner Back for either the Colorado Buffs or the Denver Broncos
- He wanted to…live the life only Chris could!!!

Tears—The Lifeblood of Love!

When Chris and Tim were young, I remember it always puzzled them when I would cry. They never saw me "cry when you were hurt," but I would cry when I was 'happy'—which made no sense to them when they were growing up. But as they got older, they started to understand. And after Chris got to know ODA 316, it made even more sense to him. For tears are most often an expression of love, not of pain. Chris told me in one of our road trips back "home" that he finally understood because even his biggest, toughest, meanest and most furious brothers on ODA 316, were not 'afraid' to cry when that was the emotion that was needed.

I have shed my share of tears over the past three years. In fact, there were many times writing OUR book that I had to stop to 're-supply my tear ducts' before I could continue the mission! But, Eric Herzberg, a great friend of mine, and the Gold Star Father of Lance Corporal Eric Herzberg, USMC who was killed in Iraq in 2006, and is interred two rows in front of Chris at Arlington, said this in his eulogy for his son:

We've cried for him many times each day, at the most unexpected thoughts or memories. Eric, when I think of why we cry so hard for you— It's not because you are in pain. We know that now you are at peace now.

It's not because you were unprotected and alone when you died. Not only were you with your friends, your brothers, but you had legions from across America praying for you.

We cry for you not because you were unprepared. You had the best training in the world, the best equipment, and the best leadership. And you prepared yourself by deepening your relationship with the Lord who made you. I believe you knew how temporary this world is and you prepared yourself for the next world by reading His word every night.

And we certainly don't cry because we think of you as a victim. The victim's right at this moment are us—your friends and family. We feel almost immobilized with grief right now—but we know you would not want us to remain in this state too long. We know that you want us to continue to serve others as you did.

No, we don't cry for you because of those things.

We cry for you because of the huge sense of loss we feel, which is also felt by our community of family and friends. And we grieve because of all those whose lives you now won't touch here on earth. Eric, we all needed your presence here. Today we feel that sense of loss for what you won't accomplish on this earth.

Yet still, through all this, we remember the Marine with compassion who turned thoughts of hate and division into love, affection and unity—one Iraqi at a time. We remember the son who always spoke the truth, and can help heal wounds—even those within his own family. We remember the friend who is always loyal and faithful.

And the spiritual warrior who never shied away from necessary battles but always brought his faith and humanity with him.

Eric, we cry because we know you would have been a dad who would have raised kids just like you. Yes, we came here to honor you, Eric, but we had it all backwards. It is you who have honored us. We feel honored just to have known you as long as we did, and to have seen the example of your life. You were tested under the most trying of circumstances and your character and integrity never went unnoticed.

Thank you, Eric—your words describe so well what we all feel when we think about living the rest our lives without our heroes, our warriors, our sons.

I still cry every day for Chris, and I am sure I will for the rest of my life. One of the things that writing OUR book has done for me, is it has allowed me to talk about Chris without getting so emotional. One of the mantras of not only SF, but most of the military, as it relates to the Global War on Terrorism, is, "Never Forgive—Never Forget!" And trust me Chris, you will NEVER be forgotten! Your life has touched mine and so many people.

You have made us better people, and having you in our lives gives us the strength to continue here without you. But there are some things that are so special, so emotional, so amazing to me, they will ALWAYS bring tears to my eyes as they have such an impact and influence on my life even now:

- Seeing Chris' stone at Arlington for the first time and every time since then when I arrive in Section 60
- Thinking about Chuck running back amongst all those bullets to get his brother Chris down from the turret
- Thinking about Shawn insisting on going over to be with 316
- Thinking about JT constantly being by Tim's side
- Thinking about Dan giving me his bracelet
- Thinking about Big Al giving each of us our 3rd SFG (A) Challenge Coins
- Thinking about Jim at his Silver Star Ceremony in Baghdad
- Thinking about Big Ron's smile at the JFK Chapel Memorial
- Thinking about the smile on Tony's face when Chris and Malia were born
- Thinking about Scott giving me Chris' SOTIC coin

- Thinking about Markus taking care of Tim at his house, and all Markus has been through this past year and the way he has attacked his cancer like the warrior he IS
- Thinking about Big Al having to make the call and his professionalism to bring the rest of OUR family home
- Thinking about Buzz calling out the Final Roll Call at the Memorial
- Thinking about Chief sitting at the alter in the chapel after the Memorial
- Thinking about LTC (P) opening Chris' casket with me, staying there to be with me when I needed him and his strength the most
- Thinking about Tim laughing at Chris the last time Chris was on skis
- Thinking about seeing the falcon with Scott when we first played golf together
- Thinking about Jimbo's eyes when he first got off the escalator in the Denver airport
- Thinking about our last phone call

…and I am sure I will cry about these things for the rest of my life. But that is OK—it is the way it should be. Chris' brothers and I cry together because we love Chris, we love what he meant to us, and we love each other as Chris loved us.

So, to my dear friends who have asked me how I get through this—there is an easy answer now—I get through it because Chris would want and DEMAND that I get through it. I have lived my life in pain—42 surgeries and surviving 3 types of cancer can do that to you—but the pain of not having Chris here with OUR family is the greatest pain I have ever experienced, and it is a pain I will have in my heart until I cross over to be with Chris, my dad, Jay, and the rest of the warriors waiting on the banks of the river for me and the rest of Chris' brothers.

But until that day, I will miss Chris:

- Every minute of every day
- Every time I go skiing
- And all of our phone calls
- Opening my email 50 times a day to see if there is one from Chris
- "Watching" Bronco games on the phone with Chris

- Hearing the movie lines Chris had for every situation
- Training with him
- Talking "shop" with him
- Getting his advice about what I should do
- Giving him advice before he did things on his own
- Watching him grow as a man and a warrior
- Growing older with him instead of because of him
- Watching him teach his children what my dad taught me and I was so very lucky to be able to teach Chris
- I read somewhere that to truly honor the sacrifice of those warriors that gave their all for us, we owe them a sacred debt to live EACH day to its fullest—and that is what I try to do. So, how do I do this …?

I realize how lucky I am to have ALL my memories of Chris because those of us that miss him the most are also the ones who have the BEST memories of Chris.

I try to live my life as he would want me to.

I have OUR 316 family to share my life with.

I try to take care of Tim and Chris' other brothers.

I share Chris' life with others because it was indeed a very Special life.

I see in the eyes of OUR family the love that they have for Chris and I will honor that for the rest of my life just as Chris honored OUR lives with his.

Chris knew what I needed him to know…and I know I will be with him again!

31

Epilogue: Where We Go From Here...

Every Gold Star Family deals with the loss of their loved one in a different way. For me, it was a 'no-brainer!'—in more ways than one!

Chris only contributed to one charity—the Special Operations Warrior Foundation (SOWF). The SOWF was created in 1980 and is dedicated to providing a college education to every child of a Special Operations warrior who have served in the Army, Navy, Air Force and Marine Corps that was either killed in action or during a training mission. To date, 119 children of our fallen Special Operators have graduated from college, but there are over 700 other children who need and WILL receive the support of the SOWF for their college expenses.

OUR family decided that the proceeds from the sale of The Making of OUR Warrior will be donated to the SOWF for the children of Chris' brothers.

If you would like to donate to the Special Operations Warrior Foundation, or would like more information, please contact them at: www.specialops.org

I have also started two other companies to not only honor Chris, but to support both the SOWF and the families of our fallen heroes.

Chris was always trying to make different things out of bullets—after all, he was a Weapons Sergeant! But, he never figured out how to make a pen out of a bullet. Well, Dad did, and I started Junior's Bullet Pen Company on Chris' birthday, 24 September 2007. We make pens out of .308 shell casings, and 25% of the proceeds from the sale of EVERY bullet pen are donated to the SOWF. If you would like more information about Junior's Bullet Pen Company, please visit our website at: www.juniorsbulletpens.com

But, I felt I needed to do something else to honor Chris. Writing OUR book has been more than a labor of love. It has been emotionally draining and uplifting. It tore me apart and helped heal the hole in my heart at the same time. It was the hardest thing I have ever done, and yet, it is the best thing I have ever written. And, I am so glad OUR family convinced me to write OUR book.

To that end, I want to help other families tell the story of THEIR hero, THEIR loved one, THEIR warrior. I was discussing my plans to help others as OUR book has helped me with one of my dearest friends, who is also the publisher of some of my other projects in the world of exercise physiology and sports medicine. And he came up with the perfect name for what I want to do—I want to help other families tell the story of their loved one that is, indeed, More Than A Name!

The More Than a Name Foundation is dedicated to providing a platform for raising public awareness of the fact that young men and women who have given their lives in service to their country were more than a name. This platform will involve several formats, including book publishing, DVD production, commemorative products, and public service announcements. We are so very excited about this Foundation, and we look forward to telling the stories of so many amazing Americans that are TRULY More Than A Name!

If you are interested in the More Than A Name Foundation, or would like us to help you tell the story of your loved one, please contact us at: www.morethananamefoundation.org

And, if you are a Gold Star family, or you know of a Gold Star family that does not have one of Michael Reagan's portraits of your fallen hero, please contact Mike at www.fallenheroesproject.org to receive a free portrait of your loved one. Michael is truly one of the most amazing men I know, and his gift of love to me, and the thousands of other families who have lost their warriors in the Global War on Terror, is perhaps the greatest gift I have ever been given.

Thank you for reading and sharing OUR story of SSG Christopher Matthew Falkel. Thank you for opening your heart and hearing OUR story of love, valor, dedication, joy and sorrow. And thank you for remembering the sacrifice that not only Chris and his brothers have made, but that EVERY member of our Armed Forces and their families make every day for EVERY American. So, the next time you see someone in uniform, please go up to them—shake their hand—and thank them for ALL they do for ALL of us! I will NEVER forget all OUR family has done for our country, and I sincerely hope no other American ever will either!